High, Wide, and Handsome
An American Journey

Julian Bishop

Published by Travellers Press

ISBN: 978-1-7364460-0-3

To Lorna

Thank you for accompanying me on life's journey

Acknowledgments

Editing is harder than writing. I would like to thank a number of people who helped me during the editing process. Sarah Maguire did a spectacular job at the development editing stage. Her diligence, wit, and bravery helped me to improve the structure and voice of the book. Mati Warner and Lorna Bulpin also gave feedback at the first draft stage. I learned many things from them, including that I knew so little about when to use a hyphen. Stephen Bland copyedited the book and gave a line-by-line critique. Few people are more British than Stephen, and I know that the use of US English must have been hard for him. Finally, I would like to thank Johannes Terblanche for help on the audiobook editing. Despite all of the above help on the book's editing, any remaining errors or mistakes are mine and mine alone. I will correct them in the second edition.

I have a theory that many first-generation immigrants to the USA have a clearer perspective on America than its longer-term residents. These recent immigrants are more likely to reflect on things that are different from their previous norm and, therefore, more likely to ask the simple question "why?"

Rather than burden you with solely my view on America, I interviewed thirty first-generation immigrants. I talked to them about the culture shock they experienced when they arrived, their own personal journey to becoming more American, and their understanding of the US now. I would like to thank Petter Andersson, Joseph Ashade, Lorna Bulpin, Marvin Campbell, Sam Garmon, Paul Jenkins, Antonia Johnston, Agnes Krischik, Irene Kulyk, Ana Tavares Lattibeaudiere, Luda McQuillin, Laurence Mourasse, Shankar Nair, Alicia Paterson, Nuno Goncalves Pedro, Ben Soppitt, Johannes Terblanche, David Walsh, and ten others who, shrewdly, preferred to retain their anonymity.

I also interviewed my own daughters extensively on their perspectives of growing up in America. Some readers may feel I have occasionally been insolent towards them. This is a British thing; I do love them and think that they are great. In any case, as university students and Snapchat advocates, they are unlikely to read something as long as a book.

Contents

Introduction

I've written this book as an antidote to the volume of negativity recorded about America in recent years. While much criticism is a fair comment intended to help the USA improve, some is undoubtedly polemic based on partisanship, jealousy, and ignorance. This book describes why many other immigrants and I love America. This isn't to say we believe everything in the USA is perfect. Just like any other country, many aspects are still works-in-progress. In particular, America has not yet resolved its iniquitous history with Native Americans and slavery. My view is that America's story is still substantially net positive for humankind. At the USA's core is the primacy of individual rights. The USA remains the only country specifically designed to protect the rights of each of its citizens and the only country where the government's purpose is to guarantee these individual rights rather than tell citizens what they must do.

By most metrics, the USA has been very successful. Since independence, its population has grown from 2.5 million to 331 million. It has achieved this mainly by welcoming immigrants from other countries and encouraging them and their children to flourish. America dominates global trade, with 24 percent of the world's economic output from only 4 percent of its population. The market value of the US's largest company is greater than the biggest one-hundred UK companies combined. America is also home to most of the world's top universities. It has pioneered diverse technologies, from the car, plane, and spaceship to inventions in electricity, photography, medical science, and computing. To the chagrin of some but the delight of many, America successfully exports its culture worldwide. Its movies, TV, and music are ubiquitous, its literature dominates both literary prizes and airport bookstands, and its technology solutions and social platforms are predominant in every free market.

This book attempts to explain where, why, and how the USA has been so successful. Even though we are in the throes of an election campaign as I write these words, this book deliberately does not focus on the machinations of modern-day politics. That is a different book for that rare person who is not already satiated by media coverage of this madness.

This is a story of two American journeys. The first is of how America came to be where it is today. The second is the story of my own family's American journey, told mainly through a coast-to-coast road trip we made during the summer of 2020. We witnessed some of America's beauty and reflected on the characteristics and culture of its diverse people. Obviously, this book reflects our own specific experience as immigrants. This may contrast with experiences of different immigrants to different parts of America, which are, of course, equally valid. I look forward to reading these other stories and perspectives.

Julian Bishop, October 2020

Chapter 1 – A Paddle up the Chattahoochee

It had been an unexpected two months. In early March, we had retreated from a Covid-rampant European vacation to our then relatively Covid-free American home. Later that month, I had been laid off from my work into a probable premature retirement, and we had spent the last two months in relative isolation in our suburban Atlanta home.

Although the isolation was irritating, we knew we were lucky. People in New York City or cities in Italy, Spain, or the UK had died in large numbers. In particular, we were glad we did not live in a care home. As with many other countries, some US care homes seemed to have installed "Heroes Work Here" signs before they got round to restricting visitor access or introducing health protocols for their staff. A good friend who has ALS was confined to his care home. He had been inspirationally optimistic since his diagnosis in 2017, but this total isolation had hit him hard. Although he was intellectually as sharp as ever, he was now quarantined in his suite indefinitely with no visits of any type allowed.

Daughter #1's college campus had closed, and her classes had moved online. She chose to remain in her apartment with her roommates. Daughter #2 would be attending the same university in August. She notionally still lived with us, but, as with most US teenagers, had her own car and was seldom at home. The shelter-in-place order – which they call lockdown in Europe – had been incredibly hard on the highly social. She was taking the lockdown the hardest. Some of her teenage behavior had deteriorated, but when we raised it with her, she said, "What are you gonna do? Ground me?"

Our US citizenship application had stalled when the country went into lockdown, just as we reached the final hurdle. As the country exited lockdown, the forthcoming presidential election seemed likely to delay approval further. We had applied for US citizenship at a time when a record number of US citizens were terminating their relationship with the country.

I knew I had become a little more American. I wore Hawaiian shirts but had not yet succumbed to slip-on shoes or sweat pants. I was also happy to tip an extra 20 percent to ensure servers had a living wage. I was still not clear on what being an American meant. One would meet someone from, say, New York, and they would tell you they weren't really American; they were a New Yorker. You could have similar discussions with somebody from San Francisco, LA, Chicago, DC, or some random person in the Mid-West. Maybe, the average American was just this one guy with a baseball cap in Peoria, with everyone else multiple standard deviations away.

To me, the core of being an American is a strong belief in personal freedom, excessive trust in democracy, intimate knowledge of the Constitution, and biblical respect for Washington, Hamilton, and Jefferson. Americans are hardworking, optimistic, and compassionate. Sure, I can tick most of these boxes.

Incidentally, no issue is more contentious amongst Americans than constitutional politics. If you think the left and right disagree on, say healthcare, it's nothing compared with constitutional disagreements. At times, it seems impossible for four or more educated Americans to congregate without some fundamental disagreements on the finer points of the Constitution's meaning. I know several people who carry around with them – like a bible – a small booklet which sets out the Constitution and its amendments. Indeed, I have been given these booklets by friends who believe I should be more educated. Ask yourself how common it is for you to meet someone in the UK who happens to be carrying around a facsimile of the Magna Carta just in case they need to refer to it.

Like all people moving to a new country, we knew we had to do all the changing if we wanted to fit in. Your new country won't change one iota for you. We had changed, and overall, we liked these changes.

We had done hundreds of simple things differently. We had learned to pronounce the words water, butter, or Atlanta with a soft "t." You tired of the waitress not understanding what beverage you wanted, the shop assistant not appreciating what you wished to spread on your bread, or a fellow Atlantan not knowing where you lived when you said you lived in Atlanta rather than a-lan-a. We also had thousands of new words to learn and even more changes in spelling.

By now, you will have noticed that I have decided to use American English for the UK version of this book. The eagle-eyed amongst you would have feared this at the acknowledgments. Shouldn't that have an extra "e" in it? Your heart probably sank when you saw the u-less behavior and the word beverage, where surely drink would have sufficed.

As readers with an interest in America, I hope you won't mind. Of course, deep down, I know you do mind. We British invented the language. Everyone should use our version.

This is the way I see it, though. I figure that you are reading a book about the USA because you have some interest in America. I suspect you have read many American novels before and gotten used to the (incorrect) spelling after only a few pages. And, yes, I am aware that gotten has just annoyed you.

It has taken me a while to adapt to US English and US grammar. For the first few years, I resisted the change. I was able to stick with British English because I worked for a company that mandated UK English in its formal communications, but a boss – let's call him American Boss #3 – preferred me to use American English.

Now that I am committing to the USA, I need to practice writing in American English. I want to make it clear that my choice in using American English is related to this need for practice and not because I'm too lazy to change my default spell checker. From time to time, I will use the UK English word rather than the US one if I don't think you will understand what I'm saying. You might think the two versions would be relatively similar, but almost every page has at least one change.

As I'm sure you know, neither spelling version is incorrect. The two versions have just developed differently. Much of this development happened before any spelling codification existed on either side of the Atlantic.

I am going to take a big detour away from our journey for a couple of pages to explore some of the differences. British English spelling rules were created by Samuel Johnson in his 1755 British dictionary. He and his team were assiduous in choosing the most closely correlated spelling with that word's source. Noah Webster, the author of the first and still the most famous American dictionary, opted for the simplest spelling in use at the time. However, he also decided to simplify the spelling of many words in his 1828 dictionary so that their spelling reflected the way they sounded.

Accordingly, most UK English spellings that have been absorbed from other languages keep the spelling of that original language. Words ending with "–our" in UK English are spelled "–or" in American English. In the original Latin, they were ubiquitously "–or." but the French added a "u" to some but not all. All American words of this type end in "–or," except the inevitable exceptions of contour, paramour, troubadour, and velour, which retain the "u" in American English. This isn't a big deal, though, as you are particularly unlikely to use any of these words in normal day-to-day writing. Americans also sometimes use a "u" for glamour because this comes from a Gaelic rather than a French word. Finally, the Space Shuttle Endeavour had a "u" in it because this was the spelling for Captain Cook's ship.

In former, more consistent times, British English used to spell a range of words like ambassador, chancellor, emperor, error, governor, inferior, mirror, superior, terror, and tremor with a "u." Nobody knows why the London train station is called Honor Oak, other than this was how Shakespeare spelled it. Shakespeare, who spelled his own name in multiple different ways, used "–or" and "–our" almost interchangeably until they were standardized by later generations to "–our" in the Fourth Folio. On the other side of the Atlantic, Honor was spelled honour in the original Jefferson draft of the Declaration of Independence before someone did a spell check.

Then it gets complicated. Both British and American English spell honorary, honorific, humorist, humorous, invigorate, rigorous, and vigorous the same way without the "u." If these words were spelled with a "u," they would just look weird. However, honorable has the "u" in British English.

For French-originating words ending in "–re," Americans swap the final two letters as in center while the British always keep the French spelling. Except, of course, when they don't in multiple months of the year, chapter, enter, letter, member, minister, monster, number, offer, oyster, powder, proper, sober, and tender. Americans don't like either meter or metre, preferring "about three feet" instead.

Words ending "–ogue" are changed to "–og" in American, for example, monolog, except when they aren't (like demagogue, pedagogue, and synagogue). Greek and Latin words like anaesthesia or paediatric are simplified to anesthesia or pediatric. I think this is a pity because it looks pretty having multiple vowels so close together. As I write this paragraph, I am thinking that the audiobook version of this section will be quite challenging.

British English words ending with "–ise" or "–yse" are spelled "–ize" or "-yze" in America, even though "-ize" is much the older. There is a whole chunk of American English words that end "–ise" too (advertise, chastise, and circumcise, to name but three).

British English has "–ce" for nouns and "–se" for verbs. American English also uses advice/advise and device/devise, but license and practice as both the noun and the verb. This could confuse a stupid person. Don't take offense or go on the defense in British English, but in both versions, you must be defensive and offensive.

American English typically doesn't double its consonants, especially when traveling or quarreling. In British English, it might be libellous or marvellous not to use the double ll, but it would be perilous or scandalous to use the single l. When in doubt, American English always prefers the single l unless they enroll, distill, instill, or enthrall.

In Britain, you apparently make a formal inquiry but enquire in general conversation. In the USA, you merely inquire unless it's the tabloid National Enquirer. Even though the Americans invented it in the twentieth century, it's an aeroplane in Britain and an airplane in the USA. Don't get me started on aluminum. You could ask Humphrey Davey, who discovered it. He called it alumium. Canadians call it aluminum like the Americans, except the metal's trade association, The Aluminium Association of Canada.

I prefer getting into a furore because you get to pronounce the final "e" like an Italian, but Americans just get into a furor. Where's the fun in that? I do not enjoy having jumped headfirst into a swimming pool in America, lest anybody says that he has just dove in.

It's a kerb in the UK, but a curb in America. You may be skeptical about all of these differences, but only in America. In the UK, you would be merely sceptical. There are literally thousands of differences, and, yes, that is an unusually correct usage of the word literally.

Indubitably, American English is now more popular than British English. One analysis of fifteen million digitized books published between 1800 and 2010 and another analysis of thirty million geotagged tweets show that American English vocabulary and spelling are becoming increasingly dominant. The word "center," for example, overtook its British alternative spelling in 1913. This is probably caused by a mixture of the dominance of US entertainment and the more recent spell checker, which is defaulted to American English in most countries. It isn't a one-way street, though. Americans are also influenced by British creators, whether Downton, Potter, or Sherlock. With so many British actors and late-night chat show hosts, it is inevitable some Anglocreep infiltrates into American English.

Punctuation can be different too. America doesn't have full stops, just periods. It prefers the double quotation marks for speech, which I swear was the original way I was taught in the UK. They also like the Oxford comma, called by some the Harvard comma, which you insert when you have a list of stuff before the final "and" or "or."

Most English-speaking Commonwealth countries elect for British spelling. New Zealand is identical apart from the word fjord, where Britain takes the Norwegian spelling and New Zealand – which actually has these geological features – spells as fiords. More American spellings have crept into the Australian language lately, but it's generally the British version that is used. Canada takes some British and some American spelling depending on their mood.

I never understood George Bernard Shaw's "The British and Americans are divided by a common language." I prefer Andrew Jackson's belief: "it is a damn poor mind indeed which can't think of at least two ways to spell any word."

Try as I might otherwise, I will naturally write with English syntax rather than in an American way. In my view, the average educated American writes well. Sentences are as simple as possible. I recall reading American literature for the first time at school. It dealt with themes that were complex but in language that was easy to read. Digital analysis of books through the ages shows that American sentences are, on average, one word shorter than seventy-five years ago.

Americans devote considerable time at school to writing. My children spent their formative years in the UK education system and were surprised to find that much of their English classes in the USA were spent on grammar and sentence construction. Daughter #1 learned long descriptive prose in the UK and how to communicate effectively in the USA. My children know about subordinating conjunctions, parallel construction, and implicit transitions. Whether this is helpful or not, I don't know. However, they both write well.

It isn't just spelling that is different; sometimes, it's the words too.

There is one mistake you make just once as a Brit in America. You order a meal with chips and are truly disappointed when your meal arrives with a packet of crisps. My wife, Lorna, once told a fifteen-minute shaggy dog story joke to some Americans, the punchline of which had something to do with crazy paving. Unfortunately, the joke did not work well with the target audience when what they heard was deranged sidewalks.

All immigrants have their favorite wrong word story. A friend's son asked his female teacher whether he could have a rubber when he meant eraser. Another friend with an Eastern European accent avoids using the word pennies, which is what they sometimes call cents here.

Some environments are challenging for a British English speaker. Certain American places fill me with fear, notably the hardware store or car repair shop, where it seems that almost half the words are different in these environments.

When I go to Home Depot, it should be familiar. Their logo has a similar orange shade to B&Q, and the store's layout is suspiciously similar. Home Depot has the same peculiar set trolleys to carry your purchases, and the store assistants are all grandparents, if not great-grandparents. What fills me with anxiety is that I will not know the American word for something I want to purchase in the heat of the moment.

Taps here are called faucets, wood is lumber, and rawl plugs are unknown here because they are called anchors. Plugs that go in your (bath)(tub) are called stoppers, while electrical plugs on your wall are called outlets. Spanners are wrenches, and drawing pins are thumbtacks. Cutlery is silverware, even if made from plastic. Rubbish bins are trash cans, glue is adhesive, and I can no longer remember what the British word is for caulk, but it's the stuff you put into a wall if you have made a hole. Outside, it's no better: a garden is a yard, a torch is a flashlight, and a barbecue is called a grill here, especially those made by George Foreman.

I have often found myself burbling to some senior associate, who should be at home in an armchair, desperately trying to describe what I want.

It is even worse in a car repair shop because you always have a sneaky feeling you are about to be fleeced. There are all the obvious ones that I use automatically now, such as bonnet vs. hood, boot vs. trunk, wing vs. fender, and windscreen vs. windshield. I also have down pat the different names for types of cars: saloon vs. sedan; and estate vs. station wagon. Will I remember that an exhaust is called a tailpipe, and a silencer a muffler? That they call indicators, turn signals, or blinkers? Brake lights are tail lights and reversing lights backup lights. It's a parking brake, not a handbrake, and a tachometer, not a rev counter. I know I will get lost in the mechanics of the engine. I barely understand what these words are in British English. It's a transmission, not a gearbox. It's a lug nut, not a wheel nut; this might confuse a petrol head, whom they call gearheads here. However, it does make sense that crocodile clips in America should be called alligator clips.

All of this is why I send Lorna to the car repair shop.

I could go on, but do you want me to? In any case, my American spell checker has squiggly lines under so much of this section. English – whether the British or American version – is a difficult language.

I will also use imperial measurements throughout, but with their metric equivalents in parentheses where necessary. Incidentally, Americans only use brackets to describe those [square-cornered things]. As a Brit of a certain age, I'm well versed with both the imperial and metric systems. I'm from the generation that measures low temperatures in Celsius and high ones in Fahrenheit.

The USA is now one of only three countries that use the Imperial System. At least in this area, they have chosen not to dumb down to something more straightforward and more logical. As you aren't likely to visit the other two countries – Liberia and Burma – let's preserve this quaint vestige from the past.

We were at an inflection point, or should I say inflexion point? As empty-nesters, we could live anywhere in the world we wanted. As unemployed or retired, I could do anything or nothing. I was in a reflective mood.

Georgia, the state we live in, had been the first state to come out of lockdown at the end of April 2020. You were allowed to play tennis and golf with some alterations. You were allowed to see movies in a movie theater, even though no new films had been released. More bizarrely, it was now OK to go bowling and get a new tattoo. Many – even memorably the president – said that Georgia had eased restrictions too early because the infection rate had not yet subsided sufficiently.

As its name suggests, the United States of America remains one united collection of fifty individual states rather than one big country. It is somewhat analogous to the European Union and the countries that make up that union but with explicit restrictions on the governance areas that the EU can control.

The original thirteen colonies, which became the first thirteen states, were highly distrustful of a strong central government. They had seen tyranny from the King of England and did not want this repeated in their brand-new country. The thirteen colonies wanted states to have the most power, with a limited role for federal, or central, government.

These principles were written into the Constitution. The first ten amendments, collectively known as the Bill of Rights, were designed to protect the rights of individuals. These rights were intended as a prerequisite for constitutional ratification and described what the government would never be able to do. The US Constitution itemizes the exclusive and limited powers of the Federal Government. Essentially, the Federal Government has responsibility for the national economy, national security, and foreign policy. It also has shared responsibility with the states for a few activities, for instance, taxation. The Constitution also lists activities that are reserved for each state. For example, states have autonomy for providing schooling and education, policing and safety, conducting elections, health, and welfare. Significantly – and for the avoidance of future doubt – the Tenth Amendment clarifies that any other area not explicitly covered by the Constitution is deemed the individual states' responsibility rather than a federal responsibility. As you can see, the Founding Fathers were pretty determined to restrict the Federal Government's future powers.

In addition to the US Constitution, each state has its own written constitution. These state constitutions cannot conflict with the US Constitution. As states have most powers, these state constitutions are on average five times longer than the US Constitution, with Alabama's Constitution a whopping forty times longer. In practice, many of the states' responsibilities are further devolved to individual cities or counties.

The average US resident has much more contact with their state and local government than with the Federal Government. Schools, police, driving, and marriage are all governed locally. Almost all criminal cases are heard by county or state courts rather than federal courts. This is why attorneys are registered in individual states and are only allowed to practice in states where they have a registration. Moreover, states still rule over a wide array of important matters like the death penalty, assisted suicide, and sanctuary cities. When you see states with different laws, this was always what was envisaged by the Founding Fathers. It is analogous to the UK having a separate policy to, say, France.

These fundamental principles of states' responsibilities have been bones of contention since the Constitution was signed. In the late eighteenth century, the Federalist Party, which favored a more substantial central government, pushed for stronger federal power. The Democratic-Republican Party – yes, they were once one party – led by Thomas Jefferson, wanted a decentralized government with greater powers to the states in order to protect individual rights. Jefferson definitively won this argument.

Federal powers have increased since this time, often through the force of presidential personality. From time to time, the Federal Government encourages states to follow specific federal guidelines by threatening to withhold federal grants. This has happened most recently, for example, when establishing a minimum age of twenty-one for purchasing alcohol or temporarily restricting the maximum speed to 55 mph, around 89 kph, in the 1970s.

This devolution is tremendous for democratic accountability, avoidance of tyranny, and the prevention of excessive centralization. It's less successful, perhaps, in the unusual event of a pandemic.

Federal Government can make recommendations to states, and federal agencies like the Centre for Disease Control (CDC) can issue guidelines. However, political decisions rest at the state level. During this pandemic, it was therefore inevitable that individual states would make different decisions. Some locked down their state tightly to eliminate or contain the virus, while others opened up quickly to allow people to get on with their everyday business.

Like many others, I had grown bored of near isolation. The routine of the morning run, walking the dogs twice a day, and online lunches with friends around the world had become stale for me. This wasn't the retirement I had envisaged. Lorna had barely been outside, other than meals on our lake-view deck.

To take advantage of some opening up, we bought a kayak to explore the rivers and lakes near our house. About a mile from our house, the Chattahoochee River flows from the Blue Ridge Mountains (Jacks Knob if you like your innuendos) to join the Flint River, which then runs its course into The Gulf of Mexico.

Although Georgia, named after George II, sounds very English, many place names in Georgia are distinctly Native American. This is due to Georgia's rich Native American history. Chattahoochee is apparently a Muskogee Creek word meaning painted rock. Locals now call the river "the Hooch," and – fueled, appropriately enough, by vast amounts of alcohol – hundreds drift downstream in large inflated tractor tires on a typical summer's day. Until 1980, the Hooch's annual raft race was the world's largest participative sporting event, attracting three-hundred-thousand inebriated rafters. Unfortunately, a drowning in 1980 and the challenge of policing such an event caused its cancelation.

As an aside, I will use individual Native American nation names where possible throughout the book. Where a more encompassing description is required, I will typically use the term Native Americans because that is the most common collective name for this group of native nations. I will occasionally also use the term First People, for variety and because some Native Americans I know prefer this term.

Actually, no consensus on what this group should be called exists today. The many federal acts refer to Indian peoples, and some elders are also used to this description. However, the term Indian is now held to be both offensive by some as well as confusing because it also refers to people who come from the country just below Pakistan. A few people believe there should be no collective noun for the indigenous American peoples and advocate that we refer to each individual nation as a separate ethnic group. They argue that using one collective noun implies the existence of a homogeneous culture between all native nations. Western culture may have presented natives in a monocultural manner, but their languages, ethnicities, and cultures vary greatly. While this is true, it's a little impractical to have no collective noun, as there are 567 federally recognized Native American nations across the USA.

Native American languages are influential throughout much of the USA. Just more than half the fifty US states have names based on Native American origins. It is perhaps, if you are particularly bored, a fun game to guess which ones.

Eleven native tribes existed in Georgia before independence. These tribes were embroiled in multiple wars and fought on both sides during the French Indian Wars of the mid-eighteenth century. Their territories were confirmed initially by Britain and subsequently the USA, but the white settlers largely ignored these agreements. After US independence from Britain, a series of conflicts with the Cherokee erupted when the new Americans decided they wanted Cherokee territory. In 1813-14, the Creek from western Georgia and Alabama was defeated by American forces led by General Andrew Jackson. The Creek ceded their lands in Georgia to the USA in 1825.

In 1830, now President Andrew Jackson signed the Indian Removal Act. This enabled the government to negotiate fair treaties with Native American tribes. In practice, the government forced the native nations to vacate their lands in nothing like a fair negotiation. Not that fair negotiation was necessarily relevant; historians estimated that the US Government made four hundred separate treaties with Native American tribes and broke every single treaty.

In the 1830s – somewhat as a response to the 1829 Gold Rush on Cherokee Land and partly because the southern tribes occupied prime agricultural land – one of the most shameful periods in US history occurred. The five "civilized" tribes of Seminole, Cherokee, Chickasaw, Choctaw, and Creek Indians were forcibly moved from their specially designated lands to the west of the Mississippi. It's estimated that one hundred thousand Native Americans were forcibly moved from Georgia and surrounding states in the 1830s. They were marched on a five-thousand-mile trail, sometimes in chains, to new lands in what is now Oklahoma. This journey was known as the Trail of Tears. You can walk this National Historic Trail today, though I would not recommend doing so in chains. In 1907, Oklahoma became a state, and the new homeland for these Native Americans was gone for good.

Back in the kayak, which coincidentally comes from an Inuit word, we explored familiar sections of the river. We had started near a branch of the National Park System and were the only people on this stretch of water. There were no buildings, no manmade installations, and no evidence of humans. The footprints on the muddy shore were all from other mammals. We saw recent evidence of deer, coyotes, raccoons, and bobcats. Snapping turtles took their first sunbathe of the year on the boughs of the trees. The Chattahoochee birds – chickadees, woodpeckers, and tufted titmice – had become used to having no people around. The cliffs on the other side of the river, often the habitat of diving teenagers, showed no recent sign of human activity.

After two months inside, the freedom to explore was liberating. We talked about whether we wanted to kayak the whole length of the 542-mile river to the Gulf of Mexico. It's navigable, but you have to portage your canoe out of the water at multiple dams and navigate the whitewater course further south.

American poet James Harrison once said: "you can't be unhappy in the middle of a big, beautiful river," unless, of course, a hippo or crocodile has just overturned your boat. We were ecstatically happy, as this stretch of water contained neither of these animals. We paddled a few miles upriver to a recreational area and were astonished to see about a hundred college-aged kids partying in the shallow waters around a river island. The noise was as loud as a party of American tourists at the Sistine Chapel and was alien to our ears. These kids, who had been sent home from their universities in March, had reverted to what they enjoyed most, pre-gaming.

I hope you will indulge in another digression here, for I want to explain what pre-gaming is. It's not as my British editor thought, "a world before we were all addicted to our screens", but rather a term used to describe a university student party.

At university – or as they usually call it here, college – social life for almost all is founded around college football. In the South, high school football, the game played by seventeen and eighteen-year-olds, attracts crowds of many thousands. Professional NFL Football is tolerated, particularly in that rarest of seasons where the Atlanta Falcons win more than they lose. However, by far the most popular sport in the South is college football. In the past few decades, the strongest Division I college football teams hail from the Southern states. Daughter #1 and Daughter #2 attend one of the oldest Southern universities, and these Southern universities attract the best high school American Football talent from across the nation. Three years later, the best of the college talent then joins the professional NFL leagues.

It's difficult to explain how it's more popular to watch Liverpool Reserves than Liverpool, but somehow this is how it is. Fundamentally, the bonds between the alumni and their colleges are generally more robust than those between citizens and their city. There are other reasons too. Many Americans now have a negative view of the excesses of the prima donna professional sportsmen in the NFL. The athletes in college football are merely prime donne in training.

During the football season, Saturday is focused on college football. TV networks cover every game from the minute you wake up to the end of the day. Colleges give full access to these TV networks, so there is a lot of content. Sunday then brings the game's professional form, but in a slightly lower-key way.

Many colleges have seats for over one hundred thousand spectators, more than any European sports stadia, but college football is expensive to attend. For a competitive game, a non-prime ticket will cost around $250, but it's going to be tough to get hold of. Someone I used to work with had large student debts but still felt he had to donate many thousands of dollars per year to his alma mater to buy face-value tickets for home games. Neither daughter is a big fan of the game, but they love the pre-gaming and tailgating experience surrounding the football. Saturday during season will likely always be centered on their college's game, and their mood forever dependent on whether their team has won.

Accordingly, there is a lot of money in college football, but not necessarily for the athletes. College coaches, for instance, can be paid $10 million per annum. College athletes are theoretically amateur, but they play undeniably in professional environments. The best players are household names but are formally not paid. Notionally at least, they do receive a free education. In reality, most Division 1 college footballers are coaxed through the easiest and minimal number of classes on offer by a phalanx of study coaches. A friend was an educational coach for college athletes at his university. He told me that he learned patience while his pupils learned the value of 23. College footballers do work hard, though. They wake up at 5 a.m. and begin the day with a two-hour strength and conditioning workout. They then take their one class of the day and complete their homework with their personal tutor's help. In the afternoon, they practice and watch films of upcoming opponents. In the evening, they eat dinner together. They repeat this schedule every day except game days.

You might ask why this travel book tackles college football. If you recall, it's because I wanted to explain what pre-gaming was. Essentially, pre-gaming is the drinking and socializing that you do before you attend the main event. The importance of pre-gaming probably has its roots in high school, the educational establishment Americans attend between the ages of fourteen and eighteen. Friday is high school football night. School administrators hold pep rallies during the school day to encourage school spirit and celebrate their school's own participation in the sport. The pep rally is held in the school stadium, where the school band plays uplifting music, and cheerleaders lead chants and dances for the many thousands of students. The high school students themselves celebrate every game with a different form of fancy dress.

Children's sport is a big deal throughout the US. Parents give up evenings to coach elementary-level sport, like Little League baseball. At this level, participation and effort are the focus. However, all children's sport from about the age of eleven upwards is taken seriously here. College scholarships will be available to the best, and consequently, sport is unbelievably competitive. Children are expected to practice every weekday night, and, for many sports, parents will accompany them to another state to play a competitive match each weekend.

I love to watch high school football. Where we live, you can luxuriate in the milder heat of the dark fall evenings. The official match commentary over the public address system is supplemented by the observations from knowledgeable fathers, who wish they were still playing. The two-hundred musicians from the splendid school marching band try to motivate the hundred or so football players. Games are astonishingly well attended. The public schools near us attract between 5,000 to 10,000 student and parent spectators, substantially more than my English football team. Everything is bigger in Texas, of course. High schools regularly fill out their 20,000 capacity stadia, and the Texas State Championship game featuring these seventeen and eighteen-year-olds has been known to attract more than 50,000 spectators.

You can watch Georgia high school games on TV, too; they are filmed and screened live on local cable TV. But it's always better in person. You start attending games of your future high school when you are about twelve. These younger ones rarely watch the game and instead are given the freedom to play with their friends away from the stands and their parents. For the lucky ones, it will be the site of their first kiss. I love the crescendo of crowd noise as the home team tries to make the last yard on third down. I love the players' parents' tension as their son succeeds or fails in their on-field endeavors. I love participating in the crowd's reaction to the replays on the large video scoreboard.

Fathers love high school football. Some hold their male children back one year to give them a height and weight advantage when the sport becomes competitive. Full-ride scholarships, i.e. those which pay all college education costs, can be won for the best football players. However, mothers have become decidedly less keen on their sons playing football as they research the dangers of concussion from repeated shocks to the brain. The most dangerous sport for girls in the USA is cheerleading. Every year, around twenty thousand are admitted to emergency rooms from cheerleading accidents. Despite this danger, cheerleading is a booming sport. About three million people participate today compared with just over half a million in 1990. At the start of the twentieth century, cheerleading was originally an entirely male sport. In fact, girls were banned from participating until 1923 due to concerns they would develop loud voices and learn to curse. Of course, today, not all cheerleaders are girls, but 96 percent are. Incidentally, one of the few men to participate in this sport was President George W Bush, head cheerleader at his high school in Massachusetts.

At college, the football shifts up a gear. In addition to the 100,000 game attendees, a further 150,000 out-of-towners will also descend on that college town. Many come the evening before the game and they pre-game. Every bar, hotel, restaurant, and public space in every college town is packed.

Tailgating is a continuation of the pre-game experience and it starts on Saturday morning. In the college town where my children go to university, the city introduced rules so that you are no longer able to tailgate before 7 a.m. on a Saturday. At 7.01 a.m., you drop the tailgate of your truck – the vehicle of choice in the South – take out the cornhole boards, horseshoe set, and giant Jenga from the truck bed and let the alcohol flow.

The meaning of the word pre-game has been corrupted over time. It now refers to any circumstance where you are drinking and socializing. My multiple-fake-ID-owning daughters will talk about pre-gaming on an out-of-season Tuesday evening. No game will take place for many months, but they are still pre-gaming.

After that lengthy digression, we return to the college-aged students pre-gaming in the middle of the Chattahoochee River. In an environment where it should have been easy to keep the mandated six feet from others, they had chosen to do what they liked to do. There was absolutely no social distancing. At precisely this moment, I knew the second wave of Covid infections in America would be inevitable.

As a national trait, I believe Americans lack patience. They are culturally wired to get things done now, not at some point in the future. I have worked with international teams for most of my work life. The US teams invariably start work immediately and, at a later point, have to think through the tricky elements of the problem. German or French teams plan more meticulously. These European teams anticipate and debate challenges; consequently, they start the project later. In my experience, both teams take more or less the same amount of time to complete the project but they approach it differently.

I've heard people talk about a "discount rate" of what you have to be paid in the future to delay gratification now. If the discount rate is high, you have to be paid a lot to postpone your current consumption. If it is low, you value future consumption almost as much as you do current consumption.

The US's discount rate is high. You see this from the relatively low US savings ratio, where four out of every ten Americans don't have enough to cover an unplanned $400 expense; the one in five who take penalty payments on retirement accounts; and the $27 trillion national debt, more than $200,000 per household. You might also see many Americans' reluctance to take environmental action on climate change as part of this trend.

In the 1960s, Stanford researchers carried out the famous marshmallow experiment. Four-year-old American children were given a marshmallow and told they would get a further squishy, gelatin piece of corn starch in fifteen minutes if they didn't eat it. The experiment was repeated with pretzels and animal cookies in case there was something special about marshmallows. Many children ate the first marshmallow. They followed up the same children a decade or so later and found that those who waited the longest had better school scores and lower body mass indexes.

According to a Gallup survey, 96 percent of Americans have knowingly consumed hot food and drink even though they know it will burn their mouth. 63 percent have done this frequently. Amazon and Walmart know that four out of ten customers will pay an average of $10 extra for same-day delivery. Half of all callers will hang up the phone if they have to wait for longer than 60 seconds for service. Internet users are even more impatient and will typically only wait two seconds for something to download. With the USA architecting so much of the developed world's technology, we would expect this impatience to be exported to a country near you soon.

So, how does this impatience relate to Covid? For many Americans, there seems to be nothing worse than being a bit bored. A minority of Americans have shown the same resolve in avoiding Covid as that of a child who has just spotted an ice-cream truck. Obviously, this is a generalization; some Americans have shown great determination in the same way that some children have been known to delay their ice cream treat until they are next in Walmart.

A British friend in the media industry, who has lived in the USA for more than thirty years, has an interesting take on American impatience. He believes US TV has wired Americans' brains to demand regular entertainment every five minutes. His theory is that, from the 1970s, advertisers demanded that American children's shows be interspersed with frequent breaks for their ads. Mini peaks of excitement and five-second cuts became the norm for 1970's American children. In the UK, my generation grew up with the Trumptonshire trilogy, with its long, continuous shots of nothing much at all. This prepared us to be more patient. If this theory is correct, future generations from anywhere on the planet will be less patient.

Back at home, we reflected on what we had seen. We are privileged to live in a great neighborhood. This isn't unusual in the Atlanta suburbs, where the standard of living is high. We have two great wooden decks with views over the lake. During the day, we enjoy the sunshine and occasional thunderstorm. At night, the summer heat still envelopes us, and the sounds of insects, amphibians, and birds are deafening. When we lived in Surrey, we lived relatively near a main road, and Lorna complained incessantly about the road noise. In Georgia, we have next to no road noise, but the cacophony from the insect population is much louder than the UK road noise.

Crickets and katydids rub the edge of their wings together in a sound called stridulation. The noise is produced only by males as part of the mating ritual. There are apparently four different types of chirp. The first is a sound that is made to attract any nearby female. The second a call to court the female. The third a cry to ward off other males. The fourth sound celebrates successful mating.

Provided it's between 55°F (13°C) and 100°F (38°C), you can calculate the temperature by counting the frequency of the chirps via the two equations overleaf. I tried this trick the other night and was surprised to learn that it worked.

$$F = c_{14} + 40 \qquad (1)$$

Where F = temperature in Fahrenheit; c14 = number of chirps in a 14 second period

$$C = \frac{1}{3}c_{25} + 4 \qquad (2)$$

Where C = temperature in Centigrade; c_{25} *= number of chirps in a 25 second period*

Like other insects, crickets are cold-blooded. As the outside temperature rises, so does the temperature of their blood. This changes the chemical reactions in the muscles, which increases the frequency of their stridulation.

Cicadas and Grasshoppers chirp during the day. Cicadas sing by contracting and relaxing the tymbal muscles in their abdomen. They chirp as both a mating ritual and to scare off birds, whose navigation system is altered by the loud noise. The noise is loud too, up to 120 Decibels for a large cicada. Indeed, it is so loud that cicadas have a tympan membrane that closes off sound to their ears, so they do not deafen themselves.

We have regular birds that visit our back yard. A large single blue heron sits on the lakeside surveying the water for food until our dogs – let's call them Dog #1 and Dog #2 – chase or bark at it. It then flies majestically over the lake, the end of its wings brushing gently into the water. Canadian Geese, migratory elsewhere but permanent residents in Georgia, form large flocks that occupy multiple habitats in the lakes and waterways close to our house. Large numbers of male cardinals with bright red plumage play in the trees with their plainer and browner female mates. However, my favorite birds are the pair of hummingbirds who visit us on the deck every summer before flying south to winter in Central America. These tiny birds, weighing about a penny, hover around our hummingbird feeder for most of the summer. They migrate by instinct, with the zeitgeber occurring on the same day in mid-October when their bodies release hormones when the hours of sunlight fall below a certain level. These tiny birds fly five hundred miles a day until they get to their destination. They will return to the same feeder on our deck next summer, using the sun as their compass and the earth's magnetic fields to guide them home.

In addition to our deck, our neighborhood has many other facilities: a large swimming pool with water slides, gym, fishing lakes, playground, basketball court, and floodlit tennis courts, to name a few. In short, we live in the type of place where you might take a vacation. It's not enough, however, for us. We like variety and like to explore new things. We had already canceled two vacations: a tour of the national parks of Utah; and a European trip to the UK, France, Italy, and Spain. We felt we wanted a change of scenery.

I had read voraciously about the SARS-CoV-2 virus, maybe too much. I had the time, so I took an online training course on contact tracing. All of my earlier optimism had been misplaced; almost everything I had assumed had turned out much worse than I had initially predicted.

From this reading, it seemed to me that there were only two ways to manage the spread of infection. First, a state could develop a comprehensive Test and Tracing program where every new case was identified and each contagious person prevented from transmitting it to others. Second, a state could lock everyone down for months. I didn't see any evidence the USA was culturally able to do either of these measures.

The pandemic would get much worse from what I could deduce rather than better until a vaccine was in place or herd immunity was achieved. When the weather got colder, people would spend more time indoors, and the infection rate would increase. The economy would worsen, forcing people to go to work, and interest in social distancing would wane.

My analysis then was that we would be living with Covid for the long haul, or at least until a vaccine was approved and given to at least two-thirds of the population. Assuming a vaccine was feasible by the end of 2020, it would take a year to administer. This meant that we would have to live in a Covid-restricted world until at least 2022 at the earliest.

I doubted my own ability to hunker down for almost two years. I wondered if it were possible to take a Pan-American trip at this time of Covid. My calculation at that time was we would have a short period of freedom before states locked down again. If all went well, we might have an opportunity to complete a lifetime ambition.

Chapter 2 – A Bucket List Journey

In a Gallup survey of many countries, Americans come top in the belief that individuals are responsible for their own success. In this way, at least, I am definitely American. I believe that it is me who architects the life that I want to lead. I prefer to live with some intention and don't like life to meander for any lengthy period. Ultimately, I think that the daily decisions we make will determine the pattern of our lives. However, this is not a self-help book. I know not everyone is built the same way or decides to live their life with the same structure. I am aware that many others prefer to take life as it comes. They prefer to be open to any opportunities that pass their way, or they like a life filled with reflection and low levels of anxiety.

However, unlike most Americans, I believe that we have only one shot at life. Most readers will be fortunate to live in societies that are essentially free. We have the freedom to choose to live how we want, go where we want, and do what we want. We just need to do the hard stuff of deciding what makes us happy and learn how to ignore comparisons with others with different goals.

I set long-term goals that I want to achieve, and – it's from these goals every January 1 – that I write a series of annual objectives. Every month during the year, I create a To-Do list of what I need to accomplish to achieve these annual objectives. I understand that the vast majority of people are not like that, but I am.

It won't surprise you, therefore, to learn that I am partial to a bucket list. Bucket lists are a collection of goals and aspirations that you would like to realize during your time on the planet. They are a list for living, not dying. There was a fairly poor Jack Nicholson film of that name a few years ago. Ironically, while I am a big filmgoer and have watched a hundred movies per year for the last forty years, this was one of only a handful of movies that I didn't finish.

According to Gallup, 95 percent of Americans have bucket lists, and two-thirds claim they check something off every year. People say that Americans are infrequent travelers, but the most popular American bucket list subject involves travel to different countries.

Some people don't like bucket lists. They believe that you will miss opportunities if you are busy ticking off things from a list, and they fear that your life will lack spontaneity. Some say, probably with reasonable justification, that many bucket list items are meaningless pursuits. They argue that people should instead look to change the world, transform someone's life, or find a meaningful job of work. Life isn't a To-Do list, and there is no finishing line.

I like a particular type of bucket list, one which provides purpose, focus, and direction. It shouldn't be impossible, but nor should it be too easy to achieve. I see others' bucket lists from time to time and see a task like "Visit Biltmore." To me, that is too easy to be a bucket list item. If you live on the East Coast, you can just start the car and drive to Vanderbilt's 1895 house. I like goals that encourage discovery and exploration, learning, and, when completed, have required a certain level of achievement.

I have a number of bucket lists. Fourteen, to be specific. I sometimes add to them and often amend them to make them more compelling. They are all non-trivial, focus on things that I love, and required some level of determination to complete. One of the things I wanted on my bucket list was to join the Mile High Club. Unfortunately, my wife told me she didn't give a flying fuck.

I've already completed many bucket lists. As I love cricket, I set myself a goal of watching cricket at every English county cricket ground with my dad. Now the most crucial part of this goal was the last three words: "with my dad." This bucket list was an excuse for me to spend time with my dad, who is in his eighties. Every year, I would fly to the UK and spend a week of focused time with my dad traveling the country and watching cricket in some beautiful green setting. It sounds like a pretty simple ambition to achieve, but it does require planning, particularly if you live on a different continent. We completed this bucket list in 2019 and were due to start in 2020 on a new cricket-related bucket list item before lockdown prevented it.

I have a number of travel-related bucket lists: travel across Russia via various routes of the Trans-Siberian Railway; or live for six months in cities we have loved. I also have a few betterment bucket lists. Despite his spelling inconsistencies, I plan to watch every Shakespeare play. If I don't set myself this target, it's doubtful that I will see any plays other than the obvious ones. I understand that all of these will be challenging to complete in 2020 or even 2021.

If I were now retired, this might be the perfect time to make inroads into one or more of my fourteen bucket lists. Realistically, I could only consider the items that were US-based. In the summer of 2020, there were too many uncertainties about traveling outside the USA. Many countries did not permit US visitors, and some countries were either in the middle of severe outbreaks or had stringent rules to prevent them. Additionally, we had children in the USA, and it might be challenging to return to the USA without quarantine. That excluded nine bucket lists.

Five bucket lists had significant US components. I wasn't optimistic that there would be any spectators in any of the Major League Baseball stadia, nor did I think that any of the World's top twenty-five film festivals would return in their standard format in 2020. Only three bucket lists remained: drive coast-to-coast across the USA, travel to every US state, and visit every US national park. Was it possible to construct some activity around these three bucket lists?

When I first started investigating, the answer was a resounding no. Most national parks were closed; many Northern states did not permit hotels to accept guests; and Montana had quarantine measures in place where visitors to the state had to quarantine for two weeks on arrival. As indicated earlier, my hope was that a short window of opportunity for this journey would present itself as states opened up from the first wave, but before the second wave hit. I was determined to drive across the USA, visiting some new states and new national parks as soon as it was possible.

People have wanted to travel across America since colonization. Since the Lower 48 states were incorporated into the USA, people have crossed it by all sorts of vehicles. A friend completed it on a bike with three other cyclists in 6 days and 15 hours. One, presumably raw and tender, solo cyclist took just 7 days and 16 hours for the three-thousand-mile ride. Others make the trip by Greyhound bus, foot, horse, and, of course, classically by car.

To the fury of the Twittersphere in early-April 2020, a group of three anonymous drivers took advantage of the lack of traffic on the roads, particularly police cars, to beat the world record for crossing the USA in the shortest amount of time. This journey is based on the Cannonball Baker Sea-to-Shining Sea Memorial Trophy Dash, popularized in two films of the 1980s. It starts at the Red Ball Garage in New York and ends at the Portofino Hotel in Redondo Beach, Los Angeles. This anonymous group completed the 2,816-mile journey driving a white Audi A8L in only 26 hours and 38 minutes, at an impressive average speed of 106mph. The car had two additional plastic fuel tanks in the trunk and used an array of GPS devices, radios, scanners, and local spotters to avoid police interception.

You can cross the USA horizontally or vertically. There is almost an infinite number of routes that can be selected. Classically, you can take the southern route from Savannah to Los Angeles via Texas; the middle way, say from Virginia Beach through the empty states of Kansas and Oklahoma; or the northern route from New York to Seattle, hugging the Canadian border.

Many years ago, I had mapped out a plan to cross the USA by Nissan Leaf. The Nissan Leaf is an electric car with a range of about ninety miles. On ordinary mains electricity, it takes about twenty hours to recharge the battery fully. I thought this slow form of travel might be an excellent way to see America up close. Not surprisingly, this plan was never enacted. Texas would have been endless.

The shortest and quickest route is from Savannah to LA. This wasn't immediately appealing to us, as we had traveled extensively in the South and had only recently been to Texas. Also, Texas, Arizona, and Southern California are extraordinarily hot in the summer months. That route is more of a winter journey. The middle way is a popular journey. It goes through many significant US cities and has both mountains and long stretches of endless roads. The upper route is the least traveled. It's long, difficult to traverse for much of the year, and passes through small-town America.

We also had to think about safety, both ours and that of others. We didn't want to get the virus and find ourselves in a hospital far from home, nor did we want to become super-spreaders. However, we had isolated completely and were confident that we didn't have the virus.

We wanted to be as careful as a nun taking birth-control pills, so I developed a series of "rules" for a long drive from coast-to-coast across the USA. First, we would only visit places that were mostly free from people. Second, we'd only eat outside. Third, we'd stay only in accommodation with proper cleaning protocols. Finally, as inside attractions were not open, we would plan our journey around outdoor activities.

The great news about the last rule was that it fitted well with our goal to visit every US national park. This challenge is more complicated than it sounds. Although we have already visited nineteen since we have been here, I am not sure that we will ever complete it. For one thing, there are sixty-two full national parks across the USA, with four new parks established since we arrived in the US. Second, many national parks are geographically challenging to reach. This makes it both time consuming and expensive.

The National Parks System is one of America's best ideas. It really does an excellent job of preserving America's geographic heritage. It now controls eighty-five million acres of national parks, about the size of seventeen Waleses, which I understand is the widely recognized international unit of measurement for countries. The UK has some fine national parks of its own, but America has twenty-one times more in area.

In 1927, more than 2.3 million people visited US national parks every year. The National Parks Administrators at that time predicted that this figure might eventually rise by 50 percent over the coming decades. This turned out to be a massive underestimate. As of 2015, some 300 million people annually visited America's national parks.

In addition to the 62 national parks, the National Park Service and some sister agencies also care for a wide variety of other places, including 37 Waleses of national forest, 29 Waleses of wildlife refuge, 21 Waleses of wilderness area, 134 historic sites, 115 national monuments, 28 lake, river and seashores, 25 battlefields, and 57 other entities. This represents outstanding value for your annual family membership of $80.

When you have visited all of the above, a further ten thousand other parks, protected by individual states rather than the federal government, are available for your exploration. These parks, about three Waleses in total, tend to have more amenities, so they attract more than 750 million visitors every year. Some state parks are every bit as awe-inspiring as the national parks, Niagara Falls, for example.

Towards the end of May 2020, some national parks announced that they would re-open in June. States that had shuttered their hotels would also allow them to function on a limited basis again. More importantly, the states that had introduced quarantine were now abandoning it.

As June arrived, social media began to feature daily pictures of people returning to life as usual. People were tired of sheltering in place, and they wanted to do the things they normally did in the summer. I was sure that this behavior would ultimately lead to a second wave and that travel across the USA would eventually become more, not less, challenging. I felt that it was now or never.

Eighteen-year-old Daughter #2, notionally at least, still lived at home with us. We decided that we would leave her to look after the dogs and the house in the month we would be gone. I cannot stress how unusual this was in our town. In the UK and Hong Kong, where we had previously lived, we had been amongst the most conservative parents with the strictest rules. In our part of Georgia, I believe most other parents saw us as dangerous liberals. The thing is that we hadn't changed our parenting approach; we had just moved countries. We could see that our local friends thought that we were mad to trust our daughter with the house. Wouldn't she just burn it down or have illicit parties? We thought the first unlikely, as we weren't sure she knew how to operate the hob, and the second inevitable.

It may not necessarily be true in other parts of the USA, but here in the South, parenting is conservative and strict. Our children went from the most polite in their UK peer group to the least polite in Georgia. Many children call their own fathers Sir and mothers Ma'am, and almost all called their elders by the same introduction. I don't particularly like a wide-power distance between children and their elders, but I do quite enjoy being called Sir by my children's many boyfriends. It makes me trust them more somehow, even though that is patently naïve.

At the heart of Southern culture is the church. They are of many denominations where we live. On our road of about twenty houses, we have three large churches. Indeed, there are few corners of major arteries without some sort of church building. Daughter #2 had experimented with the local Southern Baptist Church in her early teens. With more than seven-thousand churchgoers, the Baptist community had a campus filled with activities: a café, an activities center, and a gym and sports fields for basketball, baseball, softball, soccer, football, and dance.

Our laissez-faire liberal influence had probably won through in the end on our now purpled-haired daughter. As lockdown was easing, Daughter #2 had joined Black Lives Matters protests in the Atlanta area. She particularly enjoyed the overwhelming amount of compassion and intimacy amongst the marchers. This was a movement without prominent leaders or agreed specific goals. However, it did have strong support from young people and growing support more generally. According to opinion polls, two-thirds of Americans now believed that black people were treated less fairly than whites by the police and the criminal justice system. Each week seemed to bring a new example of police overreaction, and increasingly, these injustices were captured on video.

Many supporters of this movement were so unhappy that they wanted to defund the police. What this means varied by person. In most cases, this didn't mean a desire to get rid of the police entirely, but rather divert a portion of police funding and reallocate it to social services organizations. This probably has some merit, not only in the USA but also elsewhere. In a previous UK life, I had worked with South London police. As part of this work, I spent time with police officers, mainly at their police stations and, from time to time, on their beat and at their training. I was always astonished by their day-to-day police experience on the street. Almost all their time was spent responding to calls from people who struggled to manage their relationships with others, usually couples or neighbors arguing with each other. It wasn't crime as such, more dangerous social work.

In a small number of cases, countries and cities have chosen to dismantle their police structure and replace it with something more appropriate. They believed that it was impossible to effect change on the existing system. The country of Georgia, which borders Russia, used to have one of the most corrupt police forces on the planet. At the beginning of the twenty-first century, Georgian leaders fired all thirty-thousand police officers and hired an entirely new police force.

In New Jersey, the city of Camden ranked as one of the US's most dangerous cities for much of the noughties, copied this approach in 2013 after years of police corruption and scandal. Incredibly, partly due to strong unionization, the police department's total cost had run so far out of control that it was then greater than the city's total tax revenue. Each increase in police expenditure had no effect on crime; indeed, the key crime statistics kept deteriorating. In an unpopular policy at the time, Camden dissolved The Camden Police Department and replaced it with a newly formed Camden County Police Department. Around a hundred officers were eventually re-hired after a comprehensive recruitment process, but most officers were new. The new police department's budget was reduced by one-quarter, mostly from cutting the overgenerous union-negotiated contracts. Ultimately, however, the new force had twice the number of officers than the old one. The new police department changed how it policed. The key metrics moved away from ticket writing to community engagement. On recruits' first day, they were required to knock on the doors of their beat to introduce themselves and ask what needed improvement. Police hosted pop-up barbecues, Mister Softee trucks, and Drive-In Movies to get to know residents. Here's the thing. Camden crime dropped by half, and complaints against the police fell by a staggering 95 percent. This disbanding of the police force and dissolving the police union is now being explored by larger cities, like Minneapolis.

Of course, here lies the predicament. Standards of policing vary significantly by locality. Federal power is deliberately weak as policing is incontestably a state responsibility. However, this deliberate devolution of power to states – and then from states to cities – also enables cities like Camden to both experiment with and effect change in a way that could never happen on a countrywide basis.

A polarized America also created a smaller countermovement, Blue Lives Matters, which rejects defunding, advocates for greater protection for police officers, and argues that it is dangerous to withdraw support for police officers. This movement argues that when the police are not supported, police will inevitably become less assertive in how they do their job, and crime will eventually increase.

One specific area of focus for Black Lives Matters was a proposal to eliminate school police officers and replace these officers with additional school counselors. When we moved to the USA, it surprised us that each high school seemed to have its own police officer. Apparently, this was almost unknown in the 1970s. However, today around two-thirds of high schools, and 90 percent of all high schools with more than a thousand pupils, had a school resource officer (SRO), essentially a police officer employed by the local police force or Sheriff's office.

High schools in the USA tend to be quite large. Most in our school district are between two and four thousand students. The SRO's role is to create a safer school environment through education, crime prevention, and security. SROs are encouraged to develop close relationships with students and teachers. At the high school my children attended, the police officer, referred to always by his first name, seemed to achieve this, despite heated disagreements with some of his political beliefs. However, Daughter #1 tells me that when a classmate brought a knife to school to aid his Xanax-dealing business, the school called the actual police rather than rely on the SRO.

While we are on this subject, I am reminded that Daughter #2 experienced her own run-in with the law when she was eleven years old. She was sleeping over at a friend's house and, at 2 a.m., the girls had decided to visit the local 24-hour Pharmacy to purchase some candy. Crawling out of the kitchen window in silence, they made their way on a dark street about a mile to the relevant strip mall when they saw the unmistakable flashing-blue lights of a passing police car. They tried to scarper in different directions but were quickly captured. The girls were returned to their respective homes by the bemused police officers. We learned that night that a permanent midnight curfew was in place for children under eighteen in the thirty metros and counties around Atlanta.

The Black Lives Matters movement has had some success in removing school resource officers. Minneapolis, Seattle, Portland, Oakland, and Denver have agreed to remove police officers from schools. They argued that students of color are more likely to be excluded from school, and that – although studies have shown no correlation between SROs at schools with increased arrests – school officers contribute to the school to prison pipeline.

In 2018, the SRO's role came into sharp focus when it was alleged that the SRO had not intervened when an ex-pupil attacked a high school in Florida. The shooter killed seventeen and injured seventeen others. A month later, an SRO from a Maryland school successfully neutralized a school shooter.

Investigations into the Florida case showed the usual level of incompetence and misunderstanding these events tend to uncover. Dozens of calls to local police from people concerned about the shooter's behavior had been made over the previous two years. The SRO and others had previously recommended that the future school shooter be committed for a mental evaluation. The school had initially banned him from wearing a backpack before later banning him from the campus entirely. The local police department had failed to take any action before the shooting. On the day of the shooting, and contrary to their training, three policemen from the local police department refused to enter the school to confront the shooter. Many local police officers subsequently resigned or were fired. The FBI too came under attack for failing to pass on a clear warning they had received a month earlier.

This Florida case does not, in my view, make a strong case for or against school officers but instead gives an indication about the general competence of some local police forces.

To understand this, you have to appreciate that police agencies in the USA are structured fundamentally differently from what you may be used to elsewhere. You will recall that most policing responsibilities are held at a county or, more often, city level. There are, therefore, eighteen thousand separate US police agencies, employing around 1.2 million full-time officers. These vary from the very large (for example, the New York Police Department, which you have seen many times on TV) to local police departments that employ only one officer. Around 60 percent of police officers are employed by local police agencies; 24 percent by local Sheriffs' offices; and about 10 percent are federal agents. This localized structure means that standards and practices vary widely. Pay also varies enormously by agency, as does training.

US Police receive an average of 761 hours of basic training in classrooms, around 4 months in total. One-third of academies had an additional average of 453 hours of training, about 3 months, in the field. No US-wide standards for police officers exist, so this varies significantly by state. Some states have minimum standards, but these can be very minimum indeed. In Louisiana, for example, recruits receive only 360 hours of training, which is four times fewer than the 1,500 hours required to be a barber. In Europe, police training is typically measured in years, not hours.

My UK experience is that police probably have more or less the same level of bias as the population from which they are recruited. However, the nature of their job is that they regularly find themselves in situations where they have to act quickly, and it's in these situations where one's biases take over. To counter this, the police in all countries probably need to have a lot more training to combat their biases. This has just not been prioritized in the US police officers' training. A report from the Justice Department showed that basic training comprised only 11 hours of cultural diversity training, compared with, say, 111 hours for firearm and self-defense training. Another issue is that poor-performing officers, even those with histories of misconduct, move from one agency to another with low or no reference checking.

With all this seriousness, perhaps we have time for one short joke?
Why do police get to riots early? To beat the crowd.

In sharpest focus for Black Lives Matters is the number of citizens killed by the police. Shockingly, 1,000 people were killed by police in the USA in 2018, in dark contrast to only 36 in Canada, 14 in Germany, and 3 in England and Wales. While there can be no excuse, there is something of an explanation. The US police officer faces a much higher risk of being shot in the line of duty, as US citizens have around 40 percent of the world's firearms. European police officers do not face the same level of risk as their US counterparts.

Anyway, Daughter #2 was active in the Black Lives Matters movement without necessarily knowing much of the above. She did understand, however, that African Americans had a rough deal and wanted more equality. Although the majority of Americans now appeared to want to change unjust elements of the judicial system, by deliberate design, no single person can deliver that change nationwide. This change has to be agreed upon with multiple parties throughout the nation.

One of the most interesting areas of my interviews with first-generation immigrants was on race relations. Starting with the black interviewees first, I have to say that I was somewhat surprised by what I heard. I did hear some statements that I was expecting, for example, "I am reminded that I am black every day," "the degree of racism depends on how black you are," and "I fear any interaction with the police." I also heard some things that surprised me. Those that had come from Europe said that racism was as bad, if not worse, in their home country and that they were stopped and searched more in Europe than in America. Of course, this may be partly explained by the fact that they were younger when they lived in Europe. However, it probably also indicates that Europe has its own issues to resolve in this area.

One friend, who now works in a senior role for a large technology company, described his arrest and trial for assault on a police officer. He and his friends were relaxing on the porch of their New York house one morning when two cops – a Black woman and a Hispanic man – came to talk to them. They answered the officers' questions as politely as possible, and – as they were leaving – my friend said, "Thank you, officers." The male officer accused him of calling him an asshole and slammed my friend against a wall. As my friend froze in surprise, the officer slipped over and stumbled to the ground. The officer arrested my friend for assault. My friend spent a night in jail, and many months later stood trial for assault on a police officer. The judge dismissed the case and told the officer that he couldn't arrest someone for calling him an asshole, something incidentally which my friend swears he never did in the first place. My friend says that all his other black friends at that time now have criminal records, but that many were for minor offenses. Life was ruined for this group after conviction, because they found it difficult to obtain loans or jobs. All the black interviewees I spoke to said that most black men were afraid of cops and thus were less likely to retaliate. The penalty for any resistance from them was likely to be much higher.

One white interviewee told me that he had worked in the District Attorney's office in New York City and, as part of his training, had accompanied the police on their duties in Spanish Harlem. He described the uncontrolled fear on both sides and said that there were half a dozen times in the evening when something could have gone wrong. The police drew their guns because they were scared, and the instinctive reaction from the black residents was to run away.

Most non-black, first-generation immigrant interviewees brought up the subject of race relations in response to the open question, "Is there anything you don't like about the US?" They pointed to the lack of ethnic integration in daily life, compared with what they were used to elsewhere. Indeed, Black Lives Matters rallies are one of the few places where there is a substantial mixing of people from different ethnicities. Another is soccer matches, which are surprisingly popular here. These interviewees were also surprised that hate groups were allowed to exist in America and that a president panders to them. Both the black and non-black immigrants I interviewed were optimistic about the future of race relations. They pointed to the increased emphasis on social change in recent years and believed that – if movements like Black Lives Matters have the stamina – racial prejudice will eventually decline.

I've tried to simplify this chapter's final section on political structure as much as possible. The US's political structure is quite different to most other countries and, therefore, also somewhat confusing if you try to understand it with your own country's political structure as a term of reference. If you know the American political system already, it will be a breeze, and you will undoubtedly lament my dumbing down. If not, stay with it and, if necessary, read each paragraph a bit slower than you usually would. The alternative to not understanding the US political system is that you will just have to pick a side and agree with everything they say or accept that US politics will forever be perplexing.

The Founding Fathers were determined not to have power concentrated in one role. They saw themselves as having fought an all-powerful British King and wanted to protect their new country from future tyrants. Therefore, the US Constitution is deliberately designed by its principal author, and eventual fourth President James Madison, to prevent tyranny, no matter how wise or charismatic the leader might seem at the time. The Founding Fathers devoted years to frame a structure that would protect people's rights from any future despot wielding too much power. The system they created is often called *separation of powers*, and the method by which they did this *checks and balances*.

The Founding Fathers divided the federal government into three separate branches with specific and more-or-less-equal powers. This was the *balance*. They were as cynical as a newsroom covering a politician's visit to a flood zone and, therefore, took the view that if any governing entity accumulated too much power, tyranny was ultimately inevitable. Any significant change in direction could only occur with the agreement from the other branches of government.

The USA was not the first country to consider this form of government, but it was the first to enact it in an organized manner. The eighteenth-century French philosopher, Montesquieu, was a crucial influence in the Founding Fathers' thinking. In *The Spirit of the Laws*, banned by the Roman Catholic Church, which only increased its sales, Montesquieu argued that "everything would come to an end if the legislative, executive, and judicial powers of government were to be exercised by the same person or authority."

The Founding Fathers also inserted multiple *checks* on others' powers. They designed the structure so that each of the three branches of government also had the responsibility to review the other two branches' work. So, at a very high level, how does this structure work in practice?

In simple terms, the legislative branch, or Congress, has the responsibility to draft federal laws. They have two checks on their power: the president can veto the laws they prepare, and the judicial branch can declare these laws as incompatible with the Constitution.

As you probably know, Congress consists of two chambers, the House of Representatives and the Senate. Either chamber can introduce a bill, though each has specific responsibilities. For example, only the House can introduce a tax bill, and only the Senate can reject a proposed international treaty.

Many foreigners, and some Americans who weren't listening in thirteen years of civics class, believe the US president is all-powerful. They think he – and to date, it has always been him – can change anything. This is not true. The president leads the executive branch and is mainly responsible for carrying out federal law. He can appoint people to direct federal agencies and can issue executive orders to make this happen. However, the legislative branch is responsible for approving all presidential nominations and budgets, and the judicial branch can declare executive orders as unconstitutional.

Additionally, Congress can also pass a law that invalidates an executive order if they disagree with it. If they really feel strongly, they can ultimately impeach the president and, in theory at least, remove him from office in extreme cases. This has not yet happened in US history, which is why it's only "in theory." The president also has a couple of other powers: negotiating foreign treaties and the granting of pardons. However, we will gloss over both of these powers in this section.

Finally, the judicial branch is responsible for interpreting the law. However, the president nominates the judges who make these evaluations as seats become vacant, and the Senate approves all federal judicial nominations. It can, again, in theory, impeach judges and remove them from office.

This means that multiple parties are responsible for government. This system requires each branch to work together to move the country forward. In a two-party environment, this also requires a spirit of compromise and collaboration. Throughout American history, this spirit has been absent reasonably frequently. This is especially true at either times of great change or in the presence of an actor of tyrannical persuasion.

The number of Executive Orders and presidential vetoes varies by president. For obvious reasons, they tend to be higher when the president is from a different political party to that which controls Congress, but sometimes they are higher because the president desires more control.

Executive orders should only push through policy changes and not create new laws or re-appropriate funds. Throughout US history, many executive orders have been found unconstitutional by the judiciary. For example, President Truman attempted to place all steel mills under federal control in 1952. Courts found this invalid because it tried to make a new law rather than clarify or execute an existing law.

The other feature of an executive order is that it can be easily changed by a new president. You will often hear that a new president has rolled back the achievements of a previous president. Usually, these are changes to executive orders for which the previous president didn't have sufficient legislative support.

Franklin D Roosevelt issued the largest number of executive orders by far: 3,522 in his 3.05 terms, almost one a day. One was to establish internment camps for Japanese Americans, now regarded unfavorably by history. Only three other presidents (Theodore Roosevelt, Wilson, and Coolidge) have issued more than 1,000.

FDR issued most presidential vetoes too. He refused to sign legislation from Congress a whopping six hundred and thirty times, or, on average, one per week. If a CNN or Fox News had aired at his time, Political Crisis would have flashed up regularly on TV screens. Presidential vetoes have returned to being relatively rare again, maybe because there is little purpose to present legislation that the president will not support. In recent times, Congress tends to work with the president to understand what he might object to in advance.

US presidents still have a lot of power, certainly more than was envisaged by the Founding Fathers. However, this power is always limited by the checks that the Founders deliberately put there. They have the most control in the relatively rare scenario when their party has a majority in both the House of Representatives and the Senate. Even then, they are not the leader of their party in the same way that a UK Prime Minister or Russian President is. The judiciary will also prevent presidents and Congress from doing anything not in line with the US Constitution. For this reason, the best US presidents are probably those who are skilled at working across party boundaries, one reason many Americans prefer someone with previous experience as a State Governor where this skill has been practiced.

This separation of powers creates *checks and balances* to guard against tyranny. James Madison, also one of the authors of the Federalist Papers designed to help states decide whether to ratify the US Constitution, wrote: "If men were angels, no government would be necessary…You must oblige the government to control itself."

If the first arc of checks and balances is at the federal level, a second arc exists at the state level. As we discussed in the last chapter, the federal government was given limited powers. At a state level, a similar set of checks and balances is in place between the state legislature, the state governor, and the state judiciary. State governors – who effectively are the Chief Executives for their state – often use executive orders, notably to declare states of emergency after some weather-related disaster. Again, these state executive orders can be declared unconstitutional by the judiciary, or the state legislature can develop a new law that overrules the executive order.

The US system of government is deliberately much more complicated than the UK system, which has grown more organically. The UK has its own peculiar set of checks and balances, such as an independent judiciary and the now very occasional independence of the House of Lords. However, it's much easier for a powerful UK prime minister to effect change, and presumably, it's also easier for a UK prime minister to be a despot, at least until the next election. The other informal balance seen in the UK is that prime ministers with despotic tendencies have typically been deposed and replaced by their party before they have to fight the next general election.

Whether the US system is sound or not, the final point of note is that the US system of government is extremely difficult to change. Any change to the US Constitution requires a two-thirds majority vote in both the House of Representatives and the Senate, as well as support from at least two-thirds of the states. Only twenty-seven amendments to the Constitution have been ratified, and the first ten of these were planned from the get-go. The last change – the Twenty–Seventh Amendment, which delayed hikes in congressional salary from taking effect until after the next election – was a bit of an oddity. It was first proposed in 1789 and took more than two hundred years to be ratified. The previous Amendment, the twenty-sixth, which reduced the voting age to eighteen, was ratified almost half a century ago. In another oddity, it was also the Amendment that took the shortest time for approval, only one hundred days.

Although rare in modern times, the US Constitution can be changed. The first three words are, "We the People." These three words convey that it is the people who set up the government and imply that the government exists solely to protect its people's rights.

Of course, none of this constitutional stuff seems relevant to our drive across America. Other than perhaps that, it was the foundation on which the USA managed to control the whole continent from sea to shining sea. But that is a story for another chapter.

Chapter 3 – Driving to the Start in Savannah

The trip was now as planned as it would ever be, and certainly more planned than I would have liked. We had a broad outline of where we would be traveling. We intended to head north until we hit the Canadian border and then turn left until we reached the Pacific coast. We planned to stay mostly inside national parks, so I had booked the scarce and expensive park accommodation until we reached the Pacific. Everything was cancellable, just in case. We would book all other accommodation along the way; there seemed to be many outstanding deals.

I am really partial to a museum; I love to learn something new and enjoy the experience of being guided around something I don't know much about. When the children were young, they whined incessantly and with passion about each new museum. However, I take pride that they now both choose a museum or art gallery when they are on vacation.

Therefore, I had painstakingly traced our likely route to the Canadian border in Minnesota on Google Maps. I explored every single museum on or near the route we were taking. Museum after museum was closed for Covid reasons. Only the Corvette Museum in Kentucky appeared to be open. While I would be happy to accept my children's displeasure at a museum, it was quite another matter to annoy Lorna. I did not think she would enjoy seeing a car lot of Corvettes. I hoped that other museums would re-open as we traveled across the USA.

All the packing had been completed, except for my walking boots, which had miraculously disappeared and had to be replaced by fake North Face shoes that I had bought in China many years previously. Lorna was as busy as a wolf at a chicken farm; she was making masks. The sewing machine that I had bought her decades ago as a present (yes, I am that romantic) was churning out basketfuls of washable masks. She did not use a template; indeed, Lorna has never come across a set of instructions that she hasn't immediately thrown aside unread. She was now on Mark 6 design, and masks of various colors were ready to be worn on each outside trip. Old shirts disappeared from my walk-in closets, and similarly colored masks later appeared in the basket.

We had decided to rent a car rather than drive our own vehicle. We wondered if we would relish the three-thousand-mile return journey home after having first driven five thousand miles. Typically, the car rental company charges a vast drop off fee if you leave your car in a different location, sometimes more than the cost of the rental. However, car rental companies were struggling to survive. Nobody was traveling for either business or pleasure. The previous week, I was astonished to see that the car lot of the local waterpark, which I knew to be closed, was packed with vehicles. The car rental companies needed somewhere to put their unused cars. In normal times, more than 90 percent of cars would be rented out at any one time. The rental companies had parking for only about 10 percent of their fleet. They needed a solution for where to put the other 90 percent. Although car rental companies may have had a parking deficit, there was no shortage of parking spaces generally. It's estimated that there are in excess of 2 billion parking spaces across the USA for the 250 million cars on the road.

The car rental companies were trying everything to arrest declining cash flows and were offering some great deals. You could rent a new car for peanuts for the weekend. Facebook was filled with opportunities to buy a relatively new rental car.

The process of renting a car is both painful and joyous. Incidentally, never say you want to hire a car in the USA. I once did this, and the guy behind the desk asked whether I wanted a higher vehicle, like a truck? I don't enjoy the paperwork part of the car rental process. The line is always too long and too slow, the upsell annoying (who actually buys the GPS option?), and the paperwork cumbersome. I do like the part where you select the car. In most US locations, you rent a vehicle within a particular category, not a specific car. This means that you choose any vehicle within a few rows of their parking lot. You are a big kid in a giant sweet shop.

We had rented countless rental cars in America on our many vacations there. I remember the first we ever rented in the early-1990s, a white four-door Buick Century. Although it was the cheapest rental on the lot, it was a huge car compared with our own vehicle at that time, a 2CV. This automatic rental had a stereo, armrests, cup holders, antennas that retracted when you left the car, leather seats, and an airbag (driver only).

As we got more prosperous, our choice of cars increased. As we were in the USA, we chose American marques: Cadillacs, Chevrolets, Dodges, Jeeps, Ford F-150s and Mustangs, Oldsmobiles, RAMs, and Lincolns. We learned later that this is actually pretty un-American. It's Japanese and German cars that have cachet here. When we moved to the USA, an immigration paperwork glitch delayed our US driving licenses. New anti-terrorism rules meant that, without a driving license, we were prohibited from buying cars. Therefore, we rented two different cars every week for two months on our UK driving licenses. It was this way that we learned that a Jeep would probably not be a wise purchase.

What car would we choose that first day of our drive across America? Each row was packed full of vehicles, some driving lanes had been reclaimed, and the painted islands, which generally prohibit parking, also housed cars. We could choose from any midsize SUV. We speedily surveyed all the vehicles in our rows. We narrowed the choice down to those with large storage space. If we were to spend four weeks in a car, why skimp on space? We discounted the Dodge Journey. We compared the features inside the car and eliminated some that were subpar in some way. Finally, Lorna dismissed the green vehicle.

We chose the four-wheel drive, 3.5 liter, 284 horsepower, V6 engine Nissan Pathfinder. It had an extra row of seats that we converted into a large storage space for our kayak. It had cameras and sensors everywhere. For $200 per week, this would be our vehicle for the next month.

To do the coast-to-coast drive properly, one has to start on either the East or West Coast. We live a little inland from the East Coast, so we started our journey by driving the wrong way towards Tybee Island on the Atlantic Ocean. It's a four-and-a-half-hour drive. You will probably notice that Americans rarely talk about how many miles a journey is but prefer to measure what they value the most: their time. They do the same with bad movies. "That's two hours of my time I won't get back," not "give me back my $10."

Before our departure, we had been busier than a fan at a funeral home after the AC has broken. Since my retirement from the world of work, we had tried to cut out unnecessary expenses. As a family, we had four cars and four drivers, two of whom are relatively young. The lack of any public transport where we lived precluded a reduction in cars. However, we could reduce our annual insurance expenses by hundreds of dollars if we all completed a defensive driving course. In normal times, this would have required us each to attend a day-long course run by an ex-policeman. Lorna and Daughter #1 had participated in one a few years earlier and found it intolerable. According to them, the ex-policeman saw no need to be pleasant to the attendees, most of whom were mandated to attend by the courts for dangerous driving. You need special attributes indeed to be the type of policeman who is run out of the police for lack of customer interaction skills.

These Covid times had thrown up an opportunity to take this course online instead of in-person, which was previously the only way that you could receive the discount. Lorna had found a course run by the senior citizen's organization, The American Association for Retired Persons, which was precisely the mandatory six hours that qualified for the discount. Discrimination laws meant that one could join the AARP at any age. It was thus how Daughter #2 became probably one of the younger members of this organization.

I have to say that this course was well-curated. The video quality was extremely high, and the structure logical. Unfortunately, it was designed for an 80-year-old person. There were extended sections on how to limber up before you drive and an entertaining and extensive segment on how you should tell your spouse/parents that they are no longer fit to drive. Now, I don't want to spoil the answer for those of you who wish to experience the whole online course, but, in a nutshell, the answer is subtly and with compassion.

The online course had been designed to make you concentrate on the material. The creators' goal was to ensure that you learned the material rather than clicked a few buttons. Videos had pop-up questions at different points, and the next section button was always in another part of the screen. I had completed similar tests at work in the past few years.

If you were paying attention in Chapter 1, you will recall that driving laws have state rather than federal oversight. You need a state license to drive a car and a county tag – or license plate – for your vehicle. Each state has its own driving laws. The Constitution, of course, was established well before the motor car's invention. When the time came to invent driving laws, it was therefore done at a state level. Most important laws tend to coalesce over time, so the bulk of rules are the same in every state. It would be unlikely, for example, that any state would allow people to drink alcohol, encourage driving on the left-hand side of the road, or mandate going straight ahead on red at traffic lights. A federal body exists that tries to align laws, but individual states are not compelled to agree. States do have different fundamental principles that influence their laws. In the spirit of freedom, motorcyclists in thirty-one states do not have to wear helmets. You don't have to wear a seat belt in New Hampshire if you are 18 or older. Montana and Nevada had no speed limits during the day until 1974 when President Nixon introduced a national speed limit of 55mph as part of a range of measures to counter gasoline shortages. Montana found a way around the federal policy by not penalizing drivers' records and awarding trivial penalties for infractions. For many years, Montana drivers would have a stack of $5 bills in their glove compartment to pay the "wasting energy" fines.

My children and my wife raced through the test as quickly as possible, paying barely any attention to the content. In truth, much content was not especially relevant to an eighteen-year-old. I had more time on my hands and explored some of the differences by state. We planned to drive through thirteen separate states on this trip, so I thought I might want to be somewhat familiar with some local state rules. You will no doubt be glad that I will not burden you with every difference. However, I want to spend a bit of time on one topic: what to do if you hit a deer.

First, hitting a deer is a common occurrence. According to an insurance company here, 1.4 million deer collisions are reported every year, leading to a $4,000 average insurance claim. The probability of a deer collision varies by state. West Virginia is the most dangerous state for deer collisions: 1 in 46 West Virginians will have a deer collision each year. This was actually an improvement on the figures from the previous year (1 in 43), perhaps because there were fewer deer after the last year's carnage. Hawaii is the safest state (1 in 6,379) for deer collisions, in the main because they have no native deer. It is less safe for volcanic eruptions, however.

Second, the general advice is that you should not swerve to avoid a deer. The dangers of swerving into oncoming traffic or a ditch are apparently much greater. What you should do is apply the brakes but not so hard that the car behind crashes into you. Some say that you should accelerate just at the point where you are hitting the deer to lessen the chance that their hooves will kill you as they come hurtling through your windshield. They are wrong; this will merely ever so slightly increase the speed at which their hooves come into contact with your head. You might be one of the two hundred or so people who die this way every year in the USA, but at least it would make an interesting gravestone.

Third, you must report a deer collision to the police in some states, but not others. I can no longer remember what the rules are for each state, but you don't have to inform the police in my state. I appreciate that this isn't useful advice to the cross-America driver, and I suggest that you dial 911 just in case.

Fourth, if the deer is dead, you should attempt to move it away from the road. If it isn't, in many states, you can take your gun from the gun rack of your truck and put the poor creature out of its misery. If you are stupid enough to leave home without a weapon, you can call the police, who will do this for you. However, they don't like to do it; apparently, the paperwork for discharging a weapon is horrendous.

Fifth, state rules conflict over whether you can keep the deer meat. In some states, it's illegal to claim a deer carcass without a permit. When the police officer arrives, you can buy a roadkill tag from them. Other states have rules that mean that the owner of the lead vehicle cannot keep the deer carcass but that the car behind can legally pick up the dead deer. If venison is your thing, I suggest you always travel in convoy. My state, Georgia, recently voted unanimously to change its rules to allow you to take home the carcass of any deer or bear collision.

As an aside, how do you cook a bear, I hear you ask? Very slowly. Apparently, you need twenty-five minutes of 375°F heat (190°C or gas mark 5) for every pound of bear meat. Now, I've seen bears in the flesh; they're huge.

I have only covered deer in this example. Other strategies, statistics, and laws apply to different ungulates, whether elk, moose, or caribou.

If you move state for more than three months, you have to retake your driving test in that new state. Fortunately, the driving test isn't difficult. I have never heard of anyone who has failed the practical part of their driving test, but if you did – in our state at least – you could just retake it the next day. Pretty much every US test of any type has a 75 percent pass rate. This allows someone to pass a test and make plenty of mistakes. I hit the plastic bollards in my parallel parking maneuver (yes, that is how it's spelled here) and passed with ease, scoring a higher pass rate than my wife. I've often wondered what you could mess up and still pass. I suspect you could probably mow down up to four people on a zebra crossing, called crosswalks here, and still pass.

My maternal grandfather once told me how he took his driving test in Malta when he was in the Navy. A whole bunch of men took turns driving a bus along a straight road. Every six hundred feet, they swapped drivers. The only person that failed was the person who guided the bus into the ditch.

You can drive in Georgia with a driver's permit from the age of fifteen. This minimum age varies by state; nine mainly rural states have younger ages, and nine North-Eastern states are sixteen. Many states have become quite savvy at amending their rules to achieve other goals. In Georgia, if you are under eighteen, you have to demonstrate a strong school attendance record and show good grades to receive your driving permit. Most people teach their own children to drive here rather than employ a driving instructor. The principle is that you are unlikely to want your own children to drive by themselves unless they are indeed safe drivers. Our state mandates that you must give at least forty hours of instruction. I developed my own even more localized driving rules, which required a minimum of sixty hours of instruction. It was certainly needed for Daughter #1.

I enjoyed teaching my children to drive. It created a bond between us. At fifteen, they were at that age where they thought both parents to be embarrassing and a bit inept. Suddenly, they had incontrovertible evidence that we could do something with ease that was a struggle for them. The first time Daughter #1 drove in a vast but completely empty church parking lot, my body was enveloped in sweat so wet that I had to dry down the seat afterward. However, you gain confidence as they gain skill. There is something life-affirming about teaching your child to drive on a busy highway when the GPS instructs your daughter to move to the outside lane, and you are on the inside lane of an eight-lane highway.

Teenagers around the world show inconsistent judgment. My daughters' high school exhibits a wrecked car at the school entrance every year as a warning to young drivers. Every year though, there seems to be a tragedy where a young driver dies on the road due to reckless driving. In 2018, on the road next to where we live, one drunk seventeen-year-old hit a curb while her passenger was perched on the rolled-down window. The passenger fell out of the car and died a few weeks later from her injuries. The driver was sentenced to three months in jail and nine months under house arrest. In a bizarre twist of fate, she was released from house arrest a few days before lockdown.

In the past, passing your driving test was a significant life moment. It was your path to independence and freedom. However, driving is becoming a bit less popular with Generation Z. Only 61 percent of eighteen-year-olds have a driving license today compared with 81 percent a generation ago. Perhaps, they see that self-driving vehicles will be a feature of their life and wonder if they need to bother. Previously, getting your driving permit was widely seen as a coming-of-age milestone.

Even those who pass the test aren't necessarily buying cars. They eschew tying large amounts of capital into something they only occasionally use. They also have choices that previous generations didn't have: car sharing, Uber, and short-term car rental. The younger generation is also more environmentally aware, and gasoline-powered cars have a negative image.

In general, Atlanta's public transport is pretty dismal. For a metro area of around six million people, only 8 percent ever take public transportation. There is essentially only one metro line of thirty-eight stations and a variable bus network. Where we live, in the suburbs of Atlanta, barely any public transport is available at all. This is by collective design, rather than misfortune.

Atlanta suburbs have consistently voted against the extension of public transport to their neighborhoods. Each public vote sends increasing majorities against greater investment. Some claim that the white folks who live in the suburbs don't want to make it easy for undesirables to come to their homes. However, I suspect that most vote against these proposals simply because they don't want to pay for better public transportation, which they will never use.

We love public transport. When we lived in Hong Kong, we saw no need for a car and loved the freedom it gave us. In summer, we love traveling to Europe and letting public transport take us from place to place. We have lived near Atlanta for almost a decade, and Lorna has still never taken public transportation. Public transport is so sporadic that it is rarely convenient.

Walking is often also not an option. As a European, I often do something un-American and choose to walk between strip malls. One friend decided to pick up her children from daycare a short distance from her house. There were no sidewalks, and she found herself dragging a stroller and her kids through knee-high grass. She did this only once.

The most American of our small family is 18-year-old Daughter #2. She had perfected the southern drawl on the plane over to Atlanta, and her teachers were always astonished to learn that she has British parents. Daughter #2 loves the car. She loves that she can fill the car with gas and drive absolutely anywhere that takes her fancy. She regularly visits friends for a weekend in nearby states many hours away, just to watch a football game.

The history of American transportation has been shaped by both states' rights and technology. The original Federalist goal was to achieve international independence but domestic interdependence. However, many states were wary of being dependent on other states, and some proposals were opposed by Congress and others vetoed by Presidents Madison and Monroe.

Waterways were the original method of traversing the country. In the nineteenth century, after the Lewis and Clark Expedition (which we will come on to later in the book), the Missouri and Columbia Rivers were the main routes for expansion into the West. Obviously, the course of these waterways restricted where you could travel to and influenced where people lived. As technology improved, travel speeds increased. For example, in the early days, it would take three to four months to travel from New Orleans to Louisville, Kentucky. After the steamboat's invention, this fell to less than a month. These quicker travel times reduced isolation and increased commercial activity. In 1819, only a hundred miles of canals existed. Within twenty years, construction had increased this to 3,330 miles of canals.

The railroads were instrumental in the development of the rest of the country. However, railroads were regional and not national. In the 1830s, railroads connected existing canals and waterways to other towns. By the 1840s, they were connecting towns to cities. Manufactured goods moved from east to west; agricultural goods from west to east. The railroads cut transport time by 90 percent, increasing domestic trade and reducing reliance on international trade. There were few railroads from north to south, which restricted trade and cultural exchange. This would be one of many factors that divided America up to the US Civil War.

The motorcar's invention at the end of the nineteenth century led to an increase in the importance of roads. Most roads were initially regional and aided the transport of goods from ports and railroad depots within the local region.

During his presidency in the 1950s, President Eisenhower ushered in interstate roads. He admired the efficiency of the German Autobahn network while he was European Supreme Commander of the Allied forces during World War II. His network of freeways in the USA took thirty-five years to complete but was instrumental in transforming the American business and cultural environment.

America now has seventy primary interstate roads and hundreds of auxiliary interstate highways in the Lower 48 states. The primary interstates have one or two digits, for example, the I-20. If the number is odd, the road runs from south to north; if even, from west to east. Taking American logic one step further, if the road number is divisible by five, it runs more or less coast-to-coast or northern border to southern border. Eight roads cross the USA vertically and six, more or less, cross it horizontally.

Auxiliary interstate highways are typically spur roads, bypasses for major cities, or ring roads, which they call beltways or loops here. These roads also receive 90 percent funding from the Federal Government. I regret that I have to report some anomalies. Five interstates have duplicate numbers; fortunately, none is in the same state.

Some American highways are long. Twenty-seven primary interstate roads are longer than the UK's longest road, the 410-mile A1. There are also twelve state roads longer than the A1, which indicates how large some US states are. The US's longest road is the Seattle to Boston I-90, which is more than three thousand miles long. However, it's nowhere near as long as the nineteen-thousand-mile Pan-American Highway from Alaska to Argentina's Fin del Mundo, albeit with a sixty-mile Darien Gap. Now, there's another bucket list idea.

Exit numbers on American interstates are calculated by the number of miles the exit is from the state's southern or western entry point. This is a pretty useful system; if you have just passed Exit 18 and the next exit is Exit 33, you know you have 15 miles until the next exit. It works the same in the other direction, though subtraction may be a little more challenging.

The USA is big, much bigger than the UK, which allows it to have more infrastructure. The USA has 18 times as many railway tracks as the UK, 17 times more roads, 13 times more navigable waterways, and 50 times more airports.

When the first car came off his production line in 1913, Henry Ford said, "When I'm through, almost everyone will have one." With 257.9 million cars on the US road today (excluding large trucks and motorcycles), he is probably through. There are four vehicles for every five people – almost as many as guns.

I have many friends who think nothing about taking a four-hour drive to see someone, roughly the time it takes to drive from London to York. However, there are signs that driving may now be on the wane. Although the average number of miles driven still goes up (around eight thousand miles a year, about double that of the 1970s), the number of people driving is now decreasing. This is caused by more young adults forgoing the car, and children learning how to persuade their elderly parents to give up their license.

The percentage of people who like driving is also falling, down ten percentage points since 2000. The main reason for this decline is the amount of traffic on the roads. Until Covid hit, average commuting times were continuing to rise and, pre-Covid, the average commute time was just under an hour per day. The worst commutes are in California. Palmdale, an LA suburb, had an average commute of 85 minutes per day, and one in three people spent longer than two hours in traffic. Another LA suburb averaged 73 minutes per day, but commuting times were the least of its worries as the town's name is Corona.

Many freeways have special High Occupancy Vehicle lanes. High occupancy here is defined as more than one passenger. Still, these lanes remain empty as most drivers travel alone in their car to and from work. As we drove on the first leg of our journey on the empty High Occupancy Vehicle lane towards the start, we played our favorite podcast. However, as usually happens, we paused it after a few minutes to chat about something or other. Suddenly, we were at our destination. You would think we would have run out of subjects to talk about after three months of lockdown, twenty-three years of marriage, thirty-two years of living together, and forty years of knowing each other.

Tybee Island, Georgia – temporarily named Savannah Beach in the 50s and 60s – is a mid-income beach destination, neither exclusive nor "kiss me quick." Its main claim to fame is that it's one of the few places where an atomic bomb has been dropped. The "Tybee Bomb" was dropped accidentally as part of a military training exercise that went wrong, and – get this – the atomic bomb was never found.

People often wonder why Americans describe a city by both its city name and its state. Europeans especially laugh when Americans call "Venice" "Venice, Italy." Where else can it be, other than Italy? Many American pioneers were seldom inventive with the names of their towns. There are five substantial Venices in the USA, but this pales into insignificance compared with other cities' repeated names. Twenty-five city names have a presence in more than eighteen states. Some are named after historical figures: for example, there are eighteen Washingtons and twenty-three Madisons. Some conurbations are named after European cities, including nineteen Chesters and twenty Manchesters. Many are named after features: twenty-eight cities have Fairviews, not good ones mind you just fair ones, and twenty-three Greenvilles. There used to be only twenty-two Greenvilles, but Buttsville, Alabama, wisely changed its name.

The Simpsons created their home as Springfield because this city name was so ubiquitous, but I have to tell you that only twenty states bear this name. The most popular city name is Franklin, after founding father Benjamin Franklin. If you say you live in Franklin, this narrows it down to only thirty states.

County names are even less original. One in eight counties is named after one of twenty-four politicians. Thirty-eight states have a county named Washington, Jefferson, or Franklin, and thirteen states have all three.

Anyway, Tybee Island is the type of place where you see a sign for Tybee's only beachfront hotel, followed quickly by another for Tybee's only beachfront resort, only beachfront motel, inn, and B&B. Parking was a challenge, but we eventually located a parking meter where, for only a few quarters, we were able to enjoy the enormous beach and broad sea horizon. Due to some beach dune remodeling, Lorna and I sat on a public swinging chair on the beach from which we couldn't see the sea. In these Black Lives Matters times, it was heartening to see black, white, and Hispanic families smile at each other as they all enjoyed the same experience. Everyone was decidedly relieved to be outside doing something familiar.

We took the obligatory start-of-journey photo and ate some food at a dock restaurant on the bayside of the island. In many ways, we prefer bay views for wildlife viewing. America's East Coast originally featured countless islands, most of which are now joined to the mainland by road. The Intracoastal Waterway runs three thousand miles from Boston to Florida's southern tip before heading north again along the Florida Gulf Coast to Texas. It avoids the ocean entirely, taking a mixture of natural waterways and artificial canals. If this waterway isn't long enough for you, the Great Loop using the Mississippi River, the Great Lakes, and some canals will take you a further three thousand miles back to near the start. You can probably imagine what I was thinking.

I don't know what it is about the USA that lends itself to a coast-to-coast road trip. This isn't particularly common in the UK or even Europe. Indeed, few books about European road trips have been written, except perhaps Don Quixote. Maybe it is that most Americans – including Native Americans but excluding most African Americans – descend from immigrants who traveled to America to find a better place to live. Somewhere in their DNA, they have a predisposition to travel to find something better. The appeal could be the vast tracts of empty land or the abundance of spectacular and diverse scenery. Maybe it's the American people's variety of attitudes, too, that makes the journey rewarding. You are sure to meet others who view the world differently from you. We had wanted to take this trip for many decades. Our coast-to-coast journey started the next day.

The only two cities we would revisit on our long drive were the first and the last stops. We spent the first night in historic Savannah, one of America's most beautiful cities. This isn't your typical travel book, where I recommend several places that you should visit. However, Savannah is lovely.

For one thing, it's quite old, at least in American terms. It was founded in 1733 by James Oglethorpe and was Georgia's first state capital. Its geography has led to it being a strategic port throughout its history. British troops captured the city in 1778 as part of the Revolutionary War and resisted the siege of Savannah for four years. It was a Confederate City during the Civil War, and, fortunately for visitors today, it was spared the fate of Atlanta after a peaceful surrender.

The immediate origin of the Revolutionary War was a series of taxes imposed by King George III on the British colonists to pay for the defeat of the French in the French and Indian Wars of 1754-1763. After the Stamp Act (1765) and the Townshend Act (1767), the Tea Act (1773) was the final straw for the colonists. In an early act of cultural appropriation, New England Patriot colonists dressed as Mohawk Indians and dumped 342 chests of loose-leaf green and black tea into Boston Harbor.

The First Colonial Congress of 1774 demanded no taxes without political representation. By 1775, the Battles of Lexington and Concord between British troops and colonist militia saw the formal start of the Revolutionary War. The conflict was a civil war until 1778, with about half British colonists supporting the revolution and 20 percent supporting the British. The remaining 30 percent tried in vain to stay out of the conflict. In 1778, the war turned into a world war with first the French, then the Spanish and Dutch, joining the American side. There was something of a stalemate until George Washington's troops defeated General Cornwallis' men in the 1781 Battle of Yorktown. Two years later, America's independence was confirmed in the 1783 Treaty of Paris.

The historic city retains the original design from Oglethorpe and features twenty-two garden squares, cobbled streets, and too-many-to-count old terraced houses. You will probably have seen it in the movie *Forrest Gump*. In normal times, the city's 150 thousand residents are dwarfed by more than 14 million tourist visitors annually. It is exceptionally well-preserved, something which is unusual in America.

In general, the USA is pretty mediocre at preserving its historical sites. With relatively few government initiatives to protect critical historic landmarks, preservation is primarily left to determined groups of individuals, who are often no match for the well-organized and well-funded developers who make their money from building something new. In any case, the average American seems to prefer their history new. In most parts of the USA, you will find some German or Swedish town built from scratch, copied from something older elsewhere. They always seem to be popular tourist destinations, complete with the full range of stores and restaurants. Winston

Churchill would undoubtedly disapprove. He argued that the "further back you can look, the further forward you can see."

Savannah isn't one of those towns, however. It has a predominantly white, historic center set inside a larger, more diverse city. Aside from tourism, its port is an important commercial center and supply chain hub. Indeed, it is the fourth-largest North American port.

General James Oglethorpe was an interesting character. By a quirk of fate, he was born in the English town of Godalming, where we lived when we were last in the UK. He was an important social reformer of his day, with a mission to reform Britain's prisons. His plan was to resettle all Britain's "worthy poor" in the New World, especially those from debtors' prisons. He wanted to give everyone lots of cotton seeds and fifty acres of land: a town plot, a garden plot near the town, and forty-five acres elsewhere.

Oglethorpe was Georgia's founder and was vehemently anti-slavery. Many other colonial settlers opposed him, as the ban on slavery restricted their economic position. While Oglethorpe was returning home to England in 1743, the settlers changed the laws to legalize slavery. Georgia's history, and maybe that of the rest of the South, might have been very different without this change.

We weren't quite sure what to expect in terms of activity. Savannah was much less busy than usual, maybe one-quarter of a typical summer weekend. This meant that the streets were delightful. It was easy to socially distance, even on the cobbled, tourist trap that is River Street. After a short downpour, we took refuge in the river-fronted Hyatt. Their restaurant was closed, but they allowed their guests – and those sheltering from the rain, pretending to be guests – to bring in their takeout and eat it on the unused loggia overlooking the river. We had a drink with a masked man sheltering from the rain like us who worked in the Savannah docks. He told us that his job consisted of driving a pickup truck from one end of the dock to the other.

With the widening of the Panama Canal, Savannah now receives a good proportion of the freight direct from Asia, and this freight is expected to almost double again over the next seven years. This meant that our river veranda vantage point afforded us a great view of the supertankers going to and from the Atlantic Ocean. One of these ships would have brought our belongings from the UK almost a decade ago.

As we meandered through Savannah's cobbled streets, we felt that same sense of freedom as the first trip out after lockdown. It was like the sense of wellbeing you had when you were well again after a bout of flu. You had adapted to a new normal but were delighted to return to the old normal.

Savannah's historic district is famous for its aforementioned squares, all of which are draped with Spanish moss that falls from every tree. The houses are mainly built of nineteenth-century brick and are similar to those in, say, Central London. We examined the statues, which dripped with history. Most were from the revolutionary period, but some slaveholders and confederate leaders were also commemorated. A few days after our visit, some of these statues were vandalized with white hoods placed over their heads, and black-power fists sprayed onto their bases. A solution will need to be found for this black-majority city.

We looked in a realtor's window and thought it might be pleasant to live here for a couple of years. We had half explored this daydream in tens of other cities, regions, and countries previously. But we were now at an inflection point in our own lives. We could do anything and we could live anywhere. Our children had left home, and it was our time again.

We had something of a direction for this next stage in our life. We knew the weather we liked, the balance we wanted between city and countryside, and the type of people we wanted to live alongside. However, when you applied these criteria, many places qualified.

We decided to forego the evening booze cruise on the steamer. If we inexplicably decided to deliberately catch Covid, it would be in a different way and at a later date. We looked for somewhere to eat. Restaurants in Georgia had transitioned from dine-in to takeout or delivery during lockdown, and dine-in had not yet returned. Startup delivery companies had been aggressive in signing up restaurants for takeout delivery, even without their permission. Many restaurants had shuttered, while others were selling more meals than ever before. Daughter #2 was working as a food delivery driver in the summer before going to college. She was one of just over one-third of teenagers who have a job, down from almost two-thirds a few decades ago.

Savannah is also home to SCAD, The Savannah College for Art & Design, which has buildings everywhere throughout the downtown area. It may surprise you to learn that Georgia produces more feature films now than California. If this did surprise you, you will likely also be astonished to find that Georgia, known as the Peach State, grows 25,000 tons of peaches compared with California's 510,000 tons of peaches. Anyway, it's SCAD that provides skilled labor required for complex media projects. A couple of years previously, Daughter #2 had enjoyed a summer course on their Atlanta campus.

Although cinema was not invented in the USA, Americans generally, and Edison specifically, were early adopters. The USA has been the dominant country for movie production since its beginnings and now produces about seven hundred commercial movies every year. America invented genre cinema, and they design movies to cater to people's individual tastes: romance, westerns, horror, Sci-Fi, and action.

Every single one of the top hundred grossing movies of all time is American. For the last ten years, the top twenty movies each year have been American. Why is this? Partly, of course, because English is widely spoken around the world. However, it probably has more to do with the fact that America has a large pool of the wide range of skills necessary for completing a movie, from financing to acting to set and wardrobe design to editing to post-production to marketing. This pool of talent keeps growing. When Hollywood sees skills they like from other countries, they entice that talent into sunny Los Angeles or, increasingly, Georgia. Hollywood's reliance on foreign talent has always been substantial. The early pioneers of movie-making were almost entirely recent immigrants. Paramount was founded by a German, Carl Laemmle; Fox by a Hungarian, Wilhelm Fried; 20th Century by a Russian, Joseph Schenk; the Warner Brothers were Polish; MGM by a Lithuanian, Louis B Mayer; and Famous Players Studios by another Hungarian, Adolf Zukor. The talent they employed was also frequently foreign. The great Hollywood directors of Capra, Chaplin, Curtiz, Ford, Hitchcock, Kazan, Lang, Laurel, Lubitsch, Vidor, and Wyler, to name a few, were all born outside the USA. This pattern was repeated for immigrants both in other behind-the-screen talent and in acting.

America has an enormous home market for its films, about $11 billion in a typical year. Overseas films perform poorly in the USA, taking less than 1 percent of the total box office. Independent US films have further squeezed the market for foreign movies. American movies also dominate overseas box offices. Most American films make more overseas than they do domestically, and American movies gross almost 70 percent of the $42 billion worldwide box office sales.

The film industry is generally driven by money in the USA. The industry's artistic merits are highlighted by the industry a couple of times per year at award shows. What really matters is, did the movie make money? Poorly made American movies, of which there are many, are saved at the eleventh hour, and marketing is put in place so that most terrible movies still make money.

Hollywood is the only market that can consistently make money from movies costing more than $200 million. The budgets for these blockbusters are a hundred times greater than those of the average overseas movie.

Does this give America any advantage? I believe so. It's part of "soft power" that co-opts others towards your ideals rather than coercing them. From interviews I've undertaken with thirty recent US immigrants, almost all said that they took their initial positive view of America from its films. Historically at least, pretty much any movie made in America has to be acceptable to its home audience, and therefore it is likely to promote the USA in some way. American movies thus promote American culture and American values to a large pool of potential immigrants. They promote the American dream of freedom, the importance of the individual, and righteousness. Now that American filmmakers make movies that are more critical of America, it will be interesting to see whether Hollywood still provides the same catnip for potential immigrants. If not, we may see a decline in immigration growth and, with it, a reduction in America's growth.

As the world changes, America has changed this industry. The number of US cinema-goers has fallen pretty much every year since 2002, but movie theater revenues have not fallen due to higher ticket prices. Hollywood transitioned successfully during the video, DVD, and streaming revolutions. Now America's industry is dominating the TV streaming world.

Lorna likes few things more than to visit an old cemetery, so we went to Bonaventure Cemetery. Savannah has an abundance of estuaries, and this Victorian last-resting place is set on a bluff on one of the many inlets. The ornate hundred-acre cemetery showcases Savannah's merchant past and the azaleas for which the region is famous. The cemetery was once part of the long-ago-destroyed Bonaventure Plantation but is now part of a much less affluent area of town. John Muir, the outdoorsman, slept in the cemetery for almost a week while waiting for money to travel to Florida on his thousand-mile walk. You can still purchase plots in this cemetery, but Lorna told me that she always wanted her ashes to be scattered in Venice's lagoons. She wasn't specific about which Venice, however. It could be Venice, Italy, which she has visited a dozen times and which she tries to shoehorn into every European trip, but perhaps she meant Venice, Illinois?

We breakfasted in one of Savannah's many parks the next morning. Savannah was already hot and humid, but it still had the air of an historic European city. We had to leave the historic part of the city for Savannah's modern suburbs, as I had an appointment with a charitable organization there.

For reasons that I cannot fathom, America is seen as a selfish nation. However, when you look at the facts, the opposite is true. In his 1961 Inauguration, JFK implored his fellow Americans to "Ask not what your country can do for you – ask what you can do for your country." This spirit of volunteering your time for a cause you believe in is common in the US.

Every five years, Gallup runs a poll of almost 200,000 people in 153 countries to establish the most generous nation on earth. They define generosity as a combination of helping people you don't know, donating money (as a percentage of your income), and volunteering your time. The UK performs well, coming in at a creditable eighth place. Britain's other former colonies of Australia, Canada, and New Zealand place well too. As you might expect, Buddhist countries also fare well. However, the number one on the World Giving Index is the USA.

Americans give $428 billion in charitable donations every year. Foundations (14 percent) and Corporations (5 percent) are generous, but 81 percent of all donations come from individuals at a level of seven times that of the average continental European. Americans are generous when they choose to be. They will happily donate towards someone's healthcare needs, but many will rail against why they have to pay for someone else's healthcare as part of general taxation.

Other research shows that Americans with strong religious inclinations donate more than those without, and not necessarily solely to religious charities. The same is true for volunteering. This accords with my own experience of volunteering in the foster care sector, undoubtedly one of the most challenging and time-consuming areas of volunteerism. In Georgia, foster parenting is dominated by Christians who feel compelled by their faith and community to help out.

In 2014, Atlanta had two inches of snow. This infrequent event brought the city to a standstill for days as the temperatures dropped, further sealing the snow into the roads. Every road was blocked by abandoned vehicles that could no longer operate on Atlanta's hilly terrain, and Georgia's four snowplows could not alleviate the situation. On the day of the snow, with all the roads blocked, I was forced to walk the eight miles home in my slippery work shoes. Many pedestrians were walking the same commute. At the entrance to every subdivision, residents handed out hot drinks, warm jumpers, and heat pads to the weary commuters.

Within the USA, the most generous are rural people with moderate income. People from the South and the Mountain regions are the most generous, and the most generous states also vote Republican. Married people donate more than single people, and single people's donations rise significantly when they get married.

American culture is notably different by region, perhaps in the same way as other countries. Each area has its own culture because it has its own subtly different history.

Those who immigrated to New England in early times were Calvinist Puritan families from North of England and Scotland, who fled from religious persecution. They were from multiple subtly different denominations. Religion for these people was more an individual experience. Conditions in New England were harsh, and the hardworking immigrants were the ones that survived and prospered. These immigrants had a private home life and, for entertainment, they enjoyed reading books.

The South had a more diverse initial colonization pool. About half of all eighteenth-century British immigrants arrived as indentured servants, either in exchange for their passage or convicts sentenced for minor offenses. In broad-brush terms, the religious groups that immigrated to the South were from much more evangelistic denominations than in New England. The Biblical doctrine was applied in the South to encompass slavery. Black people were held to be descendants of Canaan/Ham, and it was the duty of good Christians to save these heathens.

The entertainment these Southern settlers enjoyed depended on whether they were city-centered or rural. In rural settings, it was based around church socials, blood sports, and story-telling. In cities, entertainment involved theaters and minstrel shows.

Some academics conclude that today's dominant political persuasion is influenced by the origins of its immigrants, the typical work done there, and its geographic features. Accordingly, New England states are predominantly, but not wholly, Democrat. The South, but not its cities, are highly conservative. The Rust Belt states used to be strongly Democrat but have been inching Republican as traditional industries have declined. Most of Middle America is red, the color of the Republican Party. The West Coast, with its more recent immigration history, is increasingly liberal, and this liberalism has begun to encroach into nearby states of Nevada, Colorado, New Mexico, and maybe Arizona.

The thirteen states, through which we would be traveling, were a representative sample of America's political, religious, and literal landscapes. We were looking forward to the journey.

Chapter 4 – Some Mammoth Caves, Kentucky

We took the backroads to Kentucky, mainly avoiding the interstate. The journey meandered through farming communities and the occasional small town. We passed close to the Hermitage, home of seventh President Andrew Jackson.

At the age of twelve, Jackson served in the Revolutionary War and remains the only US president to have been a prisoner of war. Jackson bore a scar on his face and left hand, from when he defied a British Officer by refusing to shine the officer's boots. Jackson later contracted smallpox from the ensuing jail time. No doubt, the current presidential incumbent would prefer presidents who were not captured.

In 1806, Jackson challenged expert marksman Charles Dickinson to an illegal duel after Dickinson accused him of being a "Coward and Equivocator." He also insulted Jackson's wife, about whom we will hear more. Dickinson chose to shoot first and hit Jackson in the chest. The bullet ricocheted off the brass button of Jackson's coat, decelerated when it hit his ribs, and came to rest about an inch from his heart. Jackson stood his ground, stemming the flow of blood with his handkerchief, and – as was the convention at the time – took his time to take his turn. Both men ultimately died in the duel. Dickinson bled to death that day. Jackson's death occurred thirty-nine years later from the lead poisoning from the two bullets still lodged in his chest.

Eagle-eyed readers may wonder where the other bullet came from. The second bullet came from a later duel, where he was also shot first. Jackson fought regular duels with people he believed had slighted him. Historians estimate a surprisingly inexact number of between five and one hundred separate duels.

Jackson was appointed a General in the War of 1812, where he led US troops against British-allied Creek Indians. He later became a national hero when he won an unexpected victory against Britain in the Battle of New Orleans.

Jackson owned and ran a large cotton plantation from his home. To run this plantation, he also "owned" 150 slaves. He was initially reticent about running for office in the usual way politicians do, "I know what I am fit for. I can command a body of men in a rough way; but I am not fit to be president." However, Jackson later changed his mind when it became clear that he might win.

In 1824, he fought the presidential election as a Democrat and won both the popular vote and received most electoral votes. The Democratic Party at the time was supportive of both slavery and the removal of Native Americans. This fitted well with Jackson's background. However, Jackson did not win a clear majority of electoral votes in 1824. After a lot of wheeling and dealing in the House of Representatives, he lost a house election by one vote when the third-placed candidate, the Speaker of the House, threw his support behind John Quincy Adams in return for him becoming the Secretary of State.

1828 saw the same two candidates fight it out again. Adams won the New England states, but Jackson won elsewhere to win the election. We often think of dirty politics as a modern affliction, but this campaign was intensely personal. Both candidates attacked each other virulently in the press. With varying degrees of fact-checking, Jackson was accused of being a slave trader, war criminal, cannibal who ate Indians, and son of a prostitute. Jackson's wife was also accurately accused of being a bigamist. This caused her extreme stress, and she died of a heart attack three weeks after the election. Jackson never forgave Adams and his supporters. At her funeral, he said, "May God Almighty forgive her murderers. I never can."

Jackson believed in patronage politics, "To the Victor, Go the Spoils." Jackson's inauguration as the seventh US president was crowded like Walmart on Black Friday. So many people were seeking office that there was a near-riot, and Jackson had to spend his first night as president in a hotel. Through various trumped-up charges, he eventually purged federal officeholders replacing them with his political apostles.

Jackson pledged to sweep corruption from Washington and said he would undertake the Herculean task of mucking out the giant Augean stable. He was uncompromising in his fights with others, caring little about who was hurt in the crossfire.

Jackson was an authoritarian president, wielding the veto pen more frequently than any previous president. He regularly undermined the fragile and young federal institutions, but he also ultimately strengthened the executive branch of government that the president controlled.

Some readers may detect some parallels between the White House's current incumbent at the time of writing and Andrew Jackson. It is true that national politics polarized around both men. It's also true that Jackson's portrait hangs once again in the Oval office.

Jackson was the target of the first presidential assassination attempt. Richard Lawrence, a mentally-ill house painter, believed he was the heir to the British throne and was therefore owed money by the US Government. Lawrence aimed a single-shot gold pistol, which failed to shoot. He then tried a second pistol, which also misfired. Jackson was so infuriated that he attacked Lawrence with his cane before bystanders rescued Lawrence from the president's counterattack.

Andrew Jackson was once regarded as a great US president, though his reputation has, in recent times, been reappraised in a much more negative light. Today, he is now regarded as implicated in two crimes against humanity: the forced removal of Native Americans from their lands, which subsequently enabled the setting up of slave plantations.

Jackson's history with both groups is incriminating. His battles with Native American tribes gave rise to multiple accusations of war crimes. When he received permission from Congress in 1830 to negotiate with Native Americans to move them to the West, he imposed the US Government's will rather than genuinely negotiate. He was often quoted as urging the use of all possible means, fair or foul. Even where there was an "agreed" deal, these deals were later reneged upon. Before removal, each Cherokee was paid 45 cents per year. When they moved to the West, they received nothing.

We did not stop at the Hermitage, now a National Historic Landmark. If you are interested in American history, however, this plantation is well worth a visit. If you need further incentive, the home is also close to the fun city of Nashville.

We passed close to where our girls had gone to summer camp. It had celebrated its hundredth anniversary the previous year, but this was the first year it had ever gone dark, another casualty of Covid. We had always admired the US summer camp concept when we lived in the UK and had vowed to send our children to a traditional US camp when they were older. Fortune had taken us to live in the USA years later, and we had selected this light, religious-focused girls' camp in Tennessee for our children. Like most others, the four-week camp aimed to develop the girls' character by building skills, increasing their self-confidence, and forging a sense of unselfishness and community.

Both children had enjoyed the low-tech experience of the summer camp, and Daughter #1 had graduated to become a camp counselor working with horses, a cabin leader, and a role model for the eight-year-old girls. Set in a thousand acres of lake and forest, the overall experience was little changed since the camp's inception. The girls enjoyed pretty much the same activities as their great-great-grandmothers. This camp was founded in the same year that women got the vote in the USA, and these opportunities would have been somewhat revolutionary at the time. Girls – then and now – developed skills in canoeing, sailing, swimming, archery, glee club, hiking, camping, arts and crafts, soccer, baseball, tennis, fencing, and riflery.

The sleeping space is deliberately bare. Girls shared the 1920's lake-side cabins with two counselors. There are no windows, no en-suite bathrooms, no air conditioning, and definitely no Wi-Fi or cellular connection. In contrast to US schools, girls wear a simple uniform and belong to a tribe, either Amazon or Valkyrie. Traditional US Summer Camps often celebrate Native American traditions, such as councils, storytelling, and braiding. One wonders whether future generations might find this form of cultural appropriation offensive and demand that it is banned, or appreciate that American society is celebrating and continuing a part of Native American culture.

Tennessee's Cumberland Plateau was spectacular under the clear blue skies. It is home to stunning hikes, gorges, ravines, and waterfalls. One great experience in life is to go waterfall hunting here. Some are mighty, but others are tamer and allow swimming.

We did not stop on this occasion, as we had a reservation at Mammoth Cave National Park in Kentucky. This is one of the more accessible national parks. It's a mere five hours from our home and within a similar timeframe of some hundred million people. More importantly, it was a national park we hadn't yet visited.

Lorna and I totted up the number of cave systems we had visited in our lives. Lorna is more troglodytic than me (thirteen to eleven). Mammoth is named due to its size rather than the presence of the large, extinct woolly mammal. Three hundred million years ago, much of this area was covered by a shallow sea. Organic matter in this sea transformed into limestone hundreds of feet deep. Two hundred and fifty million years ago, a river system brought in, on top of this limestone, sand, and sediments that later transformed to sandstone and shale. Underground rivers cut passages through the relatively soft limestone which formed Mammoth's caverns and passageways.

Mammoth Caves is the world's longest cave system; 426 miles of cave have been mapped so far, with perhaps a further 500 miles undocumented. This is twice as long as the next longest cave system. Despite its relative proximity to large population centers, Mammoth Cave is lightly visited relative to other national parks. Around 0.5 million people visit in an average year.

Lorna was chastised for entering the visitor center the wrong way. It was emptier than a British church on a Tuesday. The ranger behind Perspex glass was delighted to tell her that we were the only people who had booked a cave tour that day. Masked, socially distanced rangers – some might say lone – were on hand at strategic intervals to answer questions. Rangers outnumbered visitors by five to two in this cave, which had only re-opened the previous day. We didn't see Tonto, though we understand some of his ancestors had adorned the walls with their art several thousand years ago.

Outside, the amphitheaters laid empty. Most ranger-led programs would be canceled this year. We have always enjoyed these sessions before. A few years ago, one we attended at an Arkansas State Park saw around a hundred people, including fifty boy scouts, fail to make a fire with the fire-making kit they provided. The lesson I learned from this experience was that the best way to make a fire with two sticks is to make sure that one of the sticks is a match.

The part of the cave system we visited was most conspicuous for its total absence of stalactites and mites. Apparently, this is because an impermeable membrane of capstone rock makes it difficult for water to penetrate the caves. One advantage was that there was no guide pointing out some natural piece of stalacmitery and asking if you recognized the features of some US celebrity of whom you hadn't heard

This cave system may not be pretty, but it does have a fascinating history. It was formed about fifteen million years ago. Around four thousand years ago, pre-historic First People collected crystals and salts. They also buried their dead in the caves but stopped visiting about two thousand years ago.

In 1798, the caves were rediscovered. Depending on which source you believe, a man called Houchin discovered the entrance when chasing/being chased by a wounded bear. The caves were then mined for minerals by around seventy slaves for many years.

The caves became important during the War of 1812. When I lived in the UK, I have to confess that I didn't know much about the War of 1812, other than at some point, I had a vague recollection that British troops had burned down the White House.

I guess Britain has a lot of history to cover, but it's surprising how shallowly some topic areas are covered. After her first day at a US school, my then 12-year-old Daughter #1 returned home in anger. She asked why nobody had thought to tell her that Britain had once controlled the USA and had lost the Revolutionary War. Her mood did not improve when I responded, "Well, did you ask?" Daughter #1 is well-read and curious, so the UK's history with the USA must be largely ignored in UK schools and in our culture generally. This must be doubly so for lesser-known wars, like the War of 1812.

The War of 1812 was a conflict between the USA and Britain between 1812 and 1814. The USA was angry with Britain for their support of Native Americans, annoyed about trade restrictions with Britain's enemies, and unimpressed with the British impressment of some American sailors into the Royal Navy. Some US hawks saw a possibility of the USA capturing all modern-day Canada and removing Britain from North America entirely. One hawk was former President Jefferson, who confidently predicted to President Madison that success was a "mere matter of marching."

The British were at war with the French at this time, and this American conflict was a considerable distraction from their primary focus. The British blockaded the USA and searched every ship bound for their shores. This devastated the US economy. British troops made many raids on American cities, notably on the Atlantic coast. The British had some successes in this war: famously, Savannah was captured, and the White House in Washington DC was burned to the ground. The USA also had its successes. Most notable was The Battle for New Orleans, proctored by General Andrew Jackson, which resulted in two thousand British casualties with only seventy American lives lost.

The nickname Uncle Sam purportedly comes from this war. It was common practice at the time for combatants to try to poison enemy food. Therefore, all food was inspected and guaranteed to be safe to eat. An affable US Army meat inspector, Samuel Wilson, marked each meat consignment with both a US stamp and one from Sam's company. From that moment, Uncle Sam (Wilson) was forever associated with the USA.

The War of 1812 by no means had unanimous support in Congress. The Federalist Party, in particular, were against both the war specifically and the presidential overreach generally. There was a concern that the New England states would secede from the Union. The Federalists met in secret in Hartford, Connecticut in 1814, to discuss their grievances. Their timing was terrible. A few weeks later, the USA had annihilated British troops in New Orleans. The Federalists were forever discredited.

In 1814, about two weeks before the Battle of New Orleans, both parties just agreed to stop fighting as part of the Treaty of Ghent. It was amicably decided that the war was a draw. Sadly, owing to the lengthy journey between Europe and the USA, news of the peace accord did not reach New Orleans until after the battle. The border between Canada and America was agreed upon, and two centuries and counting of friendship between the two nations have ensued.

While the war may have been a draw for the USA and Britain, it was decidedly a loss for the Native American tribes who had lost their British ally. Multiple defeats to the USA followed, along with the ceding of most of their territories.

The USA also benefited in other ways. They had fought the world's most potent power – albeit when the British were distracted by fighting the French – and had not lost. The Spanish noticed this strength and, within five years, had relinquished many territories in North America. The war also started a period of history, called by some as the era of good feelings, where most Americans felt unified behind a common purpose of expanding their country at home. Aside from the latter stages of World War II and the 1950s, this period of common purpose is rare in American history.

The other benefit to America of the War of 1812 was that it forced the USA to develop its own manufacturing industry. They learned that they could not rely on the British for their manufacturing. During the War of 1812, the British blockaded US ports and starved the US Army of gunpowder. Investors purchased the Mammoth Cave system and used the seventy slaves they had "bought" to mine calcium nitrate for the war effort. The demand for the nitrates in there rose, and the investors made a killing. Some mining is still well preserved. You can see the hollowed-out poplar trunks that ancient engineers had used as water pipes.

In 1839, John Croghan bought the Mammoth Cave Estate and the slaves that came with it. One slave, 17-year-old Stephen Bishop (presumably, no relation), led tours for thousands of visitors and mapped in detail the caves and their passages. These tours were amongst the USA's first tourist activities, so it was fitting that this was our first proper stop.

Croghan also believed that the air in the caves could be used to cure people of tuberculosis. We saw the stone houses used as mini-hospitals. Unfortunately for Croghan and many of the slaves, not only did this not cure tuberculosis, but they succumbed to the disease themselves.

In the early twentieth century, Mammoth Caves became a hot travel destination. In a period known as the Kentucky Cave Wars, multiple caves competed against each other for visitors. A railroad was built, and steamboats delivered people to the caves via the Green River. In 1926, residents first campaigned for it to become a national park, and, in 1941, Mammoth Caves was dedicated as one. At the time, only forty-four miles of caves had been discovered.

The park is above ground too. We took a couple of mini-hikes on the contours of the undulating hills, avoiding bears that might chase us into sinkholes. Lorna also resisted the opportunity to canoe down the Green River. We seemed to be the only people staying in the park in one of the historic cottages. We were told that the restaurant would stay open later for us if we asked. We regretted asking, having had one of the worst meals we have ever eaten.

Our first night was spent in a rustic park cabin, which had also only opened the day before. The cabin was basic, but, as Lorna said, it looked better inside than outside. Like most USA accommodation, the cabin had air-conditioning, and the bed and linen were outstanding.

When we first arrived in the USA, we had to purchase four new mattresses. The shopping crossroad near us boasted three mattress shops. We were surprised to find that they were all owned by the same company, with its obligatory punned name, Mattress Firm. It turned out that this oversupply was repeated elsewhere in the USA and that America had more stores that sold mattresses than Big Macs. A financial data company calculated that Mattress Firm had 43 percent of its stores located within one mile of another of its outlets. Schererville in Indiana, with a population of only 28,701, had five Mattress Firm stores less than a block apart. Assuming that every person in that Lake Michigan town had their own mattress, that they all bought a new mattress every ten years from the same company and not one of their competitors or online, this would equate to sales of only one and a half mattresses per store per day. At the time, I could not fathom out why there were so many outlets.

Five years later, Mattress Firm went into receivership. They claimed that some now ex-executives had signed up to longer, more expensive leases in exchange for personal kickbacks. These charges are still meandering through the court system.

Americans love a mattress, and you see TV advertisements for mattresses all the time. The latest one asks you for your sleep number. This piece of dubious science extends the traditional soft/medium/firm designation to a number between 0 (concrete) and 100 (bouncy). It's the water bed fad for this time. Apparently, your sleep number might change. If you switch from sleeping on your side to your back, you might want to reduce your number by five. If you put on some weight – and many Americans do – you might want to increase the number by a few notches. It's all marketing bullshit to persuade you to pay four times the cost of a standard mattress. All wasted on me too. I'm equally happy sleeping on the floor as I am on a bouncy castle. Indeed, every bed we slept on during our trip was excellent.

Mammoth Cave National Park has a post office; indeed, many national parks have post offices. Kids, well before social media, people used to boast about where they were going on their vacations just like they do online today. On arriving at their destination in these olden days, visitors would line up at the national park post office to send picture postcards to their friends to prove that they had the means to take fancy vacations.

It wasn't clear who used these national park post offices now. Of course, a few park employees lived on-site and would have the occasional use of their facilities. I guess, like the UK, the USA has universal service obligations to keep post offices that few people use open.

US post offices sell stamps for letters, packages, and collectors. They also offer premium delivery services that track your letter or package. That's about it. They don't provide the cornucopia of services a UK post office does. No banking, phones, broadband, travel, ATM, driving licenses, passports, pensions and benefits, immigration, council tax, meals on wheels etc. Despite this limited service, the US Postal Service has a more extensive retail network than McDonald's, Starbucks, and Walmart combined.

There are a couple of things the US Postal Service does well. My favorite is the mailbox at the end of your drive. It's both the place where you receive and send mail. If you want to send mail, all you need to do is place a stamped letter in the mailbox and raise the little red flag to signal to the mail carrier that letters need to be collected. Second, it costs only 50 cents to send a letter, compared with 97 cents first class and 83 cents second class in the UK. This ease and the relatively low cost to send a letter might account for why 47 percent of the world's mail is processed by the US Postal Service. The USA employs about one-tenth of the world's postal workers but delivers almost half of its mail.

I also love the little electric mail vans. They are the only vehicles in the USA with right-hand drive so that the mailman or mailwoman can easily open and close the mailbox without getting out of the van. I'm not the only one who loves the Postal Service. Nine out of ten Americans have a favorable view of it, by far the highest of any federal agency.

Despite this love for the US Postal Service, their financial position is precarious. The last recorded profit was in 2006, and the cumulative losses since then have been $81 billion. Its balance sheet is no better, with money owed to both the Treasury and unpaid contributions to its retirement funds. The fundamental reasons behind this are that mail volumes are falling by about 3 percent every year. The universal service obligations make it difficult to reduce costs by a similar amount. It's predicted that they will lose around $50bn in the next decade, and their pension deficit is already sizeable. Twitter feedback – that most unreliable source of opinion – suggests that people don't care that it loses money. After all, the military loses even more under the same rules. It is, incidentally, one of the world's mysteries that it is precisely the same people on

Twitter who are simultaneously experts on Covid, police reform, climate change, and whatever the latest issue du jour is.

Once more en route, we passed close to Fort Knox, the home to the United States Bullion Depository. This Art Deco facility was built during the Great Depression deliberately away from the coast and over the Appalachian Mountains to make it less vulnerable to foreign attack. Fort Knox now holds 4,600 metric tons of gold, about 56 percent of the US's total federal holdings.

It was a significant logistical challenge to move the gold to Fort Knox in 1937 and 1941 from their previous depositories in New York and Philadelphia. For one thing, a gold bar is surprisingly heavy. A lifetime ago, I worked at the Bank of England, which houses much of the UK's gold. Although only 7½ inches long by 3½ inches wide (that's 19 cm by 9 cm if you are metrically inclined), each gold bar weighs just under thirty pounds (fourteen kilograms). This is about fourteen bags of sugar, whether you measure it imperially or metrically. The operation was surprisingly – given their limited responsibilities – overseen by the US Postal Service. The Post Office coordinated soldiers, secret service agents, and various police departments. The gold was shipped onto ninety-four trains on 552 separate wagons over a twelve-month period. Multiple decoy trains were also deployed to deter train robbers.

Fort Knox also holds many other valuables, including rare coins and stockpiles of opium and morphine. During World War 2, Fort Knox cared for the original signed US Constitution, Lincoln Cathedral's copy of the Magna Carta, the US Declaration of Independence, multiple volumes of Gutenberg's Bible, Hungary's Crown Jewels, and Lincoln's second inaugural address and drafts of his Gettysburg Address. It was closed to visitors when we passed by, but then it always is.

We took an hour's detour instead along the country roads of rural Kentucky to see the "original" Lincoln memorial. The memorial, which receives about one-quarter of a million visitors per year, houses the supposed cabin in which Lincoln was born and preserves the farm site where he lived until he reached his majority. You can also visit the spring from which he would have first drank water.

The site and museum were empty since it was in the middle of nowhere. It made me wonder when we will get the next president from a humble background. Despite her humble background, many celebrated people are descendants of Lincoln's mother, Nancy Hanks. The actors, for example, Tom Hanks, George Clooney, and Camille Cosby, are all distant cousins of Nancy Hanks. It's then that you remember that the USA population when she was born was only 3.2 million.

Almost all past presidents have a library, museum, and perhaps monument dedicated to them. Sometimes, their families or supporters are involved in their set up, but often it is the ex-president himself who is the primary driver of the content. We have seen a few of these presidential museums during our various travels around America. It's my considered view that people should not be allowed to curate their own museums.

When Lorna is traveling, she always likes to sample local foods. She has had chicken in Kyiv, whale in Japan, fertilized eggs in the Philippines, guinea pigs in Ecuador, and birds nest soup in China. As we were in Kentucky, this meant KFC. However, the good people of Kentucky didn't seem to appreciate Colonel Saunders' special recipe of herbs and spices as much as the people in all other parts of the world, and we were not able to find an outlet.

Chapter 5 – First of the Great Lakes

When you meet someone in Florida, they invariably tell you that they come from Michigan originally. They lament that they can no longer stand their home state's long winters and tell you that, in the summer, Michigan is the most beautiful place on earth. It was for this reason that we decided to spend time in Michigan on our journey. I've been to Michigan a few times, but always on the more industrial eastern side. This time we drove up the western Michigan coast hugging the shoreline of Lake Michigan.

Michigan's Democrat Governor, Gretchen Whitmer, had locked her state down harder and longer than most other US states. She had publicly criticized the President when little federal help was forthcoming and had received the now-usual childish response to her comments. She also faced a barrage of criticism herself from the majority Republican Michigan State Legislature. Despite the stay-at-home order, American patriot rallies had protested her decisions, with security for these rallies provided by various armed militia groups. Opposition to her decisions was still visible in many parts of the state that we were driving through. "Heil Whitmer" seemed to be the favored banner, even it was not particularly original. Despite the criticism, infection numbers had fallen dramatically, but it had come at the expense of high unemployment.

The state had a complicated six-phase re-opening plan that took many readings to understand. Each Michigan county was at a different stage of this plan. We entered the state into early-phase counties that were coming out of lockdown. Hotels and restaurants on the Lake Michigan coast had just re-opened, and people were going out to play.

As you know, the USA is a vast country. It is of a similar size to Canada and China, which are just under half the size of the world's largest country, Russia. People often wonder how Middle American residents cope with being so far away from the ocean. The answer is that many Americans go to the lake for vacations. In my state, it is just as common for families and friends to go to the lake as it is to take the long drive to the Gulf or the Atlantic Ocean. However, in the middle part of North America, the ocean is mind-bogglingly distant from your home. From Chicago, for example, it's a thousand miles to a decent ocean beach. No part of Britain is more than seventy-eight miles from the beach, something that in America would probably be described as close to the beach on AirBnB.

Fortunately, the Mid-West has many lakes. The five Great Lakes of North America hold more than one-fifth of the World's freshwater. Their combined surface area is almost twelve times the size of Wales or slightly more than the UK. These Great Lakes have 35,000 islands within their shores. If the Great Lakes are not enough for you, there are around 100,000 other lakes in the region. Minnesota famously boasts 10,000 lakes on its car number plates. In fact, it over-delivers with 11,842. Wisconsin, with its slogan "America's Dairyland," and Michigan, which keeps changing its motto but is now the uninspiring "Pure Michigan" alongside a website address, make no such claims about the quantity of lakes on their number plates. However, they both have more lakes than Minnesota.

The lake beach has a couple of advantages over the ocean beach: freshwater is more pleasant than saltwater, and it is easier to indulge in motorized water sports. The meteorological features here also lower both the humidity levels and coastal temperatures. The typical summer high here is 75-80°F (25°C). In Florida, summer temperatures will often exceed 100°F (38°C). These Mid-West lakes provide the beaches for Middle America.

The Great Lakes are so vast that, when the wind blows, the water has waves. Sometimes, on a stormy day, these waves can reach up to thirty feet high. The lake waves have a shorter interval than those on the ocean and, therefore, are slightly less powerful. Surf shops offer equipment in every town along the Lake Michigan coast. With no prospect of shark attack and no reefs to lacerate your body, there are worse places to learn how to surf. However, you will need a neoprene wet suit, as the best surf days coincide with cold air and strong winds.

Chicago sits more than a hundred miles to the west over Lake Michigan. Even with Chicago's towering skyscrapers, you will never see the other side due to the earth's curvature. Seventeenth-century maps from some French explorers showed America to be only three-hundred-miles wide. The explorers reached Lake Ontario and assumed that they had hit the Pacific Ocean and the next stop was China. In some respects, this is understandable. If I transported you blindfold to a Michigan beach, I think the only way you would know that you weren't on an ocean is that the water was not salty. With hindsight, this is something that the seventeenth-century Frenchmen should have tried before they trudged the three hundred miles back to produce their inaccurate maps of the small North American island.

The eastern coast of Lake Michigan has enormous dunes, and we saw trucks transporting beach buggies to play on the sand. The beaches are plentiful and are rarely crowded. Michigan alone has 3,300 miles of coastline, and there is a beach for every taste. When you research your next summer beach holiday, consider Michigan. I don't think you will regret it.

Our first stop in Michigan was South Haven. Positioned at the mouth of the Black River, it's a typical beach community on the lower Lake Michigan shores. Wooden houses are painted white with fences to match, and the marina is packed with large boats that we could not afford. It's very tidy and quaint.

Not many people would guess that Michigan is the state with the largest number of lighthouses, about double the second state, Maine. Now that you know this, it would probably be no surprise at all that South Haven also had its own operational cast-iron lighthouse. It sits at the end of a catwalk pier.

The town of South Haven was full of good restaurants and bars, the vast majority not yet open when we visited. We chose a perfect time to visit Michigan, as the people here were coming outside for the first time after four months of brutal winter followed by three months of strict lockdown. People here were as happy as Texans at a gun show. Everyone sported a permanent smile everywhere we went, and I couldn't take Lorna's picture without some person wanting to share the background.

We chose Mexican takeout, cooked by a Chinese American. We ate it on a cold aluminum bench in the middle of the harbor with its thousand-boat docks. As I recall, I liked the food slightly more than Lorna. We both enjoyed the view of the boats and the smiles of the locals, who were out for their evening walk.

We took our postprandial walk along the glistening beaches in South Haven. The beaches here are idyllic, as indeed they all are along the Lake Michigan shoreline. They are deep and long, with dazzling white sand. The beaches have the same amenities as their ocean counterparts: ice cream cabins, elevated wooden lifeguard huts, and beach volleyball courts. We planned to view the sunset over Lake Michigan, but a sudden but equally magnificent thunderstorm came over the horizon. The waves pounded the beach with unexpected fury. We retreated with a couple of hundred students from Western Michigan University judging by their sweatshirts, all of whom had also been enjoying the freedom of the beach.

Now university is a pretty different experience in the US. Unlike in the UK, you cannot specialize in solely one subject. Instead, you have to cover each of the main areas of study at a foundation level before choosing your preferred area of specialization, or what they call a major here. Thus, degrees usually take four years in the USA rather than the typical three for the UK. One advantage this gives is that you finalize your choice of major halfway through your degree, typically at the age of twenty.

As a student, you can choose to study any course that is offered by the university. Your college will mandate compulsory subject areas; for example, everyone has to take at least one math course. Your individual faculty school will require the courses you need to take for that major. Other than that, what you choose to study is entirely up to you. Steve Jobs famously took a calligraphy course because it sounded interesting. As a direct consequence, Jobs accredited this course for Apple's famed design.

As in the lower school system, assessment is continuous rather than dependent on year-end exams. US students are used to this regular stress from high school, but this weekly testing must shock many international students.

American mothers, and maybe the occasional father, can be overprotective of their adult children. Social media abounds with examples of anxious moms who try to micromanage every aspect of their child's life. This helicoptering and bulldozing parenting style can lead to depression and anxiety, but more typically contributes to some students' low ability to cope with everyday life. A few parents rent a house for the first week of their adult child's time at college just to make sure that they are adapting appropriately. These parents have probably been highly active in all stages of their child's education, and it's hard for them to let go. This year, one mother used social media to lament that her adult son hadn't made any friends yet. She posted this four hours after he had moved in. A popular US app called Life360 can track your child's every movement. It messages the parent when their baby speeds at 55 mph on a 45 mph road and tells them when their adult child leaves the dorm room. At least one of Daughter #2's friends would sometimes leave her phone in our mailbox to fool the Life360 and her mom that she was at our house.

In their first year, students live in a single-gender dorm room, typically with another student. For some, this will be a friend they already know from high school. Others will have roommates that they met online or have been assigned randomly. These dorm rooms vary according to the accommodation block's age but are typically a double room that houses two bunk beds and two desks.

Each set of sixteen or so dorm rooms has a Residential Assistant, known as an RA, who has their own room in the block. This is a marginally older undergraduate whose role is to facilitate new freshmen's social and academic adjustment. Dropout rates in US colleges are much higher than in Europe, and it's pretty standard for students to swap universities. The RAs have an extensive job description. They are expected to get to know each freshman, assist them in adjusting to roommate and community living, ensure that they understand their academic and social responsibilities, and supervise behavior in university accommodation. They are on call pretty much all the time.

RAs receive free accommodation, free food, and $1,000 per semester for all of these responsibilities. They also receive a free phone, fridge and microwave, computer, and book vouchers. This is one way that some students pay their way through college. Of course, there are strict RAs and relaxed ones. Every freshman hopes for a relaxed RA, one who will turn a blind eye to you bringing a sexual partner back to your room or to the occasional empty vodka bottle.

One immigrant friend was an RA at his American university in the 1990s. He worked five jobs simultaneously to pay his way through college, and being an RA was just one of his jobs. He was just strict enough to keep his role but was mostly absent due to his commitments at the other four jobs. He would report those boys who brought girls into their room in an unsubtle way or were particularly brazen about their alcohol consumption. Otherwise, his charges were undoubtedly pleased that they had snared a relaxed RA.

In these Covid times, the RA's responsibilities have expanded. They oversee health and safety for their dorm rooms and are the university's primary conduit for policing Covid behavior. They are forced to be stricter, as they monitor mask-wearing and visitor access. No outside visitors are allowed into accommodation halls, and the only person now authorized in your own dorm room is your roommate. Sex for the freshman has become more difficult, but maybe also more daring.

For the helicoptering parent, who remains concerned about their child's wellbeing, the care package can come to your rescue. Care packages are a way of showing that you care, but with minimal interference. For only $160, you can purchase a "full of love care package" that will deliver a bunch of junk food to your adult child's dorm room. If you prefer your child to eat healthier food, there's a package for $190. As I see it, this is just another version of that old favorite game, "my mom is better than your mom." Lorna doesn't want her daughters to think that we don't care. She certainly doesn't want them to be the only ones without a package, but she is mindful that this food would only cost $40 when bought at Costco. She makes her own packages.

From their second year, as in the UK, most students live off-campus. At Southern and some old universities, many live with others in a fraternity or sorority house. Daughter #1 elected to live in a high-class apartment with friends. It boasts a roof-top two-tiered infinity pool, cabanas, extensive fitness center, indoor basketball court, PGA-quality golf simulator, racquetball court, gaming room, tanning room, lounges, and study rooms. It is a long way from our own UK student experience.

College is expensive, in tuition, board and lodging, and other fees. Many students take on unimaginable levels of student debt. It isn't unusual to meet someone in their twenties or thirties who has $250,000 of student debt with its 5.8 percent average interest rate. They will be paying the equivalent of a large mortgage payment for their college education for the next two or three decades.

This high cost of university attendance is the main reason many students work their way through college. Our daughters are fortunate to have parents that are able – and somewhat willing – to pay for all of our daughters' university costs and give them a handsome allowance. However, Daughter #1 enjoys working. She wants to be able to buy what she wants and to take foreign vacations. Therefore, she works a couple of days per week as a barmaid at a semi-upscale bar. She likes to be part of a non-student community.

There is a paradox that an eighteen-year-old can get themselves into $60,000 or more of student debt in their first year at college, but that same student isn't allowed to buy themselves a beer. As I suspect you know, you cannot purchase alcohol until you are twenty-one years old in America. Shops and bars lose their licenses for underage sale of alcohol. Therefore, it's normal to be asked for your ID for every adult purchase. I'm fifty-four years old and on a good – but increasingly rare – day look in my 40s. I am asked for ID every time I buy beer or wine for my wife. At first, you feel good that perhaps someone thinks you could be under twenty-one, but as with all good things, you soon get used to it.

Daughter #1 and #2 both have multiple fake IDs. They buy them via the internet from China, another example of how the Chinese have stolen business away from honest American forgers. These $100 IDs often arrive hidden under a legitimate purchase, like a tea set or chopsticks. Import statistics must significantly overestimate American demand for authentic Chinese kitchenware. While state authorities regularly update security features on their IDs, the Chinese are vigilant at keeping up. Many fake IDs replicate the perforations, microprints, and deliberate spaces. The best IDs also work on a box scanner. The penalty for using these counterfeit IDs can be high in many jurisdictions, but police typically take a remarkably relaxed attitude in college towns where the maximum penalty is merely to tear up their ID, forcing the student to use one of their backups on a future occasion.

Both daughters have joined, or plan to join, the Greek system of sororities and fraternities at their university. This was quite an alien concept for me to understand when I first arrived. Of all the topics I will try to explain in this book, I find this – and healthcare, which will come in a later chapter – challenging to present neutrally.

A sorority or fraternity is a social club that many students join when they go to college. There are 5,500 fraternity chapters and 2,900 sorority chapters across the USA. Some universities have small Greek populations; others, like the university my daughters attend, have most freshman students in Greek-letter society. Despite its inherent conservatism, Greek life membership continues to increase. Most students join a sorority or fraternity only for the first two years at college, while some students retain their membership as alumni after they leave.

Each sorority or fraternity takes two or three random Greek letters to form its name. Greek letters were initially selected by the first fraternity in 1775 – yes, that's right, before independence – because they believed it would convey a sense of intelligence. Otherwise, there is really nothing Greek about the system, other than that most chapter houses have Greek columns and Greek letters on the pediment or frieze of their façade. Greek life names are often abbreviated to their initials or a shortened version of their name. This is a form of code that separates the insiders from the outsiders.

Sororities and fraternities are given nicknames according to their reputations. These nicknames also tell you something about the Greek community. The sorority, Delta Delta Delta, is nicknamed "Tri Delta – everyone else has"; Pi Beta Phi – unzip your fly, here comes a Pi Phi; and Kappa Kappa Gamma – Katcha Katcha Gonorrhea. I'm sure you understand the pattern.

Despite their subtle attempts to keep out members of the LGBT community, most fraternities have pretty unoriginal gay slur nicknames. However, sororities have also demonized individual fraternities with whom they have had a bad experience. Sigma

Alpha Epsilon is called Sexual Assault Expected and Alpha Tau Omega, Asshole Training Organization.

Fraternities or sororities have brother or sister chapters in different universities, but I understand that the culture can vary enormously by university. Each Greek entity is part of a broader organization in multiple universities with the same Greek letters. These are governed by a centralized function called International that sets standards and has the ultimate power to grant or revoke charters. The organization is international in more or less the same way that the final of the baseball season is called the World Series.

UK universities have a freshers' week event, where new students meet others and choose to join various university societies. At many US universities, the big event as a new freshman is the selection process to join Greek life. It's called rushing, and it's the process by which students are allocated to a sorority or fraternity. This process is brutal. Think of a really big school playground, where team captains get to pick their teams, and the less able are left to the end. Now do this in your first week at university.

The process varies somewhat by university, but basically, all girls and boys who want to join Greek life are taken through a series of social events and interviews during the week. I know most about sororities with two daughters, so I will describe it in more detail. Their rushing rules are numerous and considerably more complicated than, say, the Laws of Cricket. Indeed, the process is so complicated that a manual has been produced to describe it, and the first day is spent explaining the process and the rules to the rushees. The process is carefully choreographed down to giving advice on what the putative sister should carry in her purse. For the record, should you wish to apply, this is a handheld fan, breath mints, lipstick, and deodorant.

On the second and third days, small groups of about twenty rushees visit every single sorority house in "casual" clothing. Each group is welcomed by cheering and chanting from the current sororal members. Based on these twenty-minute visits plus the extensive homework and trawling of social media that the sorority chapter has been monitoring since March, each Greek organization ranks those they want by priority. A small number of misfits may find that they have been excluded from all chapters after the first round. It's hard to imagine a more dispiriting start to your college experience. You are essentially being told that you are not wanted.

The interview process continues on the fourth and fifth days. Girls will be instructed on what color dresses they should wear for each day. Frat boys jeer and whistle at the groups of girls in their red dresses as they make their way down Greek Row. Each chapter again submits its list of potentials in order of ranking. This process continues until each girl only has two potential sororities remaining. The sorority that bids the highest for you is the one you will join. The applicant has little say in which house she will go to, other than amending her behavior slightly during the process. Daughter #1 was not keen to join one particular sorority, so she acted somewhat dismissively and was cut by them at the next stage.

The eighth day is Bid Day, and also the first day of academic classes. Bid Day is the most important celebration for the Pan-Hellenic Community. Dressed in virginal white dresses, each girl learns which house she will be joining at an early evening meeting. She and her fellow rushees make their way by party bus to their new "home." The road on which all the Greek houses are based is one large and loud street party. Despite my many misgivings on the Greek System, it's difficult not to enjoy the excitement generated by these girls as they join their new sisters.

You are not yet formally a member of the sorority or fraternity. You have to endure a pledging process that takes a couple of months. For girls, this consists of a lot of education about what sisterhood means and how you should behave. Actually, a lot of this is a pretty useful induction to university life. You have probably read about the hazing process for boys. In recent years, twenty-five sets of parents have lost their son in hazing incidents, usually from too much alcohol. Although hazing is officially banned, boys are hazed to ensure they have a suitable level of belongingness. They call the worst part "Hell Week." In this week, pledging members are deprived of sleep, spanked, forced to eat spoiled food, and ordered to clean toilets with their toothbrushes. At the end of the pledging process, new members are initiated into their Greek organization in a formal ceremony for both girls and boys.

A quick look at most sorority or fraternity pictures will reveal that these are not diverse institutions. Daughter #1's new intake picture featured forty or so white girls with long blond or long brown hair in white dresses. I have seen more diversity at a Ku Klux Klan rally. My daughter represented diversity because she was British. It's for this reason that specialist black and Jewish sororities have been founded. Although sororities may once have been groundbreaking, they are now highly-conservative organizations. It's OK if you are lesbian, but don't tell anyone, don't advertise it on Instagram, and make sure you invite a man to date night.

I haven't even told you yet what it costs. Membership varies a lot by the college. At my daughters' university, it costs more than $3,000 per year to be a member. In some other colleges, it will be twice that. Not surprisingly, this high cost puts off less affluent students, particularly those from certain ethnic minorities. There are additional expenses too. Daughter #1 will never again have to buy a t-shirt. Fraternities tend to be laidback organizations, but sororities seem to delight in setting and administering multiple rules. They derive a lot of income from fines too. If you don't turn up for the weekly meeting, you will be fined. If you disgrace yourself at a social event, you will be both disciplined and fined. If you post something inappropriate on social media – for example, drinking, drug use, nudity, or other disrespectful comments on other sororities – you will be fined. The sororities say these rules are there for everyone's health and safety. However, I suspect the young women in leadership positions like creating regulations and controlling others' lives. In this way, they are preparing for later life.

In the second year, most members will live in a Greek house. This costs around $4,000 and is exceptional value compared with the cost of your own apartment. Sadly, Daughter #1 did not take up this option.

You may ask what do these fraternities and sororities do? Fraternity houses are buildings filled with men. Most fraternities seem to spend their money on alcohol and parties for girls. Sororities are quite different in how they present themselves. They stand for service through the development of character and deep friendship. In public, they emphasize academics, leadership, and philanthropy. Sorority members typically spend their second year in the house, four or more to each room. A live-in "house mother" and cook caters all meals, and the house is decorated as a plantation house would have been decorated two centuries ago. Boys are rarely allowed in the house and certainly never upstairs.

The main activity for both fraternities and sororities is drinking. Four out of five members regularly binge drink until they blackout at one of the many parties that fraternities hold for sororities. The higher-ranked fraternities invite the higher-ranked sororities to parties on their front lawn. Fraternities and Sororities take over entire beach towns during Spring Break every year, and the beach – temporarily renamed Frat Beach – is one big party. Fraternities receive much more criticism than sororities, primarily because they are more excessive in their behavior.

How are the Greek rankings established, I hear you ask. They emerge, mainly by consensus, and are based predominantly on the average attractiveness of its members. This is not politically correct and not modern, but that is how it works.

Greek life does some worthy stuff too. Most chapters are involved in service work, and both sororities and fraternities have banks of educational content. It may surprise you that academic standards are higher for members of Greek life. They have a 20 percent higher graduation rate and appreciably higher Grade Point Averages. If you don't get strong grades, you are punished by your chapter until you have corrected your grades. It is interesting that when many US children leave their parents' world and get freedom for the first time, they form smaller groups that set rules and impose these rules on each other. This is probably truer for girls than boys, though. If a girl embarrasses herself by getting too drunk, she is punished by their chapter's Standards Committee. I suspect boys are just congratulated.

As the thunderstorms rolled into the town, we left the young college students from Western Michigan University and looked for a hotel.

Chapter 6 – Trolling up the Michigan Coast

Sleeping Bear Dunes National Lakeshore, part of the National Park System but not a full-fledged national park, was our first destination for the day. It was patched together fifty years ago, mainly from private land, and receives about 1.6 million visitors every year. The park contains thirty-five miles of Lake Michigan beach, a handful of inland lakes, forests, rivers, and some lake islands, including those of North and South Manitou.

The park is named Sleeping Bear after the Ojibwe Tribal legend. The two Manitou islands represent cubs who drown in the lake while trying to reach the shore, which resembles their mother, who waits on a bluff overlooking the lake. I've looked at pictures of the coast from the lake and cannot see it myself, though the dunes' contours may have shifted over the years.

The first activity of the day was kayaking. We chose Lake Loon and River Platte for our trip. A couple was leaving the lake as we arrived, but otherwise, we had the lake and river entirely to ourselves in our new kayak. The water was crystal clear, and you could see all the fish in the lake. The headwind meant that we took some exercise kayaking up the river but had little to do on the way back. The lake was surprisingly warm, and the freshwater swim we took both invigorating and cleansing.

We drove further up to the Glen Haven, the park's northernmost point, nestled in Sleeping Bear Bay. It used to be a commercial and tourist dock, from which timber was taken by tugs to various parts of the lake and where tourist steamships once used to stop. The Glen Haven Canning company factory, which once processed fruit from five thousand cherry and apple trees, had a prominent position on the promontory. It had since been converted into a Great Lakes boat museum, closed, of course, due to Covid.

The main feature of the park is the dunes, some 450 feet high. These magnificent dunes line the park's length and are sculpted by the lake's winds and waters. We took a short walk through the dunes to the shore. Dunes are surprisingly difficult to walk up. We were glad that we didn't take the main dunes trail, which is just over three miles in length but takes up to four hours to walk. There were a few more people here, but it could hardly be described as crowded. A few children were rolling down the dunes. I suspect they are still extracting sand from their crevices.

Schools had been closed across the USA since March, and all school events were canceled. There was online school, but this was mostly optional for our senior, Daughter #2. She had reached that young age, where she had more wisdom and knowledge than the combined experience of both parents and all grandparents. She was as carefree as a tornado in a trailer park, primarily because she was plan-free.

The seniors, the students in their final year of high school, are the group for whom most Americans felt sorry. For most, senior year is a magical time in their life. College places have already been decided based on work completed until the end of their junior year and countrywide SAT or ACT tests in the first part of their senior year. After three years of academic stress where you have daily tests that contribute towards a grade point average (GPA), the senior year for most is when you could slack off a little.

Seniors enjoy a whole slew of traditions. The year begins when you decorate your car's bodywork and apply slogans in paint that, one day, you might be able to erase from your vehicle. I guess the purpose is that everyone should know that you are a senior. You will soon graduate high school and go to college or perhaps straight to work.

A few senior skip days had been held. These are organized by word of mouth by the seniors themselves. Days are identified that might be good to skip, and when teachers learn that a particular day is a skip day, most decide to reschedule tests for another time. Many seniors participate, but some do not, preferring to keep their 100 percent attendance record intact. Daughter #2 is not concerned about her attendance record, so she participates fully in every skip day. On these skip days, students meet up together outside the school to socialize. However, once your school has closed for Covid, where is the fun in a senior skip day if every day is a skip day?

Senior photos are organized and then retakes of these pictures. Like wedding photos do for your nuptials, these provide a permanent reminder of your time in high school. The images are sent to relatives and are also placed in the school yearbook. When you see a serial killer's picture, the photo used by the media often comes from the killer's yearbook. Therefore, it's essential to get the shot just right. The yearbook itself is a significant tradition for all high schoolers. Every year, a seven-hundred-page book is produced by the seniors showcasing activity at their school. Every student is featured, and every school activity is noted. It is the record of your time at high school.

Senior prom is held. These coming-of-age events started in the late nineteenth century, at first simply, as tea dances where everyone dressed up in their Sunday best. As Americans became richer, proms became more sophisticated. Venues moved from high school gymnasia to hotel ballrooms. Students competed against each other on best dressed, best form of transportation, and even best celebrity they can invite to their big day.

A prom has a myriad of sub-traditions. It starts with the prom-posal where, traditionally, a boy asks a girl to attend the prom. As social change has spread throughout high schools, this tradition has morphed too. It's now normal for a boy to ask a boy or girl to ask a girl, though we rarely see a girl ask a boy. This prom-posal has become a significant event in itself, in the same way that marriage proposals have.

Boys dress in black tuxedos and bowties. The ones with "personality" might prefer white or colored tuxes. Girls wear formal dresses of more or less any color, though some couples take care to have matching outfits. The day of the prom is a busy one. In an area like the one we live in, where there are many high schools and hence a large number of seniors, you may find that every hair and nail salon for six weeks of prom season is booked every Saturday for months in advance.

The day starts with the last tanning session. The friend with the best YouTube makeup channel is brought in to apply the makeup. Girls wear a corsage, a small bouquet of flowers worn on their dress, given to them by their dates. Girls give boys boutonnières for the lapels of their tuxedo jackets.

Groups of friends go to a local beauty spot for pre-prom pictures, accompanied by parents, siblings, and other relatives. The most popular places have long lines. In some cases, professional photographers are procured. In general, the girls look stunning, and the boys uncomfortable.

In the past, the boy would pick the girl up from her house in his father's car. As in the movies, the boy must wait downstairs with the rest of the family, including Aunts and Uncles, who have been invited for this pivotal life moment. The girl descends the stairs to the admiration of everyone below. The father's car is a less common form of transport nowadays. Teenagers prefer to attend prom as part of a large friend group. They more typically rent a limousine or party bus to arrive at Prom, often stopping at a restaurant on the way.

The prom itself is a sumptuous but highly regulated affair. Our daughters' proms were held at the Fox Theatre in Atlanta's Midtown. Designed initially as a masonic temple, The Fabulous Fox was a former movie palace that opened on Christmas Day 1929, two months after the Wall Street Crash. It closed three years later after William Fox went bankrupt, and was bought by the movie theater company, Paramount. The ballroom was the place where the big bands played and was unusual in the South in that it allowed both white and black patrons, albeit through separate entrances.

That area of Midtown declined due to white flight during the 1970s. There was a plan to demolish the theatre, but a residents' group opposed this. They eventually persuaded authorities to have the theatre registered on the National Register of Historic Places. The campaign also persuaded the big stars of the day to protest to save the Fox, and Lynyrd Skynyrd recorded their excellent live album as part of that campaign. The city eventually bowed to political pressure and refused a demolition permit. The theater was saved. However, of the six original movie palaces in Atlanta, it is the only one that is still standing.

The Fox has two surprising architectural styles: Islamic architecture for the exterior and auditorium and Egyptian architecture for the ballroom and surrounding area. The ballroom is based on the Ramses II temple at Karnak, an impressive site that we had visited a few decades previously. The nearby ladies' lounge sports a King Tut throne and makeup tables with adorning Sphynxes. If you are ever in Atlanta, take a tour or, even better, watch a theater production there.

Proms are necessarily quite regulated events as teachers cannot condone underage drinking. As a result, many prom goers prefer to move elsewhere for their entertainment. Although Daughter #2 missed her senior prom due to Covid, she was invited to the two previous proms by seniors. She spent less than one hour in aggregate at these two proms before moving to the post-prom party.

The main event of the prom process is the after-prom party, and these have also become subject to much cost inflation. These events have now become after-prom weekends. Some hapless parent chaperones a friend group of teenagers at a rented vacation home in the mountains or by the lake to continue their year-long celebration of high school graduation. This inflation shows no sign of abating; you hear about some wealthy parents who hire celebrities, entertainers, or artists to perform at after-prom parties.

It won't surprise you that the average cost to attend prom has increased to more than $1,000 per prom. We live in an affluent area of the USA, but the same behavior pattern is repeated elsewhere. A few years ago, Lorna and I took a weekend away during prom season to Montgomery, the state capital of neighboring Alabama. Montgomery is a fascinating city to visit, but it has a different demographic; it is 60 percent African American and has a median income of one-third of our city. Our Montgomery hotel hosted the local high-school prom. The Montgomery prom's rituals were precisely the same as ours, and it was essentially the same experience. The girls looked stunning and confident in their ball gowns, their hair and nails perfect. The boys looked dorky and somewhat ill at ease in their rented tuxedos. A little less money was spent, but it was still a coming-of-age treat.

Some proms, but not that of our high school, anoint a Prom King and Queen. As with everything else American, this is done by school-wide vote. The King and Queen are literally crowned and are photographed alongside their sash-wearing prom court of other popular students.

In movies, prom is when teens have sex for the first time. This is actually rare. Only 5 percent lose their virginity this night, with more than half not losing their virginity until after high school. For this lucky one in twenty, there may be the additional cost of a red-rose-petal-covered hotel room.

Although prom is strictly speaking for seniors (and sometimes juniors), my daughters had attended multiple Proms and Homecoming Queen dances. In 2020, almost every school canceled their Prom, and a generation of students was deprived of their night of firsts. They also lost several other coming-of-age moments.

Most graduation ceremonies were canceled or morphed into sterile drive-thru experiences. Graduation parties were canceled. The long-awaited graduation trip, the reward for four years of hard work, was postponed. Daughter #2 had planned a journey with friends across continental Europe that proved impossible to take. All sport was canceled, including high-school sport. State Championships could not take place. Sophomores and juniors with scholarship aspirations could no longer demonstrate their prowess to receive a free college education. In our district, teachers delivered yard placards to the front lawn of the graduating senior. However, this was scant compensation for what they had lost.

As we drove through the country, we saw many communities make great efforts to applaud seniors. The first we saw was in Michigan, where a town's main street had large poster pictures of each high-school senior hanging from every street light. It was an expensive undertaking, but one which appropriately recognized their achievement.

Schools are a mixture of tradition and also the vanguard of social change. When children reach eleven, where we live, they are offered Cotillion classes as an adjunct to their schooling. Cotillion is a mix of etiquette and ballroom dancing classes. It was introduced into England in 1766 and to America six years later. It has disappeared from the UK but is still somewhat prevalent in the South of the USA.

School cultures have become highly socially liberal. Although we live in a religious and sometimes conservative area of the USA, we are surprised by how quickly social causes are translated into schools. Coming out at puberty is commonplace. Few kids seem concerned, and this normality appears to translate to all but the most hard-core of conservative parents. In every year at more or less every high school, a handful of students will transition from the gender assigned to them at birth. When we arrived here, one transitioning student had just been elected by her schoolmates as homecoming queen. This event made the newspapers, but the election of the second transitioning student did not.

It is probably worth taking some time to reflect on how Generation Z, those born after 1996, sees the world. As the schmaltzy song goes, children are our future; a deeper dive into America's children might give us a guide as to how this generation might shape America's future. To do this, I think it's essential to differentiate between the elemental ways in which this generation views the world and how they see the world today because they are only in their teens or early 20s. To complete the caveats, it's also possible that some future world event will transform their viewpoints.

Generation Z is a digital generation. They are always connected and have no memory of a world without smartphone and ubiquitous internet. The average young adult transmits more than three thousand text messages per month. A few years ago, I counted the messages sent by Daughter #2; she was a power user, sending more than double the average. Very occasionally, when Daughter #2 wants something, she will even communicate with her parents. This generation communicates minute by minute via a range of messaging platforms with many other people. While this is positive for many, there is growing evidence of high anxiety and depression in others. This generation will inevitably seek technology solutions to societal problems, even those caused by technology itself.

They are also ethnically more diverse than previous generations: 52 percent of Generation Z are white, compared with 61 percent of Millennials, 70 percent of Generation X, and 82 percent of Baby Boomers. Generation Z seems to be liberal on social issues and more receptive to matters of social equality. This default mindset will probably not change materially in their lifetime.

Some argue that this generation will be more conservative and more serious in other ways. As a result of seeing their parents struggle in the Great Recession, they are likely to want lower student debt and higher savings. Given what is expected to happen with Artificial Intelligence, there is evidence that they are increasingly selecting majors based on future job availability. They are more likely than any previous generation to be more entrepreneurial and carry out more freelancing-type work.

This generation will certainly be better educated than any previous generation. Like most countries worldwide, Bachelor's and Master's degree completion continues to rise year on year. Almost one in seven Americans over twenty-five now has a postgraduate degree, which will likely increase further.

Girls outperform boys at every stage of the US education process from elementary school to postgraduate study, with 41 percent of women now achieving at least a Bachelor's degree, compared with only 33 percent of men. America is following Europe's lead in marrying later. Less than one in five adults under thirty are married, under half that of the same age group in the 1980s. Sometimes-desperate Daughter #1 tells us that the expectation is that she should meet her soulmate at college, but this must now be regarded as the exception rather than the rule. In 1980, 43 percent of young women had given birth compared with only 30 percent today. This will have an impact on population growth rates as pregnancy rates continue to decline. Immigration will become more critical, but we will cover that in a later chapter.

Although two-thirds of parents say that young adults should be financially independent of them by the age of twenty-two, the reality is different. According to Pew Research Centre, only 24 percent of young adults are financially independent today compared with 32 percent in the 1980s. There is a reason for the rise in the incidence of jokes about children living in their parents' basements. More than half of adults aged between eighteen and twenty-nine now live with a parent; this is almost twice the percentage of young adults who lived with a parent in the 1960s.

We also know that 70 percent of this age group – plus 64 percent of their antecedents, the Millennials – want governments to do more to solve society's problems rather than have change executed organically via society and companies. Big government policies will likely be electorally more popular over the next decade or so. However, perhaps as in previous generations, these views might temper if there is a perception that the Federal Government does not achieve its goals.

With all of these percentages, this may be the time to point out that statistically, 6 out of 7 dwarfs are not happy.

The majority of Generation Z and Millennials believe that the earth is warming due to human activity. It's difficult to see how democratic pressure will not eventually lead to federal policy change in this area to support policies already being followed by many states and companies. It's also possible that nationalism and patriotism might decline. Only one in six Generation Z and Millennials believe that the USA is better than all other countries.

On social matters, Generation Z and Millennials are also firmly aligned. Both want same-sex marriages, believe that increasing ethnic diversity is good for society, and support trans rights. The sheer weight of these generations' electoral votes should ensure that future policies will be socially friendly. The Republican Party will likely need to become more libertarian on social issues if it wants political power.

Generation Z is often regarded as the politically correct generation. However, according to Pew Research again, political correctness is deeply unpopular amongst all US age groups. Polls show that 80 percent of all adults believe that political correctness is a problem for the USA. This is true for young people, too; 74 percent of 24 to 29-year-olds and 79 percent of those under 24 believe that political correctness has "gone too far." In case you were wondering, this is also true for African Americans (75 percent), Hispanics (87 percent), and Native Americans (88 percent). This probably indicates a significant disconnect between the PC brigade and those for whom they advocate.

Most adults fear sharing their political opinions. More than half of all Democrats, three out of five Independents, and three-quarters of Republicans report that they have political views that they are afraid to share. Many first-generation immigrants I interviewed noted that Americans are often so diplomatic in what they say that they essentially end up saying nothing at all.

There may be significant implications for the First Amendment right of free speech. In previous generations, there was an acceptance that a democracy could only be effective if people were able to share their opinions. If not, it was thought that views would not change and compromises would not be reached. Cancel culture, the practice of withdrawing support for public figures and companies after they have done or said something considered objectionable or offensive, seems alien to America's values of free speech but nevertheless popular with about one-quarter of Generation Z.

We drove past many shopping malls, which in Michigan had still not re-opened. America has exported its shopping malls to the rest of the world. However, the latest trend in US shopping may surprise you. America is beginning to import the British High Street. You will be pleased to hear that these are not the drab 1970s high streets with their uniform WH Smith, Boots, and Dorothy Perkins. Developers have recreated an idyllic form of the UK High Street in many parts of America. They are recreating communities with offices, residences, hotels, dining, entertainment, shopping, and ubiquitous Wi-Fi. These areas have a lot of outdoor space by design and are places to live, not just go to.

The other shopping element that is different in the US is the prevalence of drive-through shopping, which regrettably is often called drive-thru here. It seems that most things can be bought via a drive-thru: restaurant food, of course, but drive-thru dry cleaning, pharmacy, banks, coffee shops, florists, and liquor stores are typical here. Supermarkets, too, are beginning to experiment in this area. A few specialist drive-thrus exist: in Las Vegas, you can tie the knot at a drive-thru wedding; in many places, you can get some (not so) cheap thrills at a drive-thru strip club, and a couple of funeral homes offer a drive-thru option, where the curtains open for three minutes for you to pay your respects. You can look at the open coffin – usual here, I'm afraid – for one last time before the curtains automatically close 180 seconds later.

The planning process for new shopping centers and supermarkets is more straightforward in the US than in Europe. In Europe, it can take decades to approve a new shopping area as local authorities argue about the merits of a new development and its effect on existing merchants. In the USA, while any new development has to fit into zoning guidelines and meet the latest building regulations, the presumption is that new commercial development is good for consumers and ultimately also good for efficiency.

We drove further up the Lake Michigan coast, passing through one small coastal town after another. A pretty common sight throughout America is the half-finished house. Almost all non-mobile homes here are wood- rather than brick-framed. We saw plenty of half-built houses where you can see only the outer wood frame of what will ultimately become a three-floored McMansion. It looks insubstantial, particularly for something that will cost many hundreds of thousands of dollars.

There are few more forlorn views than a small number of wood-framed houses on a new subdivision. The subdivision will have a road and, maybe, a perimeter wall, but nothing else. Post-2008 recession, developers learned their lesson not to build houses until they had pre-sold them or, at least, sold the previous houses they had built. America is still littered with subdivisions that have never been completed from this time. Despite their insubstantial look, these wood frames will last a hundred years or maybe a bit more. Most of the brick you see on a house here is added solely for aesthetic effect. Our home is three-sided brick, but none of this brick is structural to what keeps the house standing.

In the part of the USA where we live, most homes are organized into subdivisions. The word is derived from how an area of land is subdivided into individual housing lots. Your local zoning authority will define how many houses you can fit into each acre of land, say two houses for every acre. The development company will then design a map that maximizes the number of homes to fit into their land. Each parcel of land also has to include shared facilities like floodlit tennis courts, a swimming pool, clubhouses, playgrounds, basketball courts, BBQ areas, and lakes.

As with every other house in our neighborhood, our home has a suitably large address number. House numbers in the US indicate how far a property is from a specific reference point. If you see a house number like 5680, this indicates that it almost 5.7 miles away from the city center in most municipalities.

The subdivision's primary purpose is to maintain the value of houses in that area. Under the US tax code, while land may appreciate in value, the actual houses themselves are assumed to depreciate. To keep values as high as possible, communities offer both attractive facilities and enforce strict rules on residents to protect collective value. The better the facilities are, the more likely it is that people want to live in your area and hence the higher your property value. Our pool has a large water slide that sets it apart from its rivals. Other subdivisions are gated and have security on hand to enable or prohibit access.

In the Land of the Free, there are many community-imposed rules. If you want to do anything to the outside of your property, you must seek permission from the subdivision management. The management decree a list of approved paint shades that can be used. As a male, I thought there to be only about 9 possible colors: for the record, black, white, red, blue, yellow, green, brown, orange, and pink. This being America, there are far more choices available, but you are restricted to painting your house using one of the approved hues.

It is expected that you have high standards of yard maintenance, and most houses seem to outsource this to groups of people of Mexican descent who descend on a property and tidy it up weekly. From time to time, we will receive a letter informing us that our lawn doesn't adhere to the community's standards. There are also standards of behavior that should be adhered to; for example, cars should be housed inside garages at all times. As our goal is to integrate, we accept these rules and get on with life. The individualistic part of me instinctively rails against the imposition of many of these standards, while the little islander bit of me appreciates that everything is neat and tidy.

Every household pays a subscription each year for the subdivision's services. It's noteworthy that – in a country that typically fights against any tax increase, despite colossal budget deficits – people essentially volunteer to pay this tax. This may be because they can see the evident benefit they get for their money and know and trust the subdivision leaders elected to oversee their community.

During the lockdown, I have come to appreciate where we live a bit more. It's easy to go for a run, I can walk to the tennis court or the swimming pool, and twenty supermarkets are within a five-minute drive. Many other first-generation immigrants living in the USA that I talked to in writing this book love the subdivision concept and describe it as one of the favorite things about America.

An Englishman's home may be his castle, but Americans are similarly disengaged with their neighbors. Only about half of Americans know their neighbors well, and only one-quarter know most of them well. When we moved to the USA, we made a concerted effort to get to know everyone in our enclave of six homes. On our first Christmas here, we invited all of the residents from the nearby houses for a Saturday drinks party. Nobody in the group knew everyone else, though people did know their immediate next-door neighbor. People seemed to be intrigued to attend this party, the like of which they had never seen. Even though nobody had to drive home, almost no alcohol was imbibed. We tried the Christmas drinks the year after, but a couple of houses made their excuses. By the third year, we socialized with a couple of our neighbors and nodded to the remainder.

Despite this reserve and limit on the extent of intimacy, subdivisions are friendly places. We walk our two dogs throughout the subdivision. Every passing driver slows down, opens their window, and waves at you. This happens even if you have never met them before. Incidentally, the British may see themselves as pet lovers, but – according to the market research company GfK – almost twice the percentage of Americans (50 percent) own a dog as British people. Americans are also the second most likely nationality to own a cat after Russians. 39 percent of Americans have a cat, compared with 27 percent of British people. While we are digressing, it's illegal to allow your cat to go outside your property boundary in our county. How high you have to build your boundary fence to prevent a cat from escaping isn't known.

The subdivision also creates a community, second perhaps only to that found at your church. As all those in the subdivision typically attend the same public schools, children build their initial friendship groups in their neighborhoods. Tennis teams for adults are formed around each subdivision, and children compete in regular swim meets.

The subdivision funds lifeguards for the community pool, so parents can send their children off to the pool without worry for their safety. We imagined that the ice cream van, which regularly visited the pool, was a peculiarly British icon. However, they have them here, too, complete with the exact same medley of melodies. A couple of decades ago, I heard of a TV channel called Adult Swim. I turned to it – incidentally, with great interest – and was disappointed to find that it was kids' cartoons. Only since living in Atlanta have I realized that "Adult Swim" is what the lifeguard says when she or he goes for a break. Adult Swim has become synonymous with kids taking a break.

Most subdivisions also provide meeting rooms and party venues. If you want to carry on your business from near your home, it's made easy for you. You can rent a meeting room in your community. There are regular subdivision events: garage sales for the whole subdivision, women's clubs, and many pool parties. The subdivision also celebrates events, such as the fourth of July or high school graduations. The finest time of the year is Halloween. For weeks before the event, most houses decorate their front yards with macabre Halloween paraphernalia. Pumpkins adorn each doorstep, cemeteries pop up on every lawn, and ghosts drift in the breeze. The Halloween aficionados will take it further: cages of zombies will hang from their trees, spiked skulls will be nailed onto their mailbox, and bloody, grasping hands will emerge from their lawn. In non-pandemic years, Halloween afternoon has the year's heaviest traffic as parents rush home early to take their children trick or treating. Every child dresses in some sort of costume, and most adults get into the party mood too. The younger children tour the subdivision with their parents in tow, while the older ones meet up with friends to knock on every neighborhood door. Our wealthy and non-gated subdivision has many mini-commuters who are bused in from less affluent areas of the county. They all seek candy, which almost every household has bought in sufficient quantity to give every child Type 2 Diabetes. It's a really fun evening. We usually dress Dog #1 and Dog #2 up in costumes and walk the neighborhood. Sometimes, we join other adults on their front lawns to children watch.

As we drove further up the coast, each community seemed more delightful than the last. The town of Petoskey even had its own Black Lives Matters demonstration. We honked in support and felt good about ourselves.

This group of mainly young white people had decided to showcase their beliefs to the passing traffic and ask for a change to public policy. These protestors felt morally compelled to protest that day. The First Amendment, sometimes abridged as freedom of speech, guarantees five separate freedoms: religion, speech, press, petition, and assembly. Therefore, there should be nothing more American than groups of individuals assembling together and demanding change. The summer of 2020 in the USA was a time of protest. Some protested against police violence, while other demonstrators urged politicians to open up their state from Covid restrictions.

Many foreigners questioned why protests were allowed when social distancing was warranted. The simple answer is that ultimately the Constitution guarantees freedom of speech and prevents Congress or state government from passing any legislation restricting freedom of speech, religion, assembly, press, or petition of government.

Lorna and I talked about to what extent protests worked in America. The answer is that sometimes they do work, particularly if those protests are ongoing and relentless. America is a representative democracy. You have to convince a majority that the change you advocate for is one that the majority also supports. When this majority is clear and unrelenting, people in power change priorities because they want to keep their jobs.

American history gives examples of both where protest has resulted in no change and instances where change has occurred. On the no-change side, between ten and fifteen million marched across hundreds of US cities in 2003 to oppose the American invasion of Iraq. Up to five million participated at Women's Marches of 2017 and 2018, and one million protestors in Central Park protested against nuclear weapons in 1982. None of these protests resulted in the changes being sought, though they may have radicalized some participants.

On the other side, America has multiple examples of successful protests. In 1773, colonists protested against taxation without representation, and subsequent demonstrations later took place in four other states. These protests ultimately led to the American Revolution. Women had fought for the vote for fifty years, but the 1913 Women's Suffrage Parade is reckoned to be the catalyst that enfranchised American women. The Civil Rights movement was relentless in demanding change in the 1960s. Similarly, protests against the Vietnam War eventually resulted in US military exit from Indochina.

The Black Lives Matters movement feels to me like a protest that will result in change. It is already long-lasting, and opinion polls show strong majority support for some of its aims. In a recent survey, three-quarters of Americans backed the protests, including a majority of white people and Republicans. At that moment in Michigan, I was proud of my Daughter #2's effort to protest for change.

In the Declaration of Independence, its author, Thomas Jefferson, conferred three rights to American citizens: life, liberty, and the pursuit of happiness. It was the Founding Fathers' view that freedom and individual rights were the basis for declaring independence, and that future governments existed mainly to protect these liberties.

Some Americans now fear that some freedoms are at risk. Their perception is that some prominent people like to tell others how to live their lives and want to punish others for behaviors that don't match an idealized set of behaviors to which they say they aspire. It's a paradox that, while many people like to tell others how to live their lives, most don't like it when others tell them what they should do. Many Americans I know have reduced what they will say to others. While this may have some kindness benefits, it doesn't change the way people think or vote. Ultimately, the lack of dialog on sensitive issues leads to no long-lasting change.

Freedom of speech is problematic because it also requires you to accept that others get to share their opinions and perspectives with which you disagree. The deal is that you receive your freedoms in exchange for others getting their different freedoms. When I was a visitor to the USA, it always struck me as incongruous that predominantly Christian America tolerated hard pornography and exotic dancing until I understood this was part of First Amendment rights. You have the right to say what you believe, and others have the right to criticize your views and disagree with you. Nobody has the right to say that you can't share your opinions.

These First Amendment rights have raised many issues in this pandemic. Americans know that they have the freedom to say what they want about Covid. Societal pressure may moderate some expression of viewpoints, but people have the freedom to tell you what they think, and, in recent times, the internet's nature has allowed these viewpoints to be shared more widely and more quickly than in the past.

America has a long history of prioritizing individualism over centralized government rules. This aversion to collective action is responsible for light-touch state lockdowns, premature openings, and tolerance for those not wearing masks. It's self-evident to me that mask-wearing is a sensible way to slow down the flow of this virus. However, a small minority resist wearing masks. They see it as a further restriction on their freedom and another example of someone telling them what they have to do. It's challenging for government to punish people who don't lockdown. So tricky, in fact, that many states haven't tried. The police – notoriously non-mask-wearing themselves – have been reluctant to enforce mask-wearing.

The uncomfortable fact is that people asserting their own freedoms sometimes endanger the lives of others. The freedom to smoke tobacco may cause illnesses to others around them. People will permit some free speech restrictions – for example, child pornography, inciting hatred, obscenity, and false advertising – but they do not give the government carte blanche to restrict freedoms more generally.

Our overnight stop was in the small one-thousand-person town of Harbor Springs. Given the decline of the motor industry in eastern Michigan, we were surprised by the multimillion-dollar price of the shore-fronted properties.

America is a wealthy country and has around 8.4 million millionaires, approximately 6.5 percent of all households. To qualify as a millionaire, you need to have at least $1 million in assets, excluding real estate and retirement plan assets. Most years, a further half a million net new millionaires are created. Perhaps surprisingly, New Jersey has the most millionaires per capita, almost 10 percent. Not in any way surprisingly, Mississippi and West Virginia come at the bottom of this table. These two states come at the bottom of pretty much any table that ranks US states unless it's a table for least educated, highest poverty rate, or lowest percentage of passport holders. Michigan comes in about halfway on the millionaires per capita list of states. Almost 6 percent of Michigan households are millionaires, 237,000 of them. The Michigan lottery minted 33 new millionaires in 2019 alone. Of these 237,033 rich people, eleven are billionaires. Traverse City, which we had just passed through, is the US zip code with the largest number of millennial millionaires in the country.

The wealthiest fourteen universities ranked by alumni wealth are American. Harvard has almost 14,000 alumni worth more than $30 million, and the other Ivy League colleges plus the big-name technical schools like Stanford and MIT also score highly. If money is your thing, it may pay to attend a big-name college.

My experience is that few Americans classify themselves as wealthy. Millionaires will say, "I'm not rich," because they reserve this label only for the super-rich. They may have two homes, multiple cars, their children in private school, bulging retirement funds, and stock market investments. However, they don't yet have a yacht or a private plane, just a smaller boat and a pilot license. They will eat at Michelin-starred restaurants like we do at MacDonald's, own a late model Porsche Cayenne, and still pay for a bunch of services that they no longer recall having purchased. They are not rich, though; that is always reserved for someone on the next rung up.

Of course, many poor people live in America. If you drive to most rural areas, you will quickly see people who live in near poverty. Parts of most cities also have desperately poor communities. We once drove back from Graceland to Central Memphis, and it was difficult to believe that we weren't in a South African township.

Nevertheless, this town is a fabulous spot for a night or maybe longer. Its sheltered bay is home to many high-end boats, which meant that there were high-end restaurants, luxury homes, and resorts. It was a haven for second homes for the wealthy. During the summer, the rich played with their boats. In the winter, they could ski in the nearby resorts above the town.

We got a terrific deal on a historic B&B that was just opening up at one-quarter capacity. There was a lot more self-sufficiency than usual. As with most other hotels on our trip, there was nobody to take your bags (which I hate), no room service (which I don't use), no change of towels (I will just hang mine up as I do at home), and no valet parking.

I don't remember ever using a valet parking service in the UK. In the US, pre-Covid, it was a pretty standard offering at hotels, restaurants, hospitals, airports, cinemas, and stores. In some places, it is compulsory, but usually, you can self-park too. In their never-ending quest to make life more convenient for you, any vaguely higher-end establishment will offer it. You drive up to the front entrance, collect a ticket, and a young man will drive your car away. At the end of the evening, you hope that the valet ticket will lead you to be reunited with your vehicle.

I use this service sparingly. I never know how much to tip or am too mean to pay the $10 additional charge, and so therefore habitually take the mild inconvenience of the extra hundred-yard walk. I will use it if there is torrential rain or if it's compulsory and, when I do, I feel good about the service. My life has just become a little bit easier. Some high-end cars, though not mine, come with an additional valet key. This starts the ignition and opens the driver's door but doesn't allow access to the trunk and glove compartment.

Higher-end establishments have struggled during Covid but are all offering takeout services, most for the first time. Many restaurants struggle as their markup is mostly based on a superior dining experience rather than merely food quality. We ate at a two-star Michelin restaurant in New York last Thanksgiving as a treat for Daughter #1, and I continue to receive their regular emails. I wondered if anyone would use their takeout service. Would the butter-poached lobster with Gewurztraminer Foam and venison soufflé really travel well? Would the biodegradable containers spoil the mood? I was pleased, therefore, to see that this Central Park-facing establishment had the initiative to offer a picnic set up in the park.

Most places we were to stay in on our trip had either abandoned breakfast or were dispensing breakfast in brown bags. Though breakfast was a differentiating feature at this inn, they attempted to serve breakfast as usual. Masks and disposable gloves had to be worn when collecting food, tables were spaced out, and condiments were bussed like dirty dishes to be sanitized before their next use.

This self-sufficiency had hit some women, especially hard. In some places, restrictions had meant that there was nowhere to have your nails manicured or hair done. You saw women with badger stripes on their hair, or, worse, women who had resorted to self-dying. Others of more advanced years were sporting drooping faces from the absence of Botox treatments.

We took the short walk into the well-kept town that evening along the shore. On their first weekend in their second home, teenagers explored the town with their mates on bikes, delighted to have some freedom again. We found a cheap place for a pizza, which we ate in a more upscale location overlooking the expensive boats. The higher-end restaurant on the harbor seemed to do profitable business. This was Upper-Class America. Every lakefront property here sold for multiple millions, and the restaurants catered accordingly.

On the walk back to the inn, we passed a hexagonal house built of steel. It was designed by Ephraim Shay, a self-taught railway engineer. He had designed and created tracks and trains as a way of hauling logs at his sawmill. He subsequently invented the eponymous Shay geared steamed locomotive, which sold all over the world. Shay had moved to Harbor Springs later in his life and decided to build his own house. He didn't stop there; he built boats, waterworks, freighters, and, finally, a railroad. He was your archetypal man messing around in his shed at the bottom of the garden. I am pleased to say that his name lives on in the elementary school in the town.

Back in the hotel room, Lorna found a tick at the back of her head from the day's dune climbing. She removed the tick with tweezers taking care not to leave the head embedded in her skin. She asked me to search for further ticks, but I couldn't find any. There are a dozen or so serious diseases that can be contracted from these insects. Deer ticks – maybe caught from a West Virginian traffic accident – can transmit the long-lasting Lyme disease. She discovered that June was the peak tick season in Michigan and that ticks needed to be removed within twenty-four hours. She took a picture of the tick and sent it to The Connecticut Agricultural Experiment Station at 11 p.m. that night. Within fifteen minutes, they had responded to say that this tick was a relatively harmless one. However, they could test this particular tick for disease if she sent it to them. Lorna regretted having just flushed it down the toilet.

Chapter 7 – In Awe of Mackinac

I've been looking forward to seeing Mackinac Island for several decades. I must have read about people making the journey across to the Upper Peninsula when I was a child. This place had, for a long time, been on the list of places I must visit.

Two Great Lakes, Michigan and Huron, are hydrologically just one lake separated by a five-mile-wide strait. In the 1950s, the state of Michigan constructed a bridge to join its Upper and Lower Peninsulas. This bridge also delineates the border between Lake Michigan and Lake Huron. These are large lakes, too; while they contain no whales, each lake could house Wales almost three-times over. Together they form the world's largest lake by surface area.

Mackinac Island is one of Lake Huron's thirty thousand islands, but it is its most famous one. The Ojibwe believed that the island resembled a giant turtle, or Mitchimakinak in their language. This was spelled in half a dozen different ways until the French and the British eventually mangled it to Mackinac but pronounced it Mackinaw.

The main reason for Mackinac Island's fame is probably The Grand Hotel, which overlooks the Mackinac Strait. This striking hotel is a regular feature on the list of the world's best hotels and has the world's longest porch, with the three-story veranda measuring 660 feet or 202 meters. This porch has 147 separate planting boxes containing 1,375 blooming geraniums.

The view of the pristine-white hotel as you approach the island by boat is one of the great iconic manmade views, and it dominates the backdrop of the south of the island. The grounds are magnificent, too, with more than 125,000 bedding plants and 34,000 perennial bulbs. The 220-foot-long Esther Williams swimming pool is particularly impressive; it was named after the actress and swimming advocate who starred in a movie set in the hotel. Of course, there is also a golf course where you are transported the mile and a half by horse-drawn carriage between the front and back nine holes.

The second reason for Mackinac's fame is the absence of motorized traffic. This was banned in 1898 to encourage tourism. If you want to go anywhere, you have a choice of walking, horse and cart, or bike. This means that the island is different from almost anywhere else in the US.

Lorna's confidence is impressive and occasionally inspiring. She is sure that she will be good at something, even if – some would say, especially if – she has never done it before. To be fair, she is good at lots of disparate stuff. There is nothing she can't mend, and for none of these repairs does she ever need to read the instructions. She also acts this way about some things she believes to be true. Lorna is a hundred percent confident that, when the tourists have gone for the day on Mackinac Island, a fleet of diesel trucks come out at night and make all the deliveries. On this point, she is wrong. Motorized traffic is banned on the island. Everything has to be delivered by horse and cart, bicycle, or on foot.

There are a couple of exceptions. A small number of emergency vehicles are motorized and, in the winter, snowmobiles and snowplows are allowed to drive on the island. In 2019, at the Secret Service's insistence, Vice-President Pence brought a fleet of motorized vehicles to the island for his visit to a conference at the Grand Hotel. They were flanked, on bicycles, by the Michigan State Police.

The island's people expend considerable effort to preserve and restore their heritage. We watched the decidedly average 1980 time-travel film *Somewhere in Time* that was filmed on Mackinac Island. The moviemakers had filmed there because they needed "a place that looked like it hadn't changed in eighty years."

The island has a busy history. It was a settlement for various Native American tribes since around the year 900. It later became a trade center for fur, about which we will hear more in chapter 9. The British built Fort Mackinac during the Revolutionary War. It was never attacked and was officially acquired by the USA as part of the 1783 Treaty of Paris.

During the War of 1812 – yes, that one again – it was captured a second time by the British in the war's first battle. The Americans were surprised by the attack, mostly because nobody had told them that war had been declared. The US forces failed to recapture the island in an 1814 battle, but the Treaty of Ghent saw Britain return the island to the US.

The island remained in federal hands for a few decades. During the US Civil War, the fort was used as a prisoner of war camp for confederate sympathizers. After the war, the island became a tourist destination. It was designated as the US's second national park in 1875, and many boat and railroad companies built hotels on the island. The federal lands were returned to Michigan in 1895 at Michigan Governor Rich's request, and the national park was downgraded to a state park, albeit Michigan's first. The terms of this downgrade are that, if there is too much commercialization, the land will return to federal ownership.

You reach the island by hydro-jet ferries. Ours took a detour from St Ignace via the bridge. The five-mile bridge intimidates some, as the road surface is see-through and made from meshed steel. Two speeding vehicles have fallen over the edge two hundred feet, some sixty meters, into the lake. The first was a lightweight Yugo caught by winds, and the second a suicide. Which lake you fall into depends on both which side of the road you are driving and the prevailing winds. In the case of the Yugo, it took police divers more than a week to locate the car, which was embedded in the lake floor more than one hundred and fifty feet below the water level. The bridge is designed to move up to thirty-five feet east or west in high winds. If you are nervous, in normal times, the signs indicate that you can ask a Mackinac Bridge Authority employee to drive your vehicle for you. Unfortunately, Covid had suspended this assistance, so we just braved it alone.

Before 1957, the only way to move from the Lower Peninsular to the Upper Peninsular was by ferry. Sadly, this option is no longer available. There were apparently always long lines of cars, trucks, and snowmobiles waiting to cross the straits.

When we arrived, the island was gradually opening up after lockdown. The timing of our trip across America was dependent on when this island and some other national parks opened up. We stayed for a few days in the island's oldest hotel. It had opened a couple of days previously and was obviously still training new staff.

The hotel was a rabbit warren of corridors and mini-staircases, and you felt you were playing a giant game of Snakes and Ladders – which, incidentally, they call Chutes and Ladders here – as you tried to navigate your way around. Elevators were labeled with floor numbers that didn't necessarily bear any correlation to the floor for which you were aiming. Every journey back to the hotel room was an adventure.

We spoke to some business owners from behind our respective masks. They were obviously delighted by the number of visitors to the island. They were initially unsure whether they would be permitted to open by the state of Michigan, and then whether visitors would actually travel. The Saturday we arrived was their first biggish visitor day of the year. Islanders sported a look of relief and delight on their faces as they allowed themselves to believe that they would be able to earn money this year to feed their respective families.

In normal times, the five hundred or so full-time residents and a similar number of horses are joined daily by around fifteen thousand tourists, or fudgies as the islanders call them. However, the tourist season for Mackinac Island is relatively short. In the winter, the winds increase, and the temperature falls. This causes an ice bridge to form between the mainland and the island. Islanders use their Christmas trees to delineate snowmobile routes to and from the island.

Our timing was perfect. Busy enough to be vibrant, but probably not the anti-social distancing melee it will be on the fourth of July. Our luggage was brought by bike from the dock by a young man who would probably be a lot fitter by the end of the summer.

We rented bikes from a man who, the previous day, thought that his family might have to be evicted from their home. This day was the first day of significant visitors, and he was as busy as an ant at a picnic. He was also so high on life that he could not stop talking. We cycled counterclockwise along the flat eight-mile lake road around the island, most of which is State Park. It was idyllic, with endless views of the lake on our right-hand side and hillside on our left. The roads had cracked and crumbled over the winter, so we also had to look where we were cycling. The pace that Lorna set was shown up by runners who occasionally passed us. The number of unused bikes at the cycle rental stores revealed how crowded this island would become on an average summer day. Apparently, the town usually is so cluttered with bikes, ridden by inexpert cyclists who haven't ridden in thirty years, that it is positively dangerous.

Work is essential to Americans. When you meet someone new, the first question invariably asked is, 'What do you do?" One's identity is inextricably linked to one's occupation, and Americans seem content with this. As you probably know, Americans work more hours and take fewer vacations than their European counterparts.

In the 1930s, the economist John Maynard Keynes predicted that, as the USA became more productive, Americans would barely need to work. Data supported this theory for fifty years. In the mid-nineteenth century, American workers worked around 3,500 hours per year. Working hours declined on a more or less straight-line basis until 1990 when they had fallen to about 1,850 hours per year. The decline in working hours in the USA has slowed markedly since 1990. The average American still works 1,790 hours per year, while workers in Europe are limited, in theory anyway, by EU labor law to a maximum of 48 hours per week. The Japanese (71 hours fewer), British (116), French (308), and Italians (419) all work far fewer annual hours than Americans.

The globalization of competition since 1990 means that many developing countries can compete if they work harder. Many countries now work more hours than Americans: Indians work on average 398 hours more per year, ex-pats in Dubai work 533 more hours, and the busy Hanoi citizens work a whopping 900 more hours per year than Americans.

Nevertheless, Americans self-report that they work more hours than their European counterparts. More than 86 percent of men and 67 percent of women say that they work more than forty hours per week. And we mean almost every week because Americans famously take fewest vacations of any OECD country. Vacation allocation is left to the individual company, with no legal federal minimum. On average, Americans are given 13 days of vacation every year, compared with the UK average of 28 days and France's 30 days. However, 55 percent of Americans never take their full vacation allowance, and an unbelievable 41 percent don't take any vacation at all. Of all the crazy things about Americans, this is the figure that blows my mind. Americans always look aghast at the month-long vacations we like to take. Most Americans would seldom take a vacation longer than one week.

Americans also take fewest lunch breaks, with only one in four ever having lunch away from their desk. Email and messages are always on: evenings, weekends, and vacations. My experience is that in a country where most people are employed on an "at-will" basis, workers need to show that they are indispensable to the company. From a legacy given to them by the Puritans, Americans have a fundamental belief that there is a connection between their work and the rewards they receive. When asked to rank the most important value of a new employee, two-thirds of managers say they want someone hard-working, much more than, say, the 6 percent who demand detail orientation. The corollary of this is that most Americans also have little truck with funding others' lack of hard work and are generally not supportive of the idea of a welfare state.

There is no mandatory paid parental leave in the USA. Again, this is up to the individual company, with most companies making little or no allowance for new mothers or caring for relatives. My first American boss – let's call her American Boss #1 – was back at work the day after giving birth to her first child.

The employees who work the longest are college-educated, millennial professionals. For many, as with their ancestors, there is a joy to hard work. For others, the American Dream promises that you can be anything if you work harder. Americans know that you will never get to the C-Suite without working at least seventy hours per week. If you work just thirty-five hours, you simply won't progress.

Both daughters are full-time students but choose to earn extra income. Daughter #1 enjoys working, especially when she isn't micromanaged. She likes the extra cash, meeting new people, and the prestige amongst her friends of working as a barmaid in a cool college-town bar. This job enables her to earn at least $20 an hour, which compares favorably with the jobs I had at that age. However, she can make multiple times more in tips if the bar is busy. Daughter #2 works when she has to. She can have a good work ethic but always prefers to spend time with her friends. She worked in a restaurant and hated both the management and the customers. Like many of her age, she has found most pleasure in the gig economy, where she enjoys the flexibility of working when she wants to.

It isn't unknown for privileged children, like mine, to work three or four jobs. Plenty of teenagers are simultaneously waiters, have a pressure-washing business, mow lawns, and do some babysitting. All of this is part of the process to instill the hard work culture into them.

The US work environment is also different. The professional workplace that I know is much less social than in Europe, with typically low socialization after work, too. Everything is much more proper. Political discussion is rare, and inquiries on private lives uncommon. Few non-work-related personal opinions are shared, and workmate fraternization is underground. The workplace isn't a natural place to build friendships; it's much more transactional. There is a large separation between work and personal life. If someone tells you they have a personal reason for not doing something, this is the end of the conversation.

The Dutch psychologist, Geert Hofstede, pioneered work on measuring national culture. He developed six cultural dimensions that enabled a comparison between average country cultures. One cultural dimension is individualism. As you might expect, the USA is the most individualistic nation on earth. Americans don't like others to tell them how to do their job and want the freedom to do things the way they think best. They also expect to be rewarded for their results. Almost all recent immigrants that I spoke to believe in the central tenets of the American Dream. If you work hard and are smart enough, you will be rewarded with upward social mobility for you and your family.

This predisposition for hard work and individualism doesn't naturally lead to strong teamwork. This probably did not matter too much in an agrarian world where you picked your own corn. However, in a knowledge-based technology environment, American companies have had to invest in training time to persuade people to work together and even more time in meetings to ensure that "everyone is on the same page." American workers indulge in self-promotion, talking up their results regularly, and it's more common to see ambitious workers elbow others out of their way.

The American attitude towards retirement is different from that in Europe. Many Americans never do it. Some through lack of savings and profligacy of spending, but many others through choice. Social security, available from the age of 62 in the USA, can be appreciably higher than the UK Old Age Pension. Still, many people have either never saved beyond this or have squandered any savings. Many Americans with ample savings prefer to carry on working; they enjoy the structure and meaning that work provides. It is common to see very old people in the workforce in America. This is not just at the US equivalent to B&Q and amongst American Airlines cabin crew, but a much broader set of companies. One-fifth of adults over sixty-five work.

Since I went into premature early retirement, I have enjoyed telling Americans that I am retired in response to that obligatory first question. There is a look of first surprise and then admiration. They are genuinely delighted for you that you have managed to save enough money not to need to work and always say, "good for you."

As with every generality, there are also exceptions to the never-retire rule. The FIRE movement – Financial Independence Retire Early – has many adherents here, particularly amongst Millennials. The theory behind FIRE is that you learn to live on low levels of income and save money quickly so that you can retire at the earliest opportunity. Some people retire at 40, others in their 30s, and the most aggressive reach the milestone in their late 20s. This is an example of how pockets of Americans choose to live their lives according to a radically different lifestyle to the norm, whether they be motorcyclists, members of religious groups, or traveling nomads.

The USA has been the world's largest economy since 1871, but its economic success is only partly due to its citizens' work ethic. Many other reasons exist for its financial success. First, the USA is a big market with 330 million consumers. When you have this many potential customers, it's easy to take advantage of economies of scale. This market is also comparatively culturally homogenized; 97 percent speak the same language, and 78 percent come from the same Caucasian, non-Hispanic ethnic group. America also has access to every resource type, both natural and human. In the unlikely event that they ever run out of these resources, they merely import them from elsewhere.

Second, American culture is highly entrepreneurial, and self-starting is more the norm. The USA is a society where ambition is valued, and Americans will regularly and genuinely celebrate others' success. The recent immigrants I spoke to said that this contrasted with what they saw in Europe, where many people preferred to believe that you had achieved your success through corruption or luck. Many people have a second job, or side gig as they are known here. Self-employed people set up businesses with relative ease and find that a great community supports them and wants them to succeed. Larger companies are happy to take risks too. Access to capital is high, and big companies will regularly look to grow via an expensive merger or acquisition.

As comedian and writer Ricky Gervais said:

"Americans don't hide their hopes and fears. They applaud ambition and openly reward success. Brits are more comfortable with life's losers. We embrace the underdog until it's no longer the underdog. We like to bring authority down a peg or two. Just for the hell of it … Failure and disappointment lurk around every corner. This is due to our upbringing. Americans are brought up to believe they can be the next President of the United States. Brits are told, 'It won't happen for you.'"

Third, American companies are driven to look for better ways to do things and more profitable business models. In many technology companies, anybody can develop an idea, and managers are obligated to explore that idea. Companies will also more readily change what they do in order to be in the most profitable part of the value chain. Many American companies will not hold back, waiting for government regulation to change. They will move ahead in uncertainty in the expectation that Government regulation will follow them.

Fourth, Americans have great confidence and low fear of failure. They communicate their thoughts clearly, perhaps because they have practiced their public speaking at "Show and Tells" since they were three-years-old. Many companies are built around innovation, which is fueled by their excellent university system.

Finally, people stay in their jobs longer than in parts of Europe, perhaps due to people needing health coverage. This applies to both positions in technology and in service jobs, where you can still find cashiers wearing badges boasting that they have been a Walmart associate since 1984.

The island has no other traffic, other than horses and horse-drawn carriages. If you so feel, you can rent a horse and a buggy and drive yourself around the island. We didn't feel that way inclined. We were inclined, however, to play golf on an executive putting course by the lake. The grass on the greens was too long, probably due to late opening, and Lorna, as usual, crumbled under the lightest of competition. The people in front were much more typical Americans, insisting that we go-ahead to give themselves longer shot preparation time.

The island is pristine and perfect, but not necessarily in a good way. There is little rustic or real about the island; it has the feel of a place preserved by Disney. Unlike the rest of Michigan, there seem to be fewer second homes here, just high-end hotels and Airbnb apartments. Most visitors come to the island for a day trip on one of the many express boats. With their modern clothes and huge polystyrene cups full of Coke, there are so many tourists that it's impossible to believe you have stepped back in time.

In the harbor, there was a large community of late-middle-aged boaters from nearby lake towns who socialized both noisily and not so distantly. It was their version of pre-gaming, and none would likely have passed a BUI – Boating under the Influence – test. No doubt they had been coming here on their expensive boats for many summer weekends in previous years. Many had made a weekend of it for the reasonable $30 overnight mooring fee. We enjoyed watching their joyful reunion as we sat gently swinging on the hotel veranda chairs.

The island is also famed for its fudge. The island's fourteen fudge shoppes collectively make ten thousand pounds of it daily in season, consuming around ten tons of both sugar and butter annually. We could afford the $20 for four pieces but didn't choose to because they had just exceeded the price point at which it became offensively expensive.

Chapter 8 – On our UPpers

After a few days on the car-less island, we took a seven-hour drive along the single-lane roads of the Upper Peninsula, known more colloquially as the UP. About five of these hours were along Lake Superior. Superior, of course, only by name, not necessarily by ranking.

Michigan gained most of the UP as part of a settlement with Ohio in the almost bloodless war over Toledo. For pacifistic readers, this may be your favorite type of conflict. Nobody died, and only one person, a Michigan deputy sheriff, was injured. Under a deal brokered by President Jackson, Michigan ceded the strip of land around the city of Toledo in exchange for the three hundred-mile-wide Upper Peninsula. Now I've never been to Toledo, but it would seem that Michigan did well from this deal. At the time, analysts reckoned that Michigan had the poorer side of this deal. A federal report said the UP was a "sterile region on the shores of Lake Superior destined by soil and climate to remain forever a wilderness." Within a decade, this view changed when mineral wealth in excess of that of California was discovered.

Geographically, it would make more sense for the Upper Peninsula to belong either to Wisconsin or Canada, both of which are attached by land, rather than the Lower Peninsula of Michigan, which is separated by water. Through benign Lower Peninsula neglect, the UP region has developed its own heritage and culture. Incidentally, in case you were wondering about the title for chapter 6, Yoopers call residents of the Lower Peninsular trolls because they live under the bridge.

The UP, or the Yoop as it's sometimes called, is extremely rural. Although it represents almost one-third of Michigan's land, it contains only 3 percent of its population. If it were its own state, as some have argued, there would be nine other states which were roughly half of its size, but it would be the most sparsely populated by far. The largest city in the UP has only twenty thousand people.

From the 1970s, some UP politicians have argued for the UP to secede from Michigan. They propose a new fifty-first state, usually to be named Superior. This isn't a new idea. Jefferson suggested more or less the same area be called Sylvania State, on account of its dominant forests.

It won't happen, of course, unless as part of a broader compromise. The Senate structure, where every state gets to elect two senators regardless of the state's population, means that admission of new states is a profoundly political decision. In 1820, slave-owning Missouri couldn't become a state until free-state Maine was also admitted; this was known as The Missouri Compromise, the first of many such political compromises. Washington DC is not part of any state and therefore doesn't elect senators. Republicans would never vote for its statehood because it would mean the guaranteed election of two Democratic Senators for Washington DC.

The history of how the USA formed its current boundaries is a compelling one. At the time of independence, the USA consisted of the thirteen colonies of New Hampshire, Massachusetts, Connecticut, Rhode Island, New York, New Jersey, Pennsylvania, Delaware, Maryland, Virginia, North Carolina, South Carolina, and Georgia. These East Coast colonies are represented by the thirteen stripes on the flag.

If you permit me first a little diversion on the US flag, there are many interesting things about it. The first American flag, the Grand Union Flag, had a Union Jack in the top left-hand corner. Old Glory, the nickname for the American flag in more or less its current form, was first designed in 1777. In addition to the thirteen stripes, it had thirteen white stars in a circle on a blue background. In fact, this part of the flag is strikingly similar to the current EU flag. The white on Old Glory signifies purity and innocence, the red hardiness and valor, and the blue vigilance, perseverance, and justice. The current version of the flag is the twenty-seventh version. It was designed by an Ohio high school student, Bob Heft, who was given an open-ended assignment for his American History class. In 1958, only forty-eight states were members of the Union. However, working under the assumption that Alaska and Hawaii might soon join the US, Heft set about redesigning his grandmother's flag to incorporate fifty stars. Neither his grandmother nor his teacher were impressed with his design that included four rows of five stars and five rows of six stars. His teacher gave him a B Minus grade for the project but conceded that he would bump it to an A if Heft persuaded the US Government to adopt his design. Heft wrote twenty-one letters and made eighteen phone calls to various Government Departments, but was perhaps surprised to receive a phone call from President Eisenhower to congratulate him on his winning design from more than 1,500 submissions. Heft's history grade was bumped to an A, and his grandmother forgave him. Like all new US flags, under the US Flag Code, the new flag does not become the official flag until the next Fourth of July. My last flag-based fact is that there are six flags on the moon, obviously all American. The only one which has fallen over is the one planted by Neil Armstrong.

Anyway, let's get back to the USA and its boundaries. The 1783 Treaty of Paris officially ended the American Revolutionary War and formally set the boundaries between the British Empire and the USA. The concession of the non-colony territory east of the Mississippi River was regarded as "exceedingly generous" towards the USA at the time. Britain's generosity was, of course, based on self-interest. Britain's thinking was that it would benefit from close economic ties with the USA because a large US population growth would require more significant imports from British merchants. A financial benefit could therefore be achieved without the costs of defending such a large territory.

I suspect that these countries' special relationship stems from both the colonies' founding population and this generous act. The two countries also have a common language, a similar representative-democracy and economic system, and a set of shared values and culture that are continually re-enforced throughout literature, film, and TV. The alliance between these two countries is one of the longest in modern history. Although America has taken immigrants from everywhere in the world, Britain continues to be the mother country for America in many ways.

While wars have divided the two countries in the intervening period, these conflicts have been settled ultimately in an amicable way. There is a much more extensive list of conflicts where both countries have fought on the same side.

A story I like is of a fort that the USA built on Lake Champlain on the New York and Quebec border to protect itself from invasion from Canada in the aftermath of the War of 1812. Unfortunately, it was built one mile north of Canada's border, earning itself the nickname Fort Blunder. A few years later, Britain and the USA agreed on some boundary changes to bring this fort into US territory.

Of course, the phrase "special relationship" was coined by Winston Churchill after World War II on a lecture tour around the USA. It was a development from the fraternal association concept that he had talked about in his Christmas White House broadcast in 1941 and a precursor to his more expansive geopolitical theories, which he set out in his four-volume *History of the English-Speaking Peoples.* He wrote these tomes between stints as the British Prime Minister, and Atlee wittily said the book should have been entitled "*Things in history that interest me.*" As another aside, pre-lockdown, we attended a lecture in Atlanta on Churchill and the US Civil War, about which Churchill had written extensively. Apparently, his Civil War knowledge was encyclopedic.

As the USA became more powerful, it's natural that the terms of the special relationship are determined more by the dominant party. Britain is a relatively small country and needs allies to assert its interests. The fellow-English speaking country of America makes a natural ally. Both countries benefit from the arrangement, for instance, in The Five Eyes system of sharing intelligence, which is restricted to the USA, the UK, and other British sphere of influence countries.

By the beginning of the nineteenth century – and in simplistic terms, because you didn't pick up this book for a college history lesson – the USA claimed most territory to the east of the Mississippi, except for Florida, which was still Spanish; and the Maine border, which was disputed. To the west of the Mississippi, France claimed the vast territory of Louisiana. More than a hundred times the size of Wales, it was named after King Louis XIV and ran through the middle of continental America. Spain controlled

Mexico and the modern-day states from Texas to California, while Britain administered what is now Canada. The enormous Oregon Country was disputed between Britain, France, Russia, and Spain. It was a recipe for continuous war. Outside the contiguous lands, Alaska was Russian, and Hawaii (called the Sandwich Islands until 1795) was independent.

The USA saw itself as a continental nation-state. The first half of the nineteenth century saw the United States of America gain territory across the North American continent from one coast to another. The control of this landmass is the bedrock on which America's success has been built, as well as the foundation of substantial geopolitical advantage.

America's ambitions were part of widespread colonization by Western powers that were prevalent in the nineteenth century. As with other colonizations and, as already discussed, the USA's continentalism ignored the rights of most existing residents of that colonized land.

In 1803, President Jefferson doubled the size of the United States when he purchased the Territory of Louisiana from France. This territory encompassed the present-day states of Arkansas, Oklahoma, Missouri, Kansas, Iowa, Nebraska, and South Dakota, and substantial parts of Minnesota, North Dakota, Montana, Wyoming, Colorado, New Mexico, Mississippi, and, of course, Louisiana.

It was like a giant game of Monopoly. France had controlled the Louisiana territory from the late seventeenth century until 1762, when they ceded it to Spain. In 1800, they regained the territory as part of the Third Treaty of San Ildefonso in exchange for some land in Tuscany. Three short years later, France was prepared to sell on the territory to the USA to fund future wars against Britain. The US negotiators were ready to pay up to $10 million for the land around New Orleans and were flabbergasted to learn that the whole Louisiana territory was available for $15 million. The Americans bit the hand off the French negotiators and purchased the new land for the equivalent of three cents per acre. It was one of the best bargains in history.

Although not named so until much later, thus began the era of Manifest Destiny. Manifest Destiny was a wide-held belief that the USA was destined to expand its control across the whole of the North American continent. It is built on the theory of American Exceptionalism, which believes that the USA is divinely favored to be superior to other nations and that the USA has an obligation to spread its political system and ideals worldwide. We would probably call it racism today.

There were some opponents to the scope and speed of the destiny. Federalists initially opposed much of the continentalism, and Whigs and later the Republican leaders of Lincoln and Grant also tempered some of the continental fervor. Nevertheless, the term Manifest Destiny was used by Democrats to justify many conflicts, including the war with Mexico and the Oregon border dispute. The Democrats argued that the American people deserved these territories and that America had a mission to spread their institutions worldwide. As Andrew Jackson said, "Americans are not a perfect people, but we are called to a perfect mission."

The accumulation of new territories proceeded relatively quickly. Our old friend, The War of 1812, and its subsequent Rush-Bagot Treaty of 1818, set the USA and Canada's modern-day boundaries. In 1818, General Andrew Jackson informed then-President James Monroe that he planned to invade Florida, at that time claimed by Spain. He captured much of Florida's Panhandle. The ensuing 1819 Adams-Onis Treaty resulted in the gain of Florida in exchange for the USA ceding all claims on Texas. This deal turned out to be short-lived and another example of the USA not adhering to its treaties. As part of this agreement, the USA also inherited Spanish claims to the disputed Oregon Country.

Converting territories into states was complicated by the issue of slavery. A delicate balance existed in Congress at that time between the Slave States and the Free States. Neither side of this debate wanted to give an advantage to the other side. Therefore, no new state would be admitted to the Union unless another balancing state was also recognized. So began a series of compromises, starting with the aforementioned Missouri Compromise. In 1823, President Monroe warned European powers that any colonization on the American continent would be off-limits, the so-called Monroe doctrine.

US emigration to the Mexican state of Tejas meant that US citizens outnumbered Mexicans by a factor of six to one. By 1836, Texas declared its independence from Mexico and became an independent country between 1836 and 1845. During their period of independence, Texians had five different presidents, whose terms were restricted to two years, as well as their own Supreme Court and legislatures, which mirrored those of the USA. Texas was annexed by the USA in 1845, becoming the US's twenty-eighth state. Mexico broke off relations with the USA, and a disagreement over boundaries caused the Mexican-American War of 1846-48. This war resulted in further gains for the USA, as Mexico ended up ceding the lands of present-day states of California, Nevada, Utah, and parts of Arizona, Colorado, New Mexico, and Wyoming.

Meanwhile, on the North West Coast of America, the vast Oregon Country had been jointly administered by both the USA and Britain. It comprised the present-day states of Oregon, Washington, Idaho, and British Columbia, as well as parts of Montana and Wyoming. The USA and Britain agreed on their respective borders without major war in 1846.

By the midpoint of the nineteenth century, the USA controlled the land contiguously from the East to the West Coast. It took much longer to convert this land from territories to states and required regular compromises from political leaders. The Compromise of 1850 consisted of five separate bills that saw the thirty-first state, California, admitted as a free state, and other ex-Mex territories reorganized. It also saw Texas give up territorial claims on parts of nearby states in exchange for forgiveness on a $10m debt.

It would take sixty years to give statehood to the next fifteen states before the forty-seventh and forty-eighth states of New Mexico and Arizona were admitted into the Union in 1912.

Over a century after the USA controlled continental America, Alaska and Hawaii became US states on the same day in 1959. This was the result of yet another political compromise designed to preserve political balance in the Senate. The stories of how they got there are different.

The Hawaiian Islands were inhabited by Polynesians from the eighth century. Contrary to what many think, Hawaii was never really British. The Union Jack flag is incorporated into the Hawaii flag only because the Hawaiian king liked its design. Captain Cook visited the islands three times, and on the first two occasions, received generous hospitality. On the third visit, after a sequence of disagreements, Cook died on a Hawaiian beach in 1779. He was stabbed in the neck, ironically by a knife gifted earlier by Cook to the assailant. As Cook lay in the surf, he was attacked by other islanders who crushed him repeatedly with rocks.

American traders moved to Hawaii in the eighteenth century to sell sandalwood to China, and, from 1830, these US merchants planted sugar plantations. The USA had close relations with the Hawaiian royal family and established Pearl Harbor in 1887. These relations soured from 1891 when the new Queen Liliuokalani came to the throne. Sanford Dole, a lawyer and the son of missionaries to the islands, overthrew the royal family in 1893 with the help of a few hundred American soldiers stationed there. He then set up an independent country with himself as its first president.

Democrat President Grover Cleveland appointed James Henderson Blount to investigate what had happened. Blount concluded that US diplomatic staff and military had abused their positions and were responsible for the change in Government. Cleveland said that America had inflicted a substantial wrong and should restore the monarchy. Dole refused. Meanwhile, a Senate Committee headed by Democratic Senator John Tyler Morgan produced its own report that discredited Blount's conclusions. New Republican President William McKinley annexed Hawaii in 1898 as part of the Spanish-American War and later made Hawaii a territory.

Alaska's story is different. It was controlled by Russia for about eighty years. At its peak, eight hundred Russians plundered its 300,000 sea otter population until near extinction. They also halved the number of indigenous Alaskans.

However, Russia believed that Alaska was impossible to defend. With few sea otters remaining, it was no longer profitable and was half a globe away from St Petersburg, the then capital of the Russian empire. Besides, Russia needed money to fight a war in Crimea, so it offered the territory to both Britain and the USA, hoping to start a bidding war. Lord Palmerston, the British Prime Minister, probably unwisely turned down the opportunity, saying Britain already had enough unchartered wilderness in Canada.

In 1867, the USA purchased 586,412 square miles of Alaska, roughly 73 Waleses, for $7.2m, at about two cents per acre. Most Americans were positive about the deal, believing that it would help trade with Asia. However, others thought that the territory would naturally come to the USA in time as part of their manifest destiny. The USA also "obtained" 50,000 indigenous people. They temporarily also took ownership of 583 Russians, most of whom – feeling as welcome as a porcupine at a nudist colony – left shortly afterward. In 1896, the Klondike Gold Rush started, and Alaska grew from that point. Today, Alaska has a population of 740,000 people, including a rejuvenated 120,000 indigenous population.

By the midpoint of the nineteenth century, the USA had achieved its destiny of controlling the land from the East Coast to the West Coast. It now needed people for these mostly empty lands.

With the exception of Native Americans, every American's lineage is as an immigrant. The success of America has always been founded upon its immigrants. It has consistently been open to people who want to move to the USA and make a better life for themselves. This was true when white Europeans first came to the USA and remains true today. Immigration has rarely been about America being kind; instead, it is the USA's fundamental national growth strategy.

Today's first-generation immigrants are both more innovative and are more likely to start new businesses. More than half of PhDs in STEM subjects are first-generation immigrants. Almost exactly half of the startups worth $1 billion or more were founded by first-generation immigrants, and virtually all of the largest US companies were either founded by or run by children of immigrants. Every economic study shows that immigration – particularly high-skilled immigration – benefits the US economy and positively affects low-skilled natives. Low-skilled immigrants also help the US economy because they typically perform the type of work that natives do not want to do.

However, the immigration tap – or should I say, faucet – has regularly been dialed down and up. Some years or even decades have seen minimal legal immigration, while, at other times, immigration has been in excess of one million people per year. For all of the talk of reducing immigration in recent times, legal immigration has been around one million new immigrants per year for most years since 1990. While there have been fluctuations, the percentage of new first-generation immigrants has mostly been between 10 percent and 15 percent of the total population since the mid-nineteenth century. It's currently towards the top of this range at around forty-five million, which may explain why there is some pressure to reduce immigration from some politicians. The one type of immigration that has dramatically fallen under the current administration is refugee admissions. These have fallen to around 25,000 per year, having been at least 75,000 per year since records began in 1980.

There is a large population of undocumented workers. How many is difficult to estimate for obvious reasons, but Pew Research Center estimates around ten million, about 3 percent of the whole population. They contribute to the tax base but receive few public services. They also often pay social security taxes without collecting any of their benefits.

Arrests of non-documented immigrants is a hot political issue. The current president has been widely criticized for his immigration policies, and some pictures we have seen do indeed look inhumane. However, Immigration and Customs Enforcement (ICE) arrests are roughly half those of his revered predecessor's early years. Many large American cities have recently declared themselves as sanctuary cities for undocumented immigrants and have refused to cooperate with ICE or other federal authorities.

With so many immigrants, the USA has become expert at Americanizing its immigrant population. Most studies show that immigrants assimilate at a similar rate throughout history. First-generation immigrants tend to remain somewhat culturally detached, but this effect disappears in the next generation. First-generation immigrants commit crimes at a much lower rate than native-born Americans. However, you will be pleased to read that second-generation Americans have assimilated well enough to commit crime at a similar rate to other native-born Americans.

It is impossible to escape American nationalism at school. In almost all states, every child recites a pledge of allegiance to the flag of the United States every morning with their right hand over their heart. "I pledge allegiance to the Flag of the United States of America, and to the Republic for which it stands, one Nation under God, indivisible, with liberty and justice for all." When we arrived here, our children were told that, as UK citizens, they did not need to recite the pledge of allegiance. However, both daughters took the pragmatic decision that it was easier to join in.

Patriotism is encouraged elsewhere too. In the UK, you might sing the national anthem from time to time, maybe a couple of times a year if you attend international sporting events, or the Queen has one of her many jubilees. In the USA, I find myself standing for the Star-Spangled Banner with hand and cap on heart, trying to hit its wide range of nineteen semitones a couple of times each week. Every US event features this element: every sporting contest, each school event, and most concerts. At pretty much all events, those serving in the military, or those who have served, are requested to stand and receive applause from the rest of the crowd. My dad, who served in the British military, was delighted to stand up on his visits. I've heard well-known British/Scottish singers like Rod Stewart play the anthem and praise the good work of the US Armed Services.

The Star-Spangled Banner was written during the War of 1812 on the back of a letter but not adopted as the national anthem for a further 117 years. It was the US's first official national anthem, but others served as anthems previously. One of these was *My Country, 'Tis of Thee,* which shared a melody with the UK's national anthem,

God Save the Queen. Had that anthem stuck, it would have made for a confusing Olympics.

Immigration numbered in the hundreds per year in the 1620s. Life was hard, and about half of those immigrants died. It increased into the low thousands in the 1630s and accelerated in the second half of the seventeenth century, as around 0.4 million British people sought a new life in the New World. About half of this immigration was indentured servants, some of whom were volunteers who needed to pay off the high cost of their voyage to the New World, but others included involuntary convicts. In addition to the British immigrants, 0.6 million continental Europeans also immigrated to the USA in the eighteenth century.

Immigration, still a state responsibility, accelerated markedly in the nineteenth century. Around 30 million immigrants came mainly from Northern and Western Europe. These included 4.5 million Irish escaping from famine and 8 million immigrants of German origin fleeing from their own economic hardships. The by-now six-week-long transatlantic voyages were hell, with around a 15 percent death rate on the boat. The Germanic background of so many immigrants was to significantly influence the culture of America, which we will explore in the next chapter. Towards the end of the nineteenth century, some Chinese immigrants also sought their fortunes in the California gold rush.

There was a slowdown in immigration during and after the US Civil War, but by the end of the century, the Federal Government took control of burgeoning immigration. Between 1880 and 1920, twenty million new immigrants came to the USA, predominantly from Central, Eastern, and Southern Europe.

By 1924, the USA wanted to control immigration numbers. They introduced a quota system that restricted annual immigration. Each ethnic-origin group was limited to 2 percent of the numbers from that ethnic group already living in the USA. This policy favored European immigrants who had a massive base of existing residents.

The Great Depression of the 1930s and World War II dampened demand for immigration, and net emigration occurred for the first time. The US Government also paid for a Mexican Repatriation program that resulted in the repatriation of 0.4 million Mexicans, not all of them voluntarily. After World War II, there was a steady increase in immigrants from Europe, Russia, and Cuba. However, a government program also deported a further 1.1 million Mexicans.

In 1965, the Federal Government abandoned the quota system. Individuals are now allowed to sponsor their relatives as part of the green-card process, and a lottery system was devised for other nationalities. To give it its most recent name, the Diversity Immigrant Visa Program is free to enter and open to applicants only from countries that have had a low number of immigrants in previous years. There is a one in 220 chance that you might be one of the 55,000 immigrant visas ultimately awarded each year.

There has been a marked change in the ethnic mix of new immigrants in the last fifty years, with the vast majority coming from Asia (37%) or Central/South America (42%).

Since 1965, Gallup has measured Americans' perspective on immigration. The percentage of Americans wanting decreased immigration has always been much higher than those wanting more immigration. It may surprise you to find this changed in 2020, when, for the first time, more Americans favored increased immigration. My experience is that, unlike many countries in Europe, Americans of all political persuasions generally support individual immigrants who move to the USA wanting to create a better life for themselves and their families.

Academics show a strong consensus in favor of immigration. In a survey of economists by the University of Chicago, all eighty-nine respondents believed that high-skilled immigrants were positive for the average US citizen, and only eight thought that low-skilled immigrants were harmful.

We were traveling in the UP. In the nineteenth century, miners from Cornwall, Ireland, Germany, French Canada, and Finland came to Michigan to exploit the region's copper and iron resources. At the start of the twentieth century, three-quarters of the population were recent immigrants braving the extreme UP conditions. In the twentieth century, the market for these minerals declined, and the UP reverted mainly to logging and tourism.

Over a hundred years later, there is still ample evidence of these miner immigrants. One in six Yoopers claim Finnish ancestry, and saunas abound in every town. One town even has its street signs still in Finnish.

Another part of the legacy of mining is pasties, which are for sale everywhere. When depleted mines in Cornwall in the UK closed in the mid-1800s, Cornish tin miners emigrated to find work. Many went to Upper Michigan to work in their new mines. The most famous dish in Cornwall is the pasty, which was invented to take food into the mine. Vegetables and meat were placed inside the pastry. Initials were carved onto the pasty so that the miner would know which pasty was his. In Cornwall, the pasty has a crinkly edge, a deliberate design feature. Arsenic, which is poisonous to humans, is often found alongside tin. The Cornish tin miner would hold the pastry's crinkly edge with his arsenic laden hand. When he had eaten the rest of the pasty, he would throw away the arsenic infected crust. In Michigan, the principal mines were copper, and so the pasties we ate had no crinkly edge. Lorna loved the homemade pasty, comparing it favorably to those from our native Devon and Cornwall.

Much of traditional American food is influenced by Native Americans. Pre-colonization, meats were grilled or roasted on a spit. Vegetables were either cooked in the embers of a fire or boiled in a pot of heated rocks. Many American foods popular today are either native to America, notably corn, beans, squash, or Columbian

Exchange dishes created with both pre- and post-colonial ingredients (for example, cornbread).

In the eighteenth and nineteenth centuries, British colonists and then other immigrants brought their own ingredients and cooking styles to America. In the nineteenth century, thirty million European immigrants brought a wide array of Irish, German, Italian, Swedish, Norwegian, Hungarian, and Russian cuisines.

There is also a variety of regional cuisines in the USA, caused by a wide range of factors. These include the ingredients native to that region or that could be grown in that region, the historical cooking habits of the dominant Native American tribes in that region, the heritage of the immigrant cooking styles, and the extent to which the colonists and immigrants intermingled with the Native American tribes.

The world's largest restaurant in history was thought to be the one on Ellis Island, which received new immigrants between 1890 and 1913. It provided around one million free meals a year to the incoming immigrant at the cost of approximately eight cents per meal. Initially, lukewarm soups and boiled potatoes were served in bowls with no silverware, and bowls were re-used without washing. Food was improved following a government investigation, and food contractors selected on a broader basis than just price alone. Newer immigrants were then exposed to foods they had not seen before, like bananas and white bread.

During the progressive era of 1890–1920, food production and cooking also became more industrialized. The modern can was perfected, and foods could be eaten out of season in large numbers. The milking process and milk containers were also improved so that milk was available all year round. The importance of vitamins and minerals was now understood, and these nutrients were added to food to fortify American diets. Unfortunately, artificial preservatives and additives were also commonly added for the first time.

World War II and the Korean War saw the industrial development of dried food that did not spoil. Powdered milk, powdered eggs, and potato powder became widely available to Americans. Highly processed convenience foods were developed from the 1950s; Mac and Cheese could be reconstituted with just a little milk. In the 1960s, the TV dinner could be placed in the oven; by the 1970s, most families could warm up a frozen dinner in their microwave oven; and by the 1980s, spray cheese from an aerosol can could be sprayed directly onto one's nachos.

Developments in food technology don't stop. Today, livestock are commonly treated with hormones and antibiotics; (some) dead chickens are chlorinated; and vegetables, fruit, and wheat are genetically modified.

Given the food developments in the twentieth century, it may not surprise you that I believe that, in general, food in America can be pretty ordinary even on a good day. While the larger cities have some excellent restaurants and there are still some sporadic pockets of ethnic or regional cuisine, restaurant food elsewhere is, at best, average. We have learned the hard way not to get our hopes up when an American recommends a great restaurant.

American cuisine should be a figurative melting pot of many cuisines. Some are good, but much ethnic food has been Americanized into food that is unidentifiable from its origins. Pizza has too much dough (or the dough has cheese sprayed inside it), Italian food is oversaturated with low-quality ingredients, and Indian food has no spice. Incidentally, if you invite an American to a restaurant, they will say anything except Indian. It's just too spicy for them.

There is little choice of food other than the standard fare of chain restaurants in many American towns. I remember driving down through southern Georgia shortly after we had moved from Hong Kong. I asked what food the passengers would like for lunch. Daughter #1 replied that she would quite fancy Bento Box, a Japanese food type. I had to tell her that we were probably at least two hundred miles from the nearest Bento Box restaurant.

Pizza remains America's favorite food (21 percent), followed by steak (16 percent), hamburger (13 percent), and tacos and pasta (both 11 percent). A friend once told me that they walked into a Taco Bell intending to purchase a beef taco. The person behind the counter said that minced beef wasn't available as their meat hose was broken. He has never eaten at Taco Bell again.

Only one of the first-generation immigrants I interviewed liked American food; all the others preferred the cuisine of their homeland or indeed of any other country on the planet. Common complaints were high levels of sugar and additives, over-processed food that never went off, and cost. Daughter #1 definitely likes fine dining, which is what they call pretty much any food over which even a modicum of care has been taken. Her view is that Americans are unadventurous in what they will eat. They will eat food that has come out of a hose, but won't try xiao long bao, her favorite menu item. One of Daughter #1's roommates – let's call her Room Mate #1 – eats chiefly potatoes and chicken cooked in barbecue sauce. As a special treat, she will have an occasional pot roast cooked in Dr. Pepper. Daughter #1 is disdainful of boyfriends who want to take her to Chili's – perhaps the epitome of blandness – for a special date. When I asked Daughter #2 whether she likes American food, she gave me that look that she has been perfecting since she was ten years old of someone communicating with an imbecile, and said, "Obviously, I prefer European food."

One food that is almost exclusive to the USA is the last meal given to those about to be put to death. It sadly isn't that exclusive a club elsewhere in the world because fifty or so other countries also have the death penalty. However, the USA is the only one of these countries with public interest request laws that enable us to see what each killer has ordered. The last meal is exclusive, though it may be thought that the price you have to pay for it is just too high.

Two-thirds of inmates on death row select fried food and dessert. Fried chicken, especially from KFC, is popular. The average last meal has an average of 2,756 calories, well above the FDA recommended 2,000 calories per day. Coke is popular, diet coke less so. I guess it's probably the wrong time to watch your weight.

My favorite order was from murderer Victor Fegeur, who ordered a single olive with stone before being hanged in 1963. I appreciate that, in Louisiana, the prison warder joins the condemned man at his last meal rather than having him eat alone.

Thirty-one US states have the death penalty, but not all offer the last meal. Texas – the largest killer of killers – dispensed with the practice in 2011 when someone did not eat a single morsel of what they had ordered. You have to make them learn somehow.

The topic has been well explored in recent years. You can purchase the recipe book *Meals to Die For*, by Brian Price, a Texas inmate. Lorna and I saw the art exhibition of last meal photos at the 2013 Venice Biennale, entitled *No Seconds*.

Free refills and doggy bags are very American. If you purchase a soda or coffee at a restaurant, you can take home a free refill at the meal's end, often in a new container. I am still too embarrassed to ask and too sick of the soda to care. Similarly, if you don't finish your restaurant meal – and with the size of many of the portions here, who can? – you can take the uneaten portion home with you. Some restaurants deliberately give you portions which can be used for two meals, the first half at the restaurant and the second at home later in the week. I am disproportionately impressed with anybody who has the capability of such planning. Daughter #1 does this, probably because she has adapted to US culture faster. Any food we take home remains in the fridge for a few days before being thrown out in the trash a week later.

Talking about restaurants reminds me of an American ex-boyfriend of Daughter #1. We took him around Europe with us one summer. I asked him if he found anything unusual about our family. He told me that he had never met any people before who chose restaurants on the basis of anything other than price and portion size.

In other ways, I am also un-American and particularly British. I would never ever complain about the food at a restaurant. I would undoubtedly say "very nice, thank you," and then never ever eat at that restaurant again. My wife would and does complain. She once sent back three consecutive bottles of wine at a restaurant in Zimbabwe.

Something else that Americans do is order off-menu, either by changing some of the ingredients in the meal or by asking for something that they happen to fancy. One of my wife's friends has never been seen to order a single menu item without making some sort of change to it. Sally, of *Harry met Sally* fame, was also a notoriously picky orderer.

The UP is surrounded by three of the Great Lakes: Huron, Michigan, and Superior. In the summer, tourists go there for the outdoors and lake beaches. In the winter, it's a haven for snowmobiles, dog sledding, and other winter sports. Some areas of the UP get 30 feet of snow every year, which is enough to bury most things.

We stopped on the way at Pictured Rocks National Lakeshore, part of the National Parks System and the earliest of the four US national lakeshores. It consists of forty-two miles of coastline, as well as islands, waterfalls, and hiking trails. Despite its inaccessibility, it is increasingly popular and receives close to one million visitors a year. The pictured rocks come from the natural multicolored streaks of pigment found on 200-foot-high cliffs on the shoreline. The weather has sculptured these cliffs into shapes that supposedly resemble other things. The cliffs' colors come from groundwater, which is rich in different minerals. Iron creates a red color; manganese, black and white; limonite, yellow; and copper, pink and green. They are works of art produced by nature rather than man.

The park also has many waterfalls. These waterfalls freeze in the winter, and adventurous climbers demonstrate their skills by scaling these frozen cascades. We took a short hiking trail to a forty-foot waterfall, gorge, and an old mine. It was sublime. We also walked along a stretch of Lake Superior sand. One family had the whole beach to themselves before our arrival, and their two children screamed in delight as they used a large tree as a seesaw in the shallows. Incidentally, most Americans call this piece of playground equipment a teeter-totter, which should change the lyrics of the famous nursery rhyme to *Teeter-totter, Margery Potter*.

We wished that we had time to kayak to the pictured cliff rocks. The water was calm, and the views magnificent. There was a lifeboat station on the shore. Though the lifeboat inside the boathouse looked new, the outside was overgrown, and it wasn't clear how you would quickly get the boat out onto the lake.

We drove along the southern banks of Lake Superior, and it had a surprising industrial feel in many places. We also saw a lot of roadkill on our drive, including a dozen or so dead deer. We were pleased not to have to use the deer avoidance techniques for which we had earlier planned.

Our destination for the day was Duluth in Minnesota. Duluth consists of twenty private wharves along forty-nine miles of waterway on the west coast of Lake Superior. If you chose, you could paddle your canoe 2,300 miles from Duluth to the Atlantic Ocean via the Great Lakes and St Laurence Seaway. You would have to navigate a few canals and locks on the way, but it is possible. For the lazier, you can obtain a private cabin for around $100 per night on an iron ore freighter as it makes its way across the Great Lakes and stops from time to time at other ports and locks. Maybe that is something else to add to my list of bucket lists?

Duluth is the westernmost point of the Great Lakes and has always been a vibrant port distributing whatever is required for the era: furs, iron ore and steel, coal, timber, and now grain. Duluth's zenith was in the first half of the twentieth century when it had the highest percentage of millionaires per capita in America. Its economic depression began when mining faltered, and this depression accelerated further during the steel recession of the 1970s. As Duluth's traditional industries declined, the city shifted towards tourism. It paved downtown areas and developed the Canal Park district. Some 6.7 million tourists now visit Duluth annually to enjoy its bar and restaurant scene.

Our trip has been specifically designed to cover mainly the unpopulated areas of National and State Parks. However, we selected this large town because it was one of fifty towns that one should visit in America, according to a book that a friend gave me. Normally, apparently, Duluth is a place full of vibrant bars and restaurants. In these Covid times, the trendy canal area, with its regenerated warehouses and docks, was almost empty, and most restaurants open only for takeout. The weather was also drizzly, so we decided to eat our pizza takeout back in our hotel room.

Of course, I forgot the napkins, much to Lorna's mild annoyance. The plentiful availability of napkins is one of the main reasons why my wife likes America so much. She has always been a big fan of napkins but is a mere amateur amongst American women. Americans are obsessed with napkins. Whatever you order, they offer you piles of paper napkins. My own view is that you should either learn to eat correctly, restrict yourself to non-messy foodstuffs, or – my preferred choice – use your own trousers, or pants as they call them here.

Now I kid you not, but I watched a Hells Angels biker in an ice cream line the other day ask for additional napkins. I was prepared for him to demand to use my pants to wipe off all of his debris, a request with which, parenthetically, I would readily have complied. Incidentally, the FBI and the US Justice Department consider the Hells Angels to be an organized crime syndicate. After my experience in the ice cream line, we may have to reclassify them as an anti-grime syndicate.

After a long day's driving, we watched a series-fifteen episode of Criminal Minds on network TV. We don't have cable TV at home and only watch the occasional ad-less streamed program.

We were overwhelmed by TV ads and quickly lost the will to watch TV altogether. TV ads are the number one reason people prefer streaming services such as Netflix. TV ads cover about eighteen minutes per hour of TV, compared with UK commercial TV, which is restricted to an average of seven minutes per hour. We would start watching a program, say for four minutes, only to be interrupted by two minutes of adverts. There is no delineation between the TV show and the advert, confusing me like a ruminant on AstroTurf. The dialog segues seamlessly "We have a disorganized killer here who has a dissociative identity disorder. Have you tried this cheese on your cereal?"

You then change the channel temporarily to escape the adverts. That channel then runs the same set of adverts, and you return to your original program only to discover that it goes to a new group of adverts almost immediately when you do.

The amount of time devoted to adverts has increased dramatically over the years. Advert prices have stagnated, so the easiest way for TV to make more money is to increase the number of adverts. In the 1960s, each hour of programming had 51 minutes of program content. Today that has fallen to 42 minutes. It's now common to cut old programs or movies to fit the decreasing amount of non-advert space.

As adverts have proliferated, several commercial-skipping technologies have been developed. The networks have claimed that this violates their copyright and have sued the developers of these technologies, mostly unsuccessfully. Not that these technologies help with paid programming content or infomercials. Quite a chunk of cable TV content is programming entirely produced for and created by the advertiser. Some cable channels run nothing but infomercials. These are hour-long shows praising the virtues of a dietary supplement, compilation CD, or magical cleaning product. As the critical message is essentially that you should buy this magical cleaning product, there is a lot of padding for the ensuing fifty-nine minutes and fifty seconds. If you want to lose your reason for living, I suggest you watch an evening of these programs.

Elsewhere, adverts have become much shorter but are repeated more frequently. Although America is regarded as the home of advertising, so many ads are entirely devoid of creativity. One exception to this is the Super Bowl in American Football, where advertisers launch new, creative adverts extolling their products' virtues. More than a hundred million Americans watch this game, many of whom are viewing solely to see the adverts. To give you an idea of pricing, a thirty-second ad slot in 2020 sold for $5.6m. Another exception to the lack of creativity in advertising is the billboard ad for Chick Fil'A, a chicken burger takeout restaurant. They developed a concept of having two illiterate cartoon cows try to persuade you to "Eat Mor Chikin."

The type of adverts on TV are radically different from those in the UK. It seems that about half of all US adverts are for medications. A typical advert will introduce this fantastic new drug that eradicates, say, sleep from your eye. This new drug is so much better than the existing drug that you might use. It invites you to talk to your doctor about this drug. What then follows is a list of side effects that might happen to you if you take this drug: internal bleeding, various cancers, impotence, and likely death.

Political ads are different too. They are banned in most parts of Europe but represent 3.2 percent of all TV advertising in America. This political advertising isn't equally spread. If you live in a marginal district of a swing state, you will see little other than political ads for the duration of the long election campaign.

As mentioned earlier, America has a continuous stream of elections, so this is a good source of revenue for TV channels. These adverts rarely extol the virtues of their own candidate and policies but focus almost exclusively on their opponent's perceived weaknesses. This mudslinging obeys few boundaries. Their opponent will be portrayed as a pedophile's friend because they pushed back on some detailed regulatory proposal, as ISIS's best friend because they did not support a piece of legislation that turned out to be unconstitutional, or – worse of all in some states – as an atheist. These campaign ads are often not produced by the candidate themselves, but paid for by proxy by an organization you have never heard of, posing as an independent organization. Both sides typically run these ads, then both accuse the other side of running a negative campaign.

Negative campaigning can backfire. A Senate candidate in 2008 suggested that her opponent was godless, an atheist. The advert featured her opponent's picture with the apparent quote, "There is no God." This came as a surprise to her opponent, a Presbyterian Sunday School Teacher, and the election debate moved to why the Senate candidate, in whose name this ad was published, was so dishonest. Negative campaigning has other downsides. It alienates centrist and undecided voters and reduces voter turnout. It also further polarizes voters.

Several hundred channels were available but, with a one in three chance of selecting a channel and finding an advert, it was a desolating experience. Many networks featured only one program. There might be twenty-four episodes in a row of some 1970s sitcom. They would appear one after another, but not necessarily in the order that they were made. Therefore, you could watch hairstyles change, mothers become pregnant and un-pregnant, and replacement actors introduced and then unintroduced. This off-networking syndication can be extremely profitable for both the TV makers and also their actors. Once a show has reached about a hundred episodes, a big payday ensues for everyone involved.

Although the USA still leads the way in TV viewing at roughly four hours per day, this has fallen by about forty-five minutes in recent years. With the rise in streaming services, I anticipate that this will fall further. The average total amount of daily entertainment time for the American adult now stands at a staggering eleven hours. This includes an average of two hours per day of watching video on a mobile phone and almost two hours per day listening to the radio.

We watched cable news for a short while. I don't know exactly what the chicken and eggs are here, but it was easy to see why the country is so politically polarized. Unbiased reporting of news can be found fleetingly if you look hard enough. However, on these news channels, impartial reporting is dwarfed by opinion, whether it is the two sides reciting their defensive points or whether charismatic anchors in standalone programs set out their views on the matters of the day.

Incidentally, academics have found that Americans who rarely watch or read the news are much better at understanding the views of people with whom they disagree. They misjudge the preferences of the other side by less than 10 percent. However, those who follow the news assiduously are poor at understanding others; they misjudge the views of others by more than 30 percent. So – with the news unwatched but the world mostly understood – we retired to bed and looked forward to a new national park the next day.

Chapter 9 – Les Voyageurs

The Duluth hotel had posted the arrival and departure times of the large boats by the front desk where we picked up our brown-bag breakfast. I saw that a freighter was due to leave the dock a little later that morning. As this appeared to be the most exciting diversion in Duluth that day, we took a short walk out onto the dock. Another couple from Minneapolis had seen the same entertainment option and were already at the dock's edge waiting for the boat's departure. They expressed surprise to us that nothing was open in Duluth that day. We suggested that it might be due to Covid, but they looked surprised as if hearing about the pandemic for the first time.

We sped faster than a toupee in a tornado on the three-hour drive to the town of International Falls on the Canadian border. As with our previous journeys, the scenery was generally picturesque. Although we passed the odd tiny settlement on our route, the view was a mixture of enticing hills, dense forest, and green pasture. Large farms prevailed along the initial part of the route. Some had enormous piggeries, many had infinite fields of corn or soybeans, while others cultivated hay, wheat, and barley. Every lake and pond here seemed to grow wild rice, Minnesota's official state grain. The pretty farmhouses in northern Minnesota were Germanic in style, a reminder of its residents' heritage.

Millions of Germans migrated to the Upper Midwest states in the fifty years after the 1820s. It is said that German almost became the USA's official national language, but this is a myth as America doesn't have an official national language. However, there were nearly five hundred German-language newspapers up to the early twentieth century. In 1900, New York City was the third-largest German-speaking city globally, with one-quarter of its population conversing auf Deutsch. Therefore, it is perhaps not surprising that more Americans self-identify as having German ancestry today than any other nationality, including Britain. Around fifty million Americans trace themselves back to Germany, about 17 percent of America's total population. More Americans are likely to have their roots in Britain but, since the 1980 census, many prefer to select a more stirring origin story or simply declare themselves as American.

While Britain still provides the principal source of culture and norms in the USA, German influence on America is ubiquitous. Children begin school in kindergarten. Lager is the drink of choice for most Americans, pretzels and hotdogs are sold at each sporting event, and hamburgers and sauerkraut are available in every supermarket. Nothing is more American than apple pie, except that it comes from Germany. Germans also introduced the weekend to Americans. Before their arrival, Americans were a puritanical lot who passed Saturdays at work and all Sunday at church. Germans had a tradition of recreation at the weekend, and America's weekends now resemble those of the immigrant Germans.

Two US presidents, Eisenhower and Hoover, were of German descent. German progenies have excelled in business (Boeing, Chrysler, Heinz, Hershey, Rockefeller, and Strauss); science including Einstein; sports (Gehrig, Ruth, Spitz, and Weissmuller); literature (Dr. Seuss, Schultz, Steinbeck, and Vonnegut); music (Hammerstein and Steinway), and entertainment (Dietrich, Lang, Lichtenstein, and Wilder). I could have named many more, but the paragraph was already too dull.

Our next stop was Voyageurs National Park. Voyageurs is the only national park named after a people. Les Voyageurs were a group of eighteenth & nineteenth-century French colonists who transported furs by canoe. It was a pretty hard life; most days, they had to canoe for fourteen hours a day at fifty-five strokes per minute. If one tried this for, say, five minutes, most would soon realize that fourteen hours would be unimaginable. Les Voyageurs also needed to carry about 180lbs (82kg) of furs on their backs for extended periods. Les Voyageurs died young, typically from hernias or, as few could swim, drowning.

I should give a page or so of history lesson on the early colonization of the New World. If history isn't your thing, you can pick it up again when you next see the word "Anyway." After the (post-Viking, European) discovery of the American continent and the improvement to ships that could transport people to the "new" continent, three prominent European empires attempted to colonize America.

The French empire colonized Quebec in 1608 in what is now the, still predominantly French-speaking, eastern part of Canada. The motivation for New France was principally economic, and fur was the most lucrative trade. In the second half of the seventeenth century, French explorers and some three thousand colonists explored and settled in parts of what they called La Louisiane, the middle strip of North America from Minnesota to Louisiana.

The Spanish colonized a completely different part of America. They created the first settlement in modern-day Florida in 1565. From the seventeenth century, they set up other settlements in South West North America in what is now Mexico, Arizona, New Mexico, and California. Their immigrants' motivations were substantially different; they wanted to spread Christianity and expand the Spanish Empire.

As initially mentioned earlier, Britain formed thirteen colonies on the East Coast from 1607, and it is these colonies that would become the first US states after independence. While we're on the subject, the actual date of US independence should probably be July 2, 1776, and not the fourth of July celebrated today. It took two days to write the modern-day press release and obtain the first two signatures, the first of which was John Hancock, now slang for signature. A second noteworthy aside is that, due to the long transatlantic commute times, the British didn't learn that their part of America had declared independence until August 10, 1776.

In the first sixty years of British colonization, most came to the New World to escape persecution. After two failed attempts to colonize Roanoke Island by Sir Walter Raleigh in the late sixteenth century, around a hundred Anglicans settled in Jamestown in 1607. A further hundred pilgrim dissenters arrived in Plymouth in 1620. In the first winter of 1620, half of the pilgrims starved to death, and the remainder survived in their harsh new environment only due to the kindness of the Wampanoag tribe. The first Thanksgiving, celebrated after the first harvest in 1621, was held to recognize the help the pilgrims had received from the Wampanoag people. It remains one of the few examples of harmony between European colonists and Native Americans. Life continued to be hard for these first colonists for many years, and infant mortality was a catastrophically high 40 percent. As a result, there was initially low exploration of the rest of the continent.

A few decades later, the Calvinist Puritans followed in much larger numbers and set up home in what are now the North-East states. Like so many religious groups who have been persecuted by others, they did not tolerate different views from their religious leaders. Any dissenters were banished, and these dissenters set up their own intolerant communities nearby.

The Catholics were the next religious group to escape discrimination in Britain to start a new life in North-East America. Like the previous groups, their prime motivation was to practice their religion and raise their families.

Later in the seventeenth century, Charles II gave land in the Carolinas and Pennsylvania to those who had supported him during his exile period. These supporters set up commercial activity of beef, tobacco, and rice farming in the Southern states. This work was labor-intensive, so they brought slaves with them to do most of the hard laboring; around half of all immigrants at the time in the South were slaves. Further Anglicans, German Lutherans, and Presbyterians began to come to these restoration colonies in the early eighteenth century.

This immigration pattern from different religious groups helps explain some of the cultural differences on the East Coast of America today. The Calvinist Puritans dominated New England. Government was ruled by religious leaders, and any non-Puritans had little input into the laws of the land. Their penchant for hard work created large port cities that were important trade hubs. Their hardcore brand of Christianity created close-knit, perhaps small insular communities.

Quakers settled more widely over what is now Pennsylvania, Delaware, and New Jersey. These adherents to the Friendly Society valued equality more highly. If they had had bumper stickers for their carts, these would have sported the slogan WWJD, What Would Jesus Do?

There was a broader mix of religions in the South. Most Southern immigrants came to America for commercial reasons or, in the case of slaves or prisoners, because they were forced to. The large landowners from the South of England were conservative in their thinking. They had come to America for economic opportunity and wanted things just like they were at home. The dominant religion in the South was Anglican, which post-disestablishment morphed into Episcopalian and Baptist. Unlike the Puritans and Quakers, the Baptist groups tolerated slavery, arguing only for better treatment of slaves, not its abolition. The Baptists also saw that it was their duty to convert others to their brand of religion. They worked hard to convert their slaves to their brand of Christianity. This is one reason sixty-two major Baptist denominations in the South ply their evangelical services today. The motivation for colonization and the religious background of those Europeans who first populated the South goes some way to explain why the South is culturally different today. It is still more conservative, more evangelical, and both more racially diverse and separated.

Anyway, back to Les Voyageurs. Voyageurs National Park is predominantly water with 655 shoreline miles. It consists of four large lakes, five hundred islands, some rivers, and forests. It is lightly visited, with just under one-quarter of a million visitors per year, presumably because you require a boat to see most of the park.

The park is situated in both the USA and Canada, and the border runs through the middle of the park's lakes. Our lakeside house for three nights was so close to Canada that not only could we see Canada, but our cellular devices defaulted to Canadian mobile carriers. We had a glorious view over Rainy Lake, and, contrary to its name, the view of the lake from the balcony, dock, and triple–glazed windows was pristine and clear.

We went shopping at a supermarket in town. The supermarket was like most in America; the aisles were wide, the fresh produce tantalizing, and there was a bedazzling amount of choice for each item. One feature that you can't help admiring about America is how convenient everything is. Hundreds of micro-innovations permeate throughout the store, all designed to make one's life a little bit easier.

For example, in most supermarkets, the man at the end of the packing area puts all of your purchases into bags and then helps you transport these bags to the trunk of your car. Our local supermarkets hire people with intellectual disabilities from the local community to perform this role. In the less pricey grocery stores, the cash registry areas have plastic bags ready mounted on a triangular-shaped revolving carousel so that the lady at the cash desk can scan your shopping, deposit your item into the already opened bag, and then swing the carousel around for you to transfer the packed bag into your shopping cart. Someone invented this device to make her life and your life a little bit more convenient.

Life in America is typically about the destination, not the journey. Americans are happy to spend money on services that make their journey a little easier. American men are content to pay a couple of bucks to have someone wash and iron each shirt. Every two weeks or so, American women will drop $50 to have their fingernails groomed and varnished and their toenails trimmed and painted. American families will spend another $50 to have their lawn cut and yard freed from fallen leaves. Five workers will arrive in a pickup with five blowers and then, in team formation, remove all the leaves in about five minutes.

Some innovations only make an infinitesimal difference. I'm partial to an edamame bean. They're easy to cook: you steam them, put them in a bowl, and finally sprinkle some sea salt on them. I hear you asking, Julian, how can you make that easier? Some American innovator found a way. They come pre-salted in supermarkets here.

After searching in vain for unsalted edamame, I drew a similar blank on wine and beer. The supermarket worker, who I had reluctantly consulted, told me that Minnesota supermarkets were not allowed to sell alcohol. Alcohol regulations are complicated for the cross-country traveler. As you would expect by now, rules on alcohol sales are determined at the state or county level rather than the nation as a whole. All but four states generally permit the sale of beer at grocery stores, thirty-nine states allow the sale of wine, and only twenty states allow customers to purchase liquor. Individual counties within states often have much stricter rules. There are around two hundred dry counties, mostly in the Bible Belt South. In very many places, it is illegal to purchase alcohol anywhere on a Sunday until 1 p.m. and, in some areas, doing so is banned for the whole of Sunday. When we first arrived in Georgia, our county was a dry county on Sundays. This changed within weeks as county officials realized how much tax income they would otherwise forego with Lorna's arrival.

The absence of supermarket alcohol meant that we had to go to the more heavily regulated package store. It's called a package store because alcohol must be sold in its original and sealed container and be packaged in a brown paper bag when you leave the store. In International Falls, both package stores were based in gas stations. What could go wrong with that arrangement?

The history of alcohol in America is rich. The Puritans on the Mayflower were not as puritanical in all areas as you might think. They took fourteen tons of water, forty-two tons of beer, and forty-five tons of wine. Of course, the quality of drinking water was often poor, so that early colonial residents drank alcohol from the moment they woke up to the time they went to sleep. Alcohol dependency must have been rife, as the earliest laws in colonial America prohibited the sale of certain forms of alcohol and disallowed payment for services with alcohol. By the time of the Revolution, alcohol was called the water of life, and alcoholism was widespread. Paul Revere stopped for a rum on his famous midnight ride, and Washington prescribed it for his troops. The average annual alcohol consumption at this time was almost six gallons of pure alcohol per person. By 1830, alcohol consumption had peaked at more than seven gallons of pure alcohol per person, just under two big bottles of vodka per week for each person. As there were many religious teetotalers and children, many were clearly drinking much more than this average.

The temperance movement and use of morphine during the US Civil War gradually lowered consumption. In 1893, the Anti-Saloon League was founded. It saw saloons as havens for drunkenness, gambling, prostitution, drugs, and political conspiracy. It feared social disintegration and wanted to eliminate these dens of iniquity. The League argued that crime would fall, prisons would empty, and health would improve. The League worked with other anti-alcohol organizations, such as the Women's Temperance Movement and Ku Klux Klan, to ban alcohol. By the First World War, half of US states had banned alcohol, and, in some states, the KKK were policing this ban. The unpopularity of German brewers enabled dry politicians to push for a ban on alcohol across the USA via the Eighteenth Amendment to the Constitution. It was the first constitutional amendment that took away rights from Americans rather than adding them.

The Eighteenth Amendment did not ban the consumption of alcohol. It prohibited the manufacturing, import, export, sale, distribution, or transport of alcohol. This enabled loopholes for drinking existing stocks and consumption of naturally occurring alcohol. Another loophole was that alcohol could be prescribed by doctors for cancer or depression. One state where records exist, Nevada, showed that there were 10,000 regular alcohol prescriptions for its 90,000 residents.

Alcohol consumption did drop initially, to about 30 percent of its previous levels. Consumption moved from wine and beer to the easier-to-transport spirits. In the Swinging Twenties, it was estimated that more than half of adults continued to drink, and the cocktail with its fruity masks became popular. Alcohol consumption increased to around 70 percent of the pre-prohibition levels.

In a version of the modern sanctuary city, many states refused to police prohibition. New York was said to have thirty-two thousand speakeasies, double the number of saloons pre-prohibition. In 1930, the Mayor of Berlin visited New York City and, after a week there, asked when prohibition was due to come into effect. They had to tell him that it had been the law for a decade.

In 1930, Franklyn D Roosevelt allowed the sale of low alcohol beer, less than 3.2 percent, and said, "I think this would be a good time for a beer." By 1933, it was evident that the prohibition experiment had been a failure. Contrary to what had been predicted, crime had risen, prisons were fuller, and health had deteriorated. Wet, and moist, politicians won their battle against the dries. The Twenty-First Amendment allowed the sale of alcohol again, and states gradually permitted consumption. The final state, Mississippi, of course, remained dry until 1966. The Anti-Saloon League still exists, but with a name change: American Council on Alcohol Problems.

Post prohibition, most states set their drinking age to twenty-one, but some had lower ages. In the more permissive 1960s and 1970s, most states lowered their drinking age to eighteen. Unfortunately, this led to an unintended increase in alcohol-related car accidents. By 1975, 60 percent of all US traffic fatalities were alcohol-related, and two-thirds of these involved people aged twenty or under. In 1984, President Reagan passed the Minimum Drinking Age Act that mandated states to increase the drinking age to twenty-one or face a 10 percent cut in federal funding for their highways. This law worked, with a 50 percent decline in drunk-driving accidents.

Today, the average American consumes 2.3 gallons of pure alcohol per year, about a third of what it was in 1830. The USA is the twenty-fourth most alcoholic nation on earth per capita. Along with many other European countries, the UK is in the top ten, with about a third more consumed in volume. Around 73 percent of American adults drink alcohol, an 11 percentage point increase from a decade ago. Consumption levels decline with age, marriage, income, and education, but women are rapidly catching up to men's consumption levels. Just under one-sixth of Americans drink more than four units per day, and one-quarter of adults have binge drunk in the past month. It is estimated that seventeen million Americans have some sort of alcohol dependency. Alcohol is responsible for around 88,000 deaths per year, of which 10,000 are through drunk driving.

We rented an outboard motorboat to pootle around the park. It was a basic aluminum boat with a tiny fifteen horsepower motor. I took the role of the driver, and Lorna, the navigator. My wife has many talents, but Captain Cook she isn't. She pored over the park map with a confused look on her face as if she had been given a map of Downtown Mogadishu in error. She would ask me to drive closer to a buoy so that we could read its number. When I shouted out the marker number, she would exclaim triumphantly that she knew where we were in the four hundred square mile lake. Thirty seconds later, she would be lost again, engrossed in her map of eastern Somalia.

We loved to explore the park by boat. There were hundreds of islands to reconnoiter and prices of houses on these islands to estimate. Birds of prey, such as bald eagles, osprey, and hawks, soared in the sky. There were other boats on the deep blue waters to envy: super-speedy boats, sailboats, and houseboats. There were hazards in the water to avoid: rocks, trees, and other watercraft. Finally, there were a few seaplanes, moored at docks, to admire.

Lorna likes boating when the weather is good and the waters are flat, but she becomes nervous when the winds blow. I recall that we rented our first boat about thirty years ago on Moosehead Lake in Maine. The weather turned, and the water was genuinely rough. Lorna ordered me to the side of the lake to drop her off and said that she would walk back to our hotel. She quickly got back in the boat when she realized that she had absolutely no idea how to get home. On this choppy trip on Rainy Lake, she looked as nervous as a cat with a long tail on a veranda full of rocking chairs.

At other times, we took a couple of hikes. They doubled as snowmobile trails in the winter and were pretty muddy. We repeatedly lost our shoes in the mud and, even more regularly, were bitten by insects we could not see. I am not sure that the incredible views of the full and empty smaller lakes we saw on these hikes were worth the itching.

In the evening, Lorna fished off our pier but caught nothing. We sat on the dock and listened to a different symphony of insects to the one we were used to at home. Fireflies – alternatively called lightning bugs – in their thousands buzzed here too. Incidentally, a theory exists that lightning bug is the typical US name for this insect where lightning strikes regularly, and fireflies the name where wildfires are common.

Fireflies produce their light from bioluminescence, which essentially is a chemical reaction of oxygen, calcium, adenosine triphosphate, and luciferin. They light up for two reasons: mating and warding off predators. Male lightning bugs flash to signal their desire for mating, and females reciprocate by lighting up themselves. It is perhaps the only documented case where flashing leads to sex, which reminds me of a story. When we lived in London, a flasher visited the back lane next to our apartment and did his business. When the policeman came to question Lorna, he asked for a description. The only feature that Lorna could recall of the flasher was that he was right-handed.

There is a pattern of flashing that distinguishes one species of firefly from another. Some crafty larger firefly species have learned to imitate the female's responding code of the smaller species. When the smaller male lands next to her, she eats it. The second reason fireflies flash is to ward off predators. However, I am not sure that this is so successful. Some frogs eat so many fireflies that they glow themselves.

Overall, the Voyageurs area is a great place to rent a Lake House or houseboat. If you come here and have enough spare cash, consider renting a houseboat. They are enormous fun. We rented one a few years ago in Lake Powell and spent our days torpedoing down the slide into the warm water surrounded by canyons. It was one of life's great experiences.

In winter, the lakes turn to thick ice, and homeowners on the islands can drive to their properties either by snowmobile, car, or truck. The lake is converted into winter roads, complete with speed limits. Wolf packs can also be seen crossing the iced border. Voyageurs National Park is also one of the few places in the Lower 48 where you can see the northern lights, the aurora borealis. Of course, it's most active in the long, moonless, winter nights but can be seen in any month of the year if the conditions are right.

Cold weather is really not my thing, but I was intrigued as to why people, through choice, live in the parts of America that in the winter are so desperately cold. It was a rainy morning on Rainy Lake, so I decided to go into the town to ask. Given that this remote town's hard-won nickname is The Icebox of the Nation, I thought the good people of this community would be able to answer my question.

Taking our lives into our own hands, we went masked up into the local museum in International Falls, the first museum on our journey that was open. Unlike the supermarket, everyone wore a mask here. At the entrance, Big Smokey Bear – a 1953 twenty-six-foot-tall statue representing forest protection and imploring people to prevent forest fires – wore a fetching mask. Rather unkindly, given his message, somebody had tried to set fire to his rear end.

The museum attracts around three and a half thousand visitors every year. At $4 entry per person, the admission could not have paid for the two young curators' salaries. The museum has three parts. The first is a history of local people throughout the ages; the second is artifacts from the twentieth century; and the third is dedicated to the town's favorite son, the American footballer Bronko Nagurski.

This region had originally been home to a native population and, from the seventeenth century, it was also home to some of Les Voyageurs. In the mid-1890s, a couple of the Rainy Lake islands had brief claims to fame for gold prospecting. The tag for the area was why go to Alaska when you only have to go as far as Minnesota. The answer turned out to be that you go to Alaska because there is much more gold there. The town of Rainy Lake City was founded in 1894 and by the same summer was a community of several hundred people with a school, bank, saloons, and several stores. The gold rush in these parts ended in 1898, and the city of Rainy Lake was a ghost town by 1901.

Incidentally, you may be wondering why some lakes have lake at the end of their name, for example, Rainy Lake, while others have lake at the beginning of their name, Lake Michigan. An academic study, presumably government-funded, revealed that roughly 80 percent of lakes in America are Name Lake, with only 20 percent Lake Name. Two main reasons were given for this difference: lakes with larger surface areas are more likely to have Lake first; and those lakes that are named from romance language more likely to have Lake last. There again, if you have never pondered this question, please skip this paragraph.

At the start of the twentieth century, a chap called EW Backus decided to build a paper mill. He needed electricity to power the mills. To get this energy, he dammed the river and destroyed the waterfalls after which the town had been named. However, the Canadians owned half of the rivers and lakes. To appease them, he also had to build a paper mill in Fort Francis on the Canadian side.

The paper mills became a great success and needed to import workers to this part of the country. Ancillary businesses, such as lumber and insulation companies, were set up here, and these companies required even more workers. From the beginning of the twenty-first century, the ancillary businesses began to close, and, in the 2010s, jobs were also lost in the paper mills. Today, the paper mill still employs most of the town, but it is only a fraction of the numbers they engaged in the past.

It was impossible not to see the paper industry in this town. Large elongated trucks, which each carried a hundred seventy-foot-long trees, were as common as a termite at the veritable sawmill. Enormous piles of logs were stacked for as far as the eye could see. Elsewhere huge mountains of wood shavings lay fragrant in conical mounds. Indeed, the whole town had a not unpleasant woody smell that emanated from these colossal potpourris of wood shavings.

One curator was knowledgeable about the population history of the county of Koochiching. According to her, the county had contracted by one-third since the 1990s and will reduce further in the coming years. As jobs disappeared, people of working age moved elsewhere. For every new person coming to the county today, 1.75 was leaving.

I asked if the cold weather played any part in the exodus of people. She said not and said that the fall in population was fundamentally due to the lack of work opportunity. I asked the two curators if they liked the cold. Both said they wanted the variety. It was a hundred degrees here in the summer. However, in the winter, International Falls has more than a hundred consecutive days where the temperature doesn't rise above freezing. The other curator said that it was quite severe when the temperature fell to about minus 50, but that otherwise, there were many fun things to do in the winter.

Let me tell you that minus 50 is exceptionally cold. Minus 50°F, which is minus 46°C, requires special industrial clothing. Parts of your body – ears and nose mostly – will fall off within minutes without it. For many years, the coldest temperature ever recorded in England was -17C in 1982 in Oxford. I know this because I went outside that evening to pick up a younger school friend from a party. We had coats, gloves, and all the required clothing. However, it was as cold as a witch's nipple, and we had to take refuge in the fish and chip shop on the short walk home.

Later that day, I polled a further three people at the marina (so, in total, I sampled 0.1 percent of the town's population). One told me that he didn't like the cold weather, but the other two said they looked forward to it.

The second part of the museum was a collection from the twentieth century. It was a work in progress, and I imagined that the two women curated the exhibits when they had no customers, which was probably quite a lot of the time. People from the town donated things they no longer needed, and the museum told a story from these donations. This eclectic collection had old Polaris snowmobiles, a 1910 fire engine, and a wind sled. It also had an unusual collection of electric vibrators. These were standard household devices from the early part of the twentieth century, advertised as medical devices but apparently often used for other leisure purposes.

The third part of the museum celebrated the life of International Falls' favorite son. I confess that I had never heard of Bronko Nagurski before this visit. Nagurski was a great American footballer from the 1930s, some say one of the greatest footballers of all time. He played for his high school football team for three years. In a feature that will give every budding sportsman hope, his high school team did not win a single game when he was at school. However, he did win a scholarship to his local college, which subsequently won every state championship. Nagurski was then snapped up by the Chicago Bears at one of the highest salaries of the time. The Bears had a very successful record while he was there. In offense, opposition coaches developed plans to stop him. They had one player trip him, another player tackle him as he was falling, and the rest of the team would then jump on top of him. In truth, one rival coach said, the only way to stop him was to shoot him as he emerged from the dressing room. When he retired from football, he became a national champion wrestler. When he retired from wrestling, he came home to International Falls.

The Koochiching Museum was a great museum created by people who wanted to record their isolated community's history. I recommend it wholeheartedly.

Like everything in the USA, the weather is big too. On average, six hundred people die from weather-related injuries every year. One of the most-watched cable TV shows in America is The Weather Channel. In good weather times, the channel is filled with documentaries about how bad weather can get, but the Weather Channel comes into its element when lousy weather hits somewhere on the continent.

The indigenous people of the Caribbean, the Taino, called the storms that afflicted their islands in the summer months "Hurakán," literally God of the storm. We often think of hurricanes as the most dangerous piece of weather, but residents typically get many days' warning before these storms hit. Consequently, hurricanes average a median of only forty-six deaths per year. Big hurricanes batter Florida and the southern and eastern coasts a few times a year between June and October. The fastest wind speed ever measured was 177 mph for Hurricane Andrew in 1992, but it is reckoned that 1969 Hurricane Camille was faster at around 200 mph. Unfortunately, we shall never know, as all of the measuring equipment that day was destroyed by the hurricane. The most damaging was 2005 Hurricane Katrina, which broke the levees at New Orleans. It flooded 80 percent of New Orleans, causing $81 billion in damages and killing 1,836 people.

Tornadoes are considerably more prevalent, touching down more than one thousand times per year, but usually only cause localized damage. Three-quarters of the world's tornadoes occur in the USA, so most communities have installed Doppler Radar Warning Systems to give some warnings to their residents. These early warning systems have saved thousands of lives, though seventy people or so still die in a typical year.

When you hear the tornado warning, you have about sixty seconds to get yourself into an inside room in the basement. In our first year in the USA, the alarm was activated on a bright sunny day. I was just closing the door to the basement when the tornado hit. It went completely dark outside, and a loud noise, like a passing train nearby, raced by. About a minute later, bright sunshine prevailed again. We ventured out, and, four hundred feet down our road, four houses had lost their roofs and the large trees their tops. Trees and telephone wires were littered on the road, and there was debris everywhere. Our street was closed for a week while they removed the debris. In another year, a friend twenty miles away was hit by a tornado in the middle of the night. He was descending the stairs with children in arms just as a falling tree hit his roof. I wouldn't like you to think that tornadoes here are an everyday occurrence. In the street where we live, we have a tornado warning about every three years or so. However, when the siren sounds, we move pretty swiftly to the basement.

These tornadoes are little ones compared with the 1925 Tri-State Tornadoes, which hit Illinois, Indiana, and Missouri. The three-quarter-mile-wide tornado with 300 mph internal winds twisted for three and a half hours over 219 miles killing 695 people and destroying 15,000 homes. In 2011, 262 separate tornadoes hit Mississippi and Alabama in one twenty-four-hour period, killing 348 people. These are not normal, though; most tornadoes hit the ground for about five minutes before disappearing into the sky from which they came.

Rain is a bigger average killer, with an average of 81 deaths per year. Alvin, Texas, had 43 inches of rain (109 cm) in one twenty-four-hour period. In just one hour, Burnsville, West Virginia, experienced 14 inches (36 cm), killing 23 people. It rarely drizzles where we live. It is either hot and clear or stormy.

Hailstones are big too. The largest measured was 19 inches (48cm) in circumference, a bit smaller than a soccer ball. Hailstones regularly cause damage to houses, cars, livestock, and crops. Indeed, we receive regular visits from roofers who point to the top of our home and tell us that they can get our insurance company to pay for a new one due to hailstorm damage. Hail can also ground aircraft. In 1977, a DC-9 passenger airplane lost its engines and crashed onto a road in North Georgia. Sixty-two of the eighty-five passengers and eight others on the ground died.

In the contiguous 48 states, there are roughly twenty million cloud-to-ground lightning strikes every year, mostly in the summer. The odds of a lightning bolt striking you in your lifetime is a surprisingly high 15,300 to 1. Luckily, only about 10 percent of those struck by lightning die, about fifty people per year

Snow kills too, but not in the way that you perhaps imagine. Most deaths occur not from the storm itself but from traffic accidents on icy roads, heart attacks from shoveling snow, and some hypothermia. Almost all snow deaths are males over 40 years old. One saying that is mostly true is that it is too cold to snow. When the temperature drops below 0°F (-13°C), there is usually insufficient saturated air to create snow.

At the other end of the temperature dial, the most significant weather killer is high temperature, taking an average of almost one hundred and fifty lives per year. The highest temperature in the shade was recorded at 130°F (54°C) in 2020 in Death Valley. We don't get that type of weather in Georgia, but it is regularly 90°F+ (32°C+) in the four summer months.

With the weather set fair for the remainder of our trip and no extreme temperatures in either direction, we went to bed early to prepare ourselves for a long drive.

Chapter 10 – North Dakota

While Lorna had ticked off several new US states on this trip, North Dakota was my first, virgin visit. It's the least visited of all US states by some way, and the Fargo Bureau of Commerce recently launched a marketing campaign "Save the Best for Last" to play to its lack of popularity. It's not our last state to visit, though. By the end of this trip, we will have only visited forty-five states with Delaware, Nebraska, and Kansas still to see from the Lower 48. As part of this journey, we had a fourteen-hundred-mile drive from Voyageurs to the next destination national park in Montana. We planned to break this drive up into three days and see another national park on the way.

Just over one-third of the USA is forest. This amount of forest had surprised us when we had first traveled in North and South Carolina three decades ago, but we were now used to the sylvan wilderness wherever we went. What surprised us about North Dakota was the lack of trees. The rolling plains of North Dakota yield farm after farm, and 90 percent of its land is devoted to agriculture. Therefore, it should not be surprising that North Dakota is the US's leading producer of wheat, barley, canola, flax, beans, honey, lentils, oats, peas, and sugar beets.

European settlers were rare in North Dakota until the latter part of the nineteenth century when the railroads were first laid across the state. During the first twenty years of the railroad, the white-settler population grew eighty fold. The state still only has three-quarters of a million residents, almost all of whom have northern European ancestry. It isn't crowded, though; each man, woman, and child has an average of sixty acres each. Five native tribes, representing about 5 percent of the population, also have federally-recognized reservations here, each with their own constitution and local government.

In 1889, North and South Dakota were confirmed as US states on the same day. Such was the rivalry between the two states that President Benjamin Harrison ordered that the papers be shuffled so that he did not know which state was admitted first. The then 190,000-person North Dakota is listed first only because it comes earlier in the alphabet. Even though our children were born in the UK, they have American states as their middle names. If we had had a boy, I would have wanted his middle name to be Dakota, the Sioux word for friends.

We had to decide whether to take the northerly US2 road or the more southerly I-94. I perused all of the attractions between Fargo and Medora on the interstate option. We could see the world's largest Buffalo – which I bet is a bison, but that's for the next chapter – the largest cow, the largest freestanding hockey stick, and a statue of a man caught inside a threshing machine. Or we could take the older cross-America road through the north of the state with no apparent attractions.

I considered how much enjoyment I would derive from seeing this collection of the world's largest. First, I wondered if these things were, in fact, the world's largest. Was there a proper vetting process, or were these towns not incentivized to find something bigger? Second, was there truly an aggressive competition for the world's largest hockey stick? Or was the next tallest hockey stick in the game the maximum legal NHL length of sixty-three inches? Some quick internet research revealed that competition indeed did mirror the passion for hockey between America and Canada. Unfortunately, I also learned that this Dakotan hockey stick was a mere 110 feet long and that a longer one existed in British Columbia that measured 205 feet in length. The North Dakotans haven't backed down, though. They claim that theirs is both the world's longest "freestanding" hockey stick and that this stick can actually be used in a game, presumably one played by giants.

Ice hockey, of course, was invented by neither the Canadians nor the Americans. As with almost all sports, the British created it in the eighteenth century, and there are paintings of people playing it on a frozen River Thames from 1797. Incidentally, one of the earliest players of this sport was schoolboy Charles Darwin.

With my appetite for hockey sticks satiated by this short internet interlude, we took the northerly route without attractions through small-town North Dakota. We had not been on many interstates to date, and we preferred to continue to take the road less traveled. Pretty much every small town has its own water tower, with its community's name emblazoned on the tower. The water tower can be of any shape, but the traditional one is a large sphere. They contain about a day's worth of water and are elevated high so that gravity can give sufficient pressure. The purpose of the tower is to provide water at peak morning times and water security during emergencies.

We decided to listen to the radio and found only two choices in this remote area: Christian fire-and-brimstone evangelism or country music. North Dakota is the state with the highest churchgoing attendance and accordingly has most churches per capita. We didn't fancy listening to someone preaching to us, so instead chose the country music option. One thing that surprised us about living in America is how much we like modern country music, not the geriatric crooners from the past but the impossibly good-looking stars of today.

In most of the USA, you will have considerable choice in your radio selection as the number of stations has steadily grown since figures were first collected in 1943.

Fifteen thousand radio stations broadcast throughout the USA. Despite multiple other entertainment sources, 90 percent of Americans regularly listen to the radio for an average of one and three-quarter hours per day.

After three hours of country music, we arrived in Rugby, which announced itself as North America's dead center. An unimpressive monument of this achievement marked the supposed center. In the 1930s, geographers made a cardboard cutout of North America. They then took a pin and found the point at which the map balanced itself on the pin. For many obvious reasons, this wasn't especially scientific, but, in 1931, Rugby declared itself the dead center of North America because it was somewhere near the pin. Other nearby towns in North Dakota also made the same claim, but Rugby was the one that has stuck, probably because it sits on the US2 road.

Party pooper and geography Professor Peter Rogerson from the University of Buffalo published his analysis in 2015 that showed that the center of North America was another town almost a hundred and fifty miles southwest of Rugby. As you probably know, multiple projections can be used in map-making. The most common, Mercator, distorts the size of landmasses the further they are from the equator. It makes Greenland and Africa look the same size even though Africa is fourteen times larger. Professor Rogerson's methodology rejected the use of Mercator, using the azimuthal equidistant projection instead. He found that the precise central point in North America – calculated as "the point at which the sum of the squared distances to all other points in North America would be the smallest, the mathematical definition of a geographic center" – was another North Dakota town, unimaginatively but accurately named Center.

The town of Rugby also had a prairie village museum, run by the good, but mistaken, people of the Geographical Center for North America. On TripAdvisor, all twenty-nine reviewers had rated this museum with the highest mark possible. I must add my five to this list. Indeed I would go further and say that this is one of the best non-iconic museums I have seen anywhere in the world. TripAdvisor recommends that the visit take between one and two hours, but I think that significantly undersells the amount of time needed to see everything of interest.

This group of curators had amassed fifty thousand artifacts from every aspect of the nineteenth and early twentieth-century life in North Dakota. They had moved whole schools, churches, railway station, caboose, jail, bank, telephone office, and a town hall from nearby towns to their plot at the near-center of North America. They have created a town with twenty historic buildings, including a blacksmith, baker, dressmaker, saloon, tannery, and general store. In six exhibition halls, they also have a massive collection of almost everything from 1880 to 1950: cars, Native American objects, farm machinery, telephones, and an iron lung.

America has a reputation for being profligate with its past. It seems to demolish historical buildings almost on a whim to replace them with something a bit newer. However, in most places in America, you will find vibrant communities of knowledgeable historians who attempt to understand and preserve the past. These amateurs are the unsung heroes in documenting, preserving, and interpreting America's history.

My final recommendation is that the North Dakota tourism bureau publicize this museum, rather than the world's second-largest hockey stick. I loved this museum and think that other people would do too.

I love America for a lot of reasons. I love that it is predominantly a free country, where you can say and believe what you want and follow the lifestyle that works for you. I know modern-day culture seems to expect people to think in the same way and want the same things, but I like to meet people who are different from me.

I love that America is economically strong and love that it is creativity and innovation that mainly fuels their healthy economy. My daughters both love that they can earn money easily to buy experiences that make them happy with a bit of hard work. The vast majority of Americans really do have an excellent standard of living. In the early 1990s, I recall meeting a South African in a Johannesburg township, who had just returned from an exchange visit to the USA. He told me that everyone in America was so rich. They all had TVs, cars, and anything they wanted to buy. I asked him where he had stayed, and he told me Compton, South Central in Los Angeles, at that time, one of the poorest and most violent places in the USA.

I love that everything in America is big: houses, trees, and vistas to give just three examples. The diversity of terrains in the USA is magnificent. It's rare to find a crowded beach, as the USA has around ninety thousand miles of shoreline. As previously discussed, there are so many mountains, forests, and lakes in the USA that it's simple to find ones without any other people if that is your thing.

I love the friendliness of the American people. As part of writing this book, I interviewed thirty first-generation immigrants. Every single person highlighted that extreme friendliness of Americans.

Daughter #1 loves the diversity in culture in the USA, compared with Surrey, where she spent her first decade. Everyone here is a Bosnian American or an Irish American, even if three or more generations removed. They hold on to old identities, which creates diversity. She has a theory that because of this diversity of background, everyone feels marginalized in some way. This, in turn, validates everyone to join the conversation.

I love America for shallow reasons too. I love the weather where we live. It's now the end of October, and I have worn only shorts and t-shirts since February. Other people who bizarrely like the cold can equally find a climate suitable to their needs. I love that nothing really closes here. If you want to buy something at 2 a.m. or on Christmas Day, a Walmart or multiple restaurants are open to serve your whims.

We continued to drive through mile after mile of prairie farmland when we came across a US military base in the middle of nowhere, around which were several hi-tech defense companies. It is normal to see military personnel in fatigues in the USA. At airports, people will give up their first-class seats for someone in the military. American Boss #2 taught me how to buy someone in fatigues a drink at the airport. This treatment is in stark contrast to the UK, where military personnel is sometimes told to dress in civvies to not make themselves a target.

There is a pride in serving in the US military that is much greater than in the UK. Americans seem to be able to separate the people who serve their country from the wars they fight. They recognize that the military fight the wars they are told to fight by America's political leaders. If they disagree with a particular conflict, it is political, not military leadership that is to blame. Because of this and that they pay for college education, the US military attracts many of the brightest technologists.

The separation between the military and politics isn't as distinct in the USA as it is elsewhere. Nine US Generals have gone on to be US president compared with only two who have become British Prime Minister. To be accurate, the second Earl of Shelburne was only a Colonel, and Duke of Wellington a Field Marshal, but I have averaged them out as two Generals. Twenty-six of the forty-four presidents have served in the military, and every Cabinet has at least one military leader.

The USA spends $732 billion on its military, the second-largest budget item after social security. US military spending is higher than the combined defense spending of the next ten highest-spending countries: China, India, Russia, Saudi Arabia, France, Germany, the UK, Japan, South Korea, and Brazil from second to eleventh place. It probably hasn't escaped your attention that most of these countries are US allies. Many think this $732 billion spend is actually an underestimate, as it excludes some military costs from other buckets, but I guess that could also be true for other countries.

Defense spending represents 3.2 percent of GDP, more or less a record low since 1960, which were the earliest figures I could find. By way of comparison, NATO membership requires spending of at least 2 percent, which most European countries fail to meet.

One of the more difficult things to find in North Dakota than anywhere else on your coast-to-coast trip across America is a lawyer. There are only 1,694 attorneys in North Dakota. Elsewhere in the USA, there are 1.4 million licensed attorneys. That's roughly one lawyer for every 240 Americans and much higher than the UK, which has one lawyer per 476 people; Germany one per 500 citizens; and the comparatively lawless France one per 1,200 citizens.

The professor of finance and economics, Stephen Magee, created the Magee curve that calculates the optimum number of lawyers for a country by modeling the number of lawyers with economic growth. Lawyers bring economic benefit up to a point by enforcing contracts and punishing criminals. However, each excess lawyer beyond that point knocks US$1 million off GDP. Magee calculates that America has roughly 40 percent excess lawyers. In part, this has happened due to lawyers' domination of federal and state legislatures. With such a glut of attorneys, it's perhaps not surprising that twenty-six of the forty-four US presidents were previously lawyers.

Wherever you travel, you see attorneys drumming up business on billboards for their services. When you stop at a motel, your TV will show endless attorney adverts. Apparently, in America, you should punish the driver who causes every car wreck, sue if you have a terrible haircut, and litigate if you are an idiot who doesn't know that coffee is hot.

Like judicial systems from many other democratic parts of the world, the judiciary is independent in the USA. There are two types of court system: the state court system and the federal system.

Nineteen out of every twenty legal cases go through the state court system, so let's start there. The state court system is pretty complicated, and its structure varies considerably by state and by county. Deliberately simplifying so that you might finish reading this section and taking my state and county as a reference point, there are separate county-based trial courts for juvenile matters, probate, municipal, and magistrate's court. A State Court further exists that deals with most civil actions and common traffic offenses. The Georgia Superior Court, again organized on a county basis, is both a trial court and an appeal court. It has jury trial for felony charges, where the minimum sentence is at least one year in prison, and it serves as an appeal court for juvenile, probate, and state court. Finally, at the top of the pyramid, dealing with appeals only, is the state supreme court.

Judges have to be suitably qualified. However, most, but not all, judges are elected for four or six-year terms rather than appointed. In Georgia, these positions tend to be non-partisan elections. I know that, in many other states, judges stand for either the Democrat or Republican parties. Some other legal positions are also elected, such as district attorneys and clerks.

The Federal Court System manages the other 5 percent of legal cases, notably those involving constitutionality, treaties with other countries, disputes between two or more states, and bankruptcy. It also reviews laws and executive orders and checks that they are consistent with the Constitution.

There are ninety-four US district courts, thirteen courts of appeal, and a US Supreme Court that reviews federal and state trials' decisions. All federal judges are appointed for life by the president and confirmed by the Senate. Nowadays, these appointments are made on a partisan basis; Republican presidents appoint conservative judges, and Democrat presidents appoint liberal ones. In the four-year tenure for a presidential cycle, a president will generally make around two hundred federal judiciary appointments.

The US Supreme Court, as its name suggests, has the most power. It can reject a law or executive order if it rules that it is incompatible with the Constitution. Its interpretations of federal law and of the Constitution are final.

There are currently only nine Supreme Court justices, who are also appointed for life or until they voluntarily retire. Many people think that the most important power a president has is the nomination of a new Supreme Court Justice. A president that appoints a fifty-year-old might leave a legacy for the next forty years. FDR tried to convince Congress to increase the number of justices to fifteen, and this may be attempted again with the current conservative bias on the Supreme Court.

In the past few decades, confirmation hearings in the Senate for Supreme Court Justices have been tetchy. Scrutiny of these appointments at Senate confirmation hearings has been pretty fierce throughout history and is most fierce during times of greatest partisanship. Since the first confirmation hearings in 1789, 23 percent of all nominated Supreme Court judges have been rejected. The Senate will look at every case they have ever ruled on and every complaint about that judge, including what it is alleged they did at a party when they were eighteen or whether they once employed an undocumented worker.

The first justices were appointed by Washington and Adams, and the first court convened in 1790. The first three Chief Justices were either cautious or heard no controversial cases. However, the fourth Chief Justice, John Marshall, was fiercely independent of both the president and Congress. He served as Chief Justice for thirty-four years until his death in 1835, when the Liberty Bell was rung for the last time. Marshall was instrumental in establishing the Supreme Court as the ultimate authority in interpreting the Constitution. Today, it's also accepted that the Supreme Court reviews disagreements between different parts of government and makes rulings on legal matters that are unclear, whether on abortion rights, possession of handguns for self-defense, or a whole raft of education cases. When they do this, just as in the UK, their rulings become part of common law through the principle of judicial precedent.

Relieved that we did not need a lawyer in a state with such low availability, we drove ten hours and five hundred and fifty miles through Minnesota and North Dakota before we eventually stopped in the west of the state. We stayed the night in Watford City, which sounds like one of those drab 0-0 soccer games they have on TV on Monday evening when Aguero comes on as a late substitute and then scores twice in the last ten minutes of the game well after you have turned over the TV channel to an old episode of Bake Off.

Actually, it's less enticing. The western North Dakota population has grown fourfold in the last decade as demand has risen for oil workers for the Bakken Oil Fields. Consequently, the town seems both brand new and without personality. The population of Watford City was 1,744 in 2010 but rose exponentially in the next five years to 6,708. Accommodation for such a large group of people has been problematic and expensive. Thousands live on the outskirts of the town in RV parks, which were previously pasture. Unlike the prefabricated housing in the rest of North Dakota, brand-new apartment blocks have sprung up almost everywhere.

Named after the farmer who discovered it, Bakken has about one-quarter of the US total oil reserves. Estimates vary wildly for the amount of oil that today's technology can recover from the Bakken formation, anything from two to eighteen billion barrels depending on your source. Bakken oil is not easy to extract, though, and the breakeven oil price is more or less the same as the current market price for oil. If technology improves, it's estimated that there are 167 billion barrels of oil in the North Dakotan part of the Bakken formation. If Bakken oil had the right type of oil for, say, Britain's needs, this would be enough to meet the UK's current consumption for the next 289 years.

This is small beer compared with the amounts of oil available globally, but it could be half a trillion dollars of value if the world doesn't choose renewable energy sources, which, of course, it will. Not that this necessarily helps other regions of the world with their more plentiful, cheaper-to-extract, proven oil reserves. Venezuela has 18 percent of the world's oil reserves, but its economy is in free fall.

Oil has been an integral part of US history. Native Americans extracted tar or bitumen from petroleum seeps. After the discovery of crude oil in Pennsylvania in 1859, the USA was the largest oil-producing country for more than one hundred years. The discovery of hydraulic fracturing, commonly known as fracking, in 2002 meant that the USA could extract much more oil from the earth's crust. Fracking is the process by which oil and gas are extracted from shale rocks by injecting high-pressure water mixed with chemicals, usually horizontally, into rocks. The shale rock is fractured and releases shale gas and oil.

This process enabled the USA to double its oil production and increase its natural gas production by half, and it returned the USA to the largest oil-producing country again. In September 2019, the USA became a net exporter of oil for the first time in decades.

One of the challenges North Dakota has had is how to transport oil out of its state. The pipelines have received a lot of opposition from Native American groups and environmental protestors. The Blackfeet Nation has changed its system of government to resist the pipeline. Shortly after we arrived in the USA, a train carrying seventy-seven wagons of Bakken oil to Quebec derailed and exploded in a small town in Canada. The one kilometer-radius blast killed forty-seven people and ultimately destroyed all but three downtown buildings.

North Dakota is the new Wild West, though. The latest boom has attracted large numbers of young men. In turn, this has created crime challenges for the Watford City Police Department, which has increased from four officers to thirteen. Petty theft, drug trafficking, and sexual assault have all risen. Most people arrive expecting to earn $120 per hour on the rigs to support their families in their home town for a brief period. The earnings make it too appealing to leave, and the families eventually follow, creating challenges for the town's school and health infrastructure.

The original Wild West period of history ran for thirty years between 1865 and 1895. This period of history is so prevalent in storytelling that, during its heyday between 1930 and 1954, 2,700 Western movies were released about the Wild West Period, about a minute of film for each hour of the Wild West. Even more TV shows about the Wild West were filmed. In the late 1950s, the TV viewer could watch twenty-eight separate Western shows a week on network TV.

The Wild West was also known for its bank robberies. This is pretty unfair, as a survey of bank records shows that only eight bank robberies occurred over forty years in the late nineteenth century in the fifteen Western states. The USA now has around five thousand bank robberies a year. This means that any medium-sized city in the USA today has more bank robberies in a year than in the whole of the Wild West period. Part of the reason for this is that gun laws were much more stringent in the 1880s than today. Dodge City, for example, banned guns altogether. This early gun control seemed to work quite well, as only thirty-four people were buried in the Dodge City cemetery from this period, almost all of whom perished from natural causes. Pinkerton agents were hired to bring law and order to the West. They tracked outlaws like Jesse James and Butch Cassidy and the Sundance Kid. They also provided transportation security for valuable cargo.

You might think that the Wild West was filled with nothing other than cowboys. I'm sorry to report that this isn't true either. There were only ever about ten thousand working cowboys and one thousand times more farmers.

Watford City itself was formed in 1913 by investors who knew the route of the Great Northern Railroad. Businesses and homes moved from the nearby town of Schafer, now a ghost town. It would be easy to see how Watford City might itself become a ghost town in the future when oil demand disappears.

Hotel accommodation on a Friday night in Watford City was both cheap and plentiful. Finding something to eat for a vegetarian was more challenging. We had to resort to buying a microwaveable meal from a supermarket. With my substandard egg rolls consumed, we retired to bed in anticipation of the next day's national park.

Chapter 11 – Theodore Roosevelt's Bison

As I always did, I started the day by filling our giant cooler with ice from the hotel ice machine. This plentiful ice supply kept our drinks cold and our perishables safe to eat. Ice is ubiquitous in America. Every hotel has to have an ice machine, and every room an ice bucket. Ice is more critical than cable TV. Every supermarket, pharmacy, and gas station has huge freezers packed with large bags of ice in multiple different forms. America is obsessed with ice, particularly in its beverages. The nineteenth-century author, Henry David Thoreau, railed against the ice harvesting from his Walden Pond, but even he admired the beauty of the piles of ice blocks.

I genuinely don't understand why you would choose to serve a drink at room temperature or warmed up as they do in Asia. I have become thoroughly American in my desire for ice and will go into paroxysms of despair if our home ice maker ceases giving birth to its marvelous cubes of civilization. Every cold beverage I have has to include ice and lots of it. Lorna doesn't understand this and, in this respect, is utterly un-American. She will ask vendors to serve her beverages with little ice to extract maximum value from the soda.

We had overnighted at the Roosevelt Inn, named after Theodore Roosevelt, one of America's great presidents. US presidents haven't all been great, but Roosevelt made a lasting impact. He is one of the four sculptured into the rocks at the surprisingly impressive Mount Rushmore in South Dakota.

Roosevelt first visited the North Dakota badlands in 1883 to hunt bison. He fell in love with the lifestyle and bought his first ranch there. His wife and mother died on the same day on what turned out to be a very miserable Valentine's Day in 1884. That day's diary entry contains only eight words "The light has gone out of my life." He returned to North Dakota to give himself time to heal. He built another ranch, Elkhorn, which you can still visit today.

Theodore Roosevelt wrote many books on the wilderness of the West. The most crucial camping trip in history was probably the one he took when president with John Muir, whom we met briefly in Chapter 3. On a three-night camping trip to Yosemite,

Roosevelt and Muir talked about conservation during the day and slept under the stars at night. When he returned to Washington DC, Roosevelt doubled the number of parks in the National Park System and became known as the Conservation President. Hence, it's only fitting that he has a park named after him.

Roosevelt was the first US president to dine with an African American, the educationalist Booker T Washington. This simple act was a sensation in the then-segregated world. Roosevelt was decried in many parts of the USA for this meal, but this simple artifact ultimately changed the national debate.

Roosevelt is most famous, however, for giving his name to a children's toy. He went hunting in Mississippi in 1902 with other men. Most others had already killed a bear, so Roosevelt's attendants managed to capture a bear and tie it to a tree. They presented it to Roosevelt to shoot so that he could catch up with the other hunters' tallies. Roosevelt refused because he felt it was unsportsmanlike. This scene was captured in a Washington Post cartoon, and it was this cartoon that inspired a Russian-born businessman to create a soft toy of a bear. The toy bear was named Teddy Bear after Roosevelt's nickname, which incidentally was a name he hated.

Some US presidents have left almost no footprint on America from their presidency, other than answers to obscure quiz questions. How many of us could really recall Zachary Taylor, Millard Fillmore, Franklin Pierce, Chester A. Arthur, or either of the Harrisons? Unless we have deliberately learned it, do we know when they were president, which party they represented, or what they achieved?

William Harrison, ninth US president, is renowned for having been president for the shortest time. This Whig refused to wear a coat to his inauguration on a cold January day and then went on to deliver the longest inauguration speech ever given. He died a month later from pneumonia he caught that day.

Zachary Taylor was a slave-owning general who never voted in a single election, not even for himself when he became president. Like the current White House incumbent at the time of writing, he was an unqualified, crude, and wealthy outsider at inauguration. Unlike him, Taylor was a war hero who rarely wore uniform and was so scruffy that he was often mistaken for a farmer. Taylor had a vague electoral platform and was selected by the Whig party as, what turned out to be, the last-elected Whig president when he became the twelfth US president some 160 years ago.

He interpreted the role of president in the way that it was initially intended. He believed the president should defer to Congress and use executive orders sparingly. He also thought that the president should not use his veto unless the law was unconstitutional. Taylor's short presidency was spent on protracted discussions on admitting California and New Mexico as states. Ultimately, California's accession was left to his successor. Taylor's lasting contribution is that he first coined the phrase the First Lady.

Taylor died from gastroenteritis after sixteen months in office from overeating too many raw vegetables. He was undoubtedly getting his thirty a day. Doctors treated him with what we now know to be the inadequate treatments of ingesting mercury and bloodletting. Some believed him to be the victim of arsenic poisoning, but a 1991 exhumation showed a relatively low arsenic level in his body.

Millard Fillmore took over as president from Zachary Taylor. If you ever get on the UK TV program, Pointless, where you have to guess the name of a US president that nobody else would have listed, Millard Fillmore would be a clever name to choose. He was born into poverty but taught himself to read while working for a cloth maker. He later studied law and married his teacher. He was selected as vice president by Taylor to balance the ticket and, like many vice presidents, was left out of decision making. He was most famous for introducing the Compromise of 1850, which delayed a civil war by a decade. Modern-day historians typically place Fillmore at or towards the bottom of presidents. Yale history professor, Robin Winks, said of Fillmore and Arthur, who will come onto a little later in this chapter, that "even to discuss Chester Arthur or Millard Fillmore is to overrate them."

Millard was so poorly regarded by his own party that they selected Winfield Scott as their 1852 election candidate. His opponent was Democrat Franklin Pierce, who had been Scott's subordinate in the Mexican-American War. Nicknamed Handsome Frank, Pierce was an alcoholic who struggled with depression following the death of all his children. He died of cirrhosis of the liver in 1869. Pierce is generally regarded by historians as one of the worst presidents.

A surprisingly high proportion of US presidents – eight out of forty-four – have died in office and have been replaced by their vice presidents. In addition to Harrison and Taylor, Harding and Franklin D Roosevelt also died in office. The four US presidents to have been assassinated were Lincoln, Garfield, McKinley, and Kennedy, in case you get this question in a quiz. Garfield and McKinley ultimately died from secondary infections caused by the unsanitary conditions of the time. Some argue that Lincoln, too, could have been saved, though he may have had injuries to his brain.

Chester A. Arthur, named after the doctor who delivered him, was a Republican president in the early 1880s who never fought a single election. He often comes bottom of polls of most famous presidents, or – if you want to be more positive – top of the most forgettable presidents. However, he sounds like he was a pretty decent man.

Earlier in his career, Arthur had been a New York lawyer who defended multiple civil rights cases for African Americans that led to New York transport's desegregation. He also served as a Brigadier General on the Union side during the US Civil War, albeit in non-frontline roles. Arthur was a surprise vice president pick by James Garfield, himself a last-minute compromise candidate. President Obama was not the first presidential candidate to have his citizenship questioned. With about as much evidence as the more recent case, Arthur's opponents had speculated that he was born in Ireland.

Four months after winning the election, President Garfield was shot at a train station. Garfield died from various infections eleven weeks later, and Arthur was sworn in as the US's twenty-first president. Actually, he was sworn in twice, owing to some uncertainty over whether the first swearing-in was legal. Arthur was one of five presidents never inaugurated. Tyler, Fillmore, Johnson, and Ford – stepping in for deceased or resigned presidents – were the others, since you ask.

Arthur was known as Elegant Arthur, partly because he owned eighty pairs of pants, which doesn't sound too impressive until you remember that they call trousers pants here in the USA. He was also the first president to have a personal valet. Arthur's other nickname was Walrus, after his elegant handlebar mustache. When he moved into the White House, he held a big yard sale for all of its contents – some twenty-four wagonloads of furniture – to raise money for new furniture that Art Nouveau designer, Louis Comfort Tiffany, was installing for him.

Arthur's main achievement was Civil Service reform. This mandated that specific jobs should be based on merit rather than political connections and also established the bipartisan Civil Service Administration. Despite low expectations at the beginning of his presidency and the opinions from Robin Winks earlier, Arthur became a fairly respected president. Mark Twain wrote, "It would be hard indeed to better President Arthur's administration."

Arthur's wife, Ellen Herndon, died a year before he was elected president. Arthur placed a new rose by his wife's picture every day. His sister, Mary McElroy, took the First Lady duties while he was in office. On his last day in office, four women offered to marry him, but he turned them down. Arthur chose not to stand for re-election. He had Bright's disease, a form of nephritis. A year after leaving the White House, he died and was buried next to his wife.

Great-grandson to one of the signatories to the Declaration of Independence and grandson to the short-lived ninth US president, Republican Ben Harrison was a colonel on the Union side in the US Civil War. Nicknamed Little Ben on account of his stature or the Human Iceberg due to his formal manner, this last-bearded president was part-time and worked only until noon each day. When he left office, he told his family that he felt that he had been freed from prison.

With all of these forgettable presidents from the 1840s onwards, why is it that the USA was so successful during this period? The answer might be that the very lack of strong presidential personalities, except Lincoln to Grant during the US Civil War and its aftermath, may have helped the USA grow exponentially. The USA had established strong-enough institutions elsewhere, and the mass of motivated immigrants powered America forward with little interference from the federal government.

We planned to spend most of the day in Theodore Roosevelt's National Park. It is divided into two main units seventy miles apart: North and South. Confusingly, even though they are at the same longitude, they are in different time zones. By longitude, most of North Dakota should logically be in Mountain Time. However, in the late nineteenth century, the railroads lobbied North Dakota to make their timetables less confusing to their customers. Accordingly, the part of the state that they operated in was decreed to be in Central Time Zone, and the other areas in which they did not have tracks would remain in Mountain Time. Twelve other US states are also in more than one time zone. In some Florida areas, your phone changes time zone back and forth multiple times as you drive on the panhandle.

We arrived in the lesser-visited North Unit at 8 a.m. on a Saturday morning and, for the first couple of hours, were one of only three cars in the park. The other two vehicles were occupied by park rangers. The emptiness was surprising because the entire park usually has 0.7 million visitors every year. The visitor center was closed, and nobody was collecting park fees.

This park had one winding road which followed the land's contours avoiding the many canyons. The vistas, largely unpunctuated by trees, were of impressive canyons, albeit much smaller than those further in the West. The (not so) Little Missouri River meandered through both the North and South Units.

One of the park's great attractions is the bison or buffalo, as they are popularly known here. What is the difference between a buffalo and a bison? Almost everyone from the UK knows that the answer to this question is that you can't wash your hands in a Buffalo. In the USA, however, this joke doesn't work so well because one typically washes one's hands in a sink. In the UK, the British call the porcelain receptacle in which you wash your hands, a basin. This sounds a bit like bison if you say it in a cockney accent.

Buffalo and bison are different species, albeit from the same animal family. Contrary to the song *Home on The Range*, buffalo do not roam in the American West. They roam in Africa and Asia. It's bison that roam in parts of the American West, but it just doesn't scan as well. William Cody, who was said to have shot five thousand bison for Kansas Pacific Railroad, should surely have been called Bison Bill. To emphasize or labor the point further, the Latin name for the American Plains Bison is *bison bison bison*. Nothing about Buffalo at all.

The park itself knows that these animals should be called bison but has to use the word buffalo in the warning signs so that Americans know to what they are referring. A recent newspaper article was titled "Bison gores teen in Theodore Roosevelt National Park." It was accompanied by an image of a bison, whose picture title read "Buffalo."

Fellow sometime-travel writer, Bill Bryson, is almost perfectly named. However, if he were more American and slightly less British, he would probably be called Bill Bruffalo.

As a genuinely wild aside, linguist Dimitri Borgmann constructed a famous American sentence in 1967. It has eight consecutive buffalos and is grammatically correct. To make sense of this sentence, you need to know that Buffalo is a city in New York State; that there is a rare verb "to buffalo," which means "to bully"; and that – contrary to the second sentence of this paragraph – the plural of buffalo is indeed buffalo. You also should be aware that the restrictive clause of the third to fifth buffalo requires no commas. Therefore, the sentence reads, "Buffalo buffalo Buffalo buffalo

buffalo buffalo Buffalo buffalo." ...spellchecker breaks down, and the reader loses the will to live. This translates more simply as "Buffalo bison, that other Buffalo bison bully, also bully Buffalo bison." It has to be admitted that I have rarely had the cause to use this sentence in everyday speech, possibly because I know that the animals should be called bison, and the only bison in Buffalo are found at the Buffalo Zoo.

Why all this stuff about buffalo and bison, I hear you ask? This park has several hundred bison. We did the usual thing of taking photos of bison herds three hundred feet away or more. Later as we drove down the park road, a one-ton male bison trudged excessively slowly, one step every four seconds right past our stopped car. We even have a video of it, complete with Lorna screaming at me to shut the window. Exactly how the six-foot-tall bison would enter our car by the window isn't recorded. He trudged peacefully, but very closely, past our car, not looking at us once. About a month before our visit, a bison charged at a woman walking in the park. It knocked her down, breaking her vertebrae and facial bones. She called 911 while on the ground, and a Park Ranger had to shoot the bison to protect the injured hiker.

Pre-colonization, bison were plentiful. The Great Plains alone were thought to have around sixty million. In the nineteenth century, bison began to be prized for their meat, hides, and bones, which were used for refining sugar and making china. Peak bison slaughter was in the 1870s when the USA experienced heavy industrialization. One railway engineer said that it was possible to walk a hundred miles along the railroad between Kansas and New Mexico without touching the ground by stepping from one carcass to another. By the end of the nineteenth century, the bison was almost extinct.

Many Americans at the time thought extinction was a good thing. The empty prairies made it easier to build towns and railroads. Some US military leaders felt that near extinction was a "triumph of civilization over savagery" because the absence of bison deprived Native Americans of their food source, making it easier to relocate them to their reservations. Not that there were too many Native Americans remaining by the end of the nineteenth century. The Native American population likely fell to less than one-quarter of a million.

Fortunately, not everyone agreed. Our friend, Theodore Roosevelt, was one of a group of wealthy philanthropists who arranged for fifteen bison from the Bronx zoo to be sent by train to Oklahoma to repopulate the bison herds. Some Comanche met the train; the children from the tribe marveled at their first sight of a bison. I am pleased to report that America is today home to around half a million bison and that, in 2016, the bison was named the USA's official national mammal.

We thought our visit could not be improved after our close encounter of the bison kind, but we were wrong. We went on a few short hikes in the park near the Little Missouri River. In many places, there was total silence. I explored a cave in the canyon walls, but Lorna did not join me. She had seen the bear-proof garbage receptacles and was fearful that bears may have over-hibernated.

The best of these hikes was one to the Prairie Dog Village. Let me start by saying that I'm not going to go into a diatribe about their name – they are squirrels, not dogs – but William Clark, about whom we will hear more in the next chapter, more accurately named them ground rats. We have the French to blame for the name prairie dogs. They called the animals *petits chiens*. They also gave America the word prairie, an old French word for meadow.

We had seen a Prairie Dog village a few years ago in the Badlands National Park in South Dakota. However, the Badlands' experience was unsatisfying, as we were sitting in a car looking at these prairie dogs from a long line of traffic. Incidentally, multiple badland formations exist across the whole of the West. Theodore Roosevelt National Park is also a badland. The Lakota tribe are probably responsible for the name; they call them *mako sica*, eroded land. Les Voyageurs picked up the term from them, calling these lands *les mauvaises terres*. Many movies are set in the desolate badland terrains. The best is the Terence Malick's debut, Badlands, based on a real-life murder spree of a man and his girlfriend in South Dakota.

In Theodore Roosevelt National Park, we walked into the prairie dogs' "village" after a short hike through a canyon with its beautiful yellow cactus flowers and fragrant prairie sage. It was a stiflingly hot day. These canine, rat-like squirrels emerged from their burrows and surrounded you. It was a mind-blowing experience, as we were entirely alone in the national park.

Prairie dogs were once more prevalent. At the beginning of the twentieth century, a naturalist surveyed one prairie dog community in Texas that covered 25,000 square miles and contained an estimated four hundred million prairie dogs. It's the black-tailed prairie dog that lives in Theodore Roosevelt National Park. Prairie dogs live in family groups (or coteries), comprising one male adult, a few females, and their many children. Each family unit builds a large tunnel complex in the sandy soil with around fifty entrance and exit points. These tunnels are constructed to provide airflow, and the warren has separate areas for nurseries, sleeping, and toilets. Multiple coteries of prairie dogs live alongside each other but in separate one-acre territories.

Prairie dogs have their eyes and tiny ears at the back of their head and spend much of their time standing up on their hind legs, scouring the prairie and the sky for dangerous predators. Many animals enjoy the taste of these prairie dogs: badgers, bobcats, coyotes, foxes, snakes, and multiple birds of prey.

Prairie dogs communicate with each other via indecipherable squeals, called barks but sounding more like faraway meows. Prairie dogs are incredibly chatty, talking to each other more or less incessantly. Mothers make one noise when they want their children to follow them and another if a child is straying near the territory edge. Apparently, prairie dogs have distinct sounds for different predators. Each type of predator has its unique call, including one for a human with a gun. When a prairie dog sees something it doesn't like, it sounds out a loud warning sound, and all the other prairie dogs disappear into their warrens via one of the many nearby holes. When it's safe to come out again, an all-clear is sounded.

The prairie dogs seemed happy to see us and were highly inquisitive. These national park prairie dogs obviously don't regard humans as predators, and a number scurried over to our boots to say hello. We watched these fascinating creatures for some time. We loved how family members greet each other like the French do with a prairie dog kiss. We came to the park when many babies were emerging for the first time from their burrows. These babies stuck close to their mothers, occasionally stopping to groom each other.

We could have abused the prairie dogs' hospitality by staying all afternoon, but we had other places to be. We said goodbye to our hosts and got on the road.

Chapter 12 – Speeding into Montana

The drive in North Dakota may have been longer, but the road in Montana was straighter. Following our day in the Theodore Roosevelt National Park, we needed to drive 440 miles to our next destination, 426 of them in a straight line on the same road. To give you a perspective on Montana's size, the drive from its eastern border with North Dakota to its western border with Idaho is a hundred miles longer than that of the twelve-hundred-mile drive from Washington DC to Chicago. From an earlier chapter, you will recall that our perennial "loser" state, West Virginia, was #1 in the nation for deer collisions. Montana is #2, with one in fifty-seven drivers colliding with a deer every year. Therefore, we drove carefully.

This was probably sensible because Montana has the most traffic fatalities per capita. Unlike in North Dakota, this Montana road is only one lane in each direction. The road is incredibly straight, with the occasional detour around someone's property lines. The roads here have rumble strips in the middle, which shake you awake when you stray beyond the central line. The undulating nature of the countryside also means that it's difficult to overtake as oncoming vehicles invariably hide in the brow of a hill.

Montana was pretty though, staggeringly beautiful indeed with huge lakes, rivers, prairies, forests, and mountains wherever you look. Montana has everything except ocean beach. The east is mainly prairie, but the remainder of the state is mountainous, and its name derives from this feature. The name Montana was debated heavily at the time of statehood, and the Indian name of Shoshone was also proposed. We will learn more about the Shoshone shortly. Many mountains, and the valleys that accompany them, boast large, unpolluted lakes which, in turn, are fed by one hundred and seventy thousand miles of river. The book and subsequent movie, *A River Runs Through It*, was written and filmed here. Montana is renowned for its big, blue skies and, for this reason, its car license plates sport the tagline Big Sky Country.

Montana is the USA's fourth-largest state by area, a smidgen bigger than Japan. Japan has 127 times as many residents, though. Only Alaska and Wyoming are less crowded than Montana on a per capita basis. Forty-six of the fifty-six counties in

Montana are designated as frontier counties, i.e. they have fewer than five thousand people.

At independence, the USA had around two and a half million people and, by 1800, the population had doubled to more than five million. From this point, population growth was exponential. The USA reached the size of the UK today by around 1890, and 100 million by 1920. Since then, the population has grown by double-digit percentages more or less every decade. It took until 1970 for the US population to hit 200 million and until 2009 to hit 300 million. The USA now has the third-largest population in the world, after China and India. The current projections are that the USA will reach 400 million sometime in the 2050s.

From time to time, you will hear some Americans say that the USA is full up and can't take any more immigrants. This is patently untrue. America is enormous, and its population density is still low. This is especially true in Montana. Of course, this is also true for the UK. If you divided the land of the UK equally, every person would have 0.9 acres. The figure for the USA is quite a bit higher at 7.4 acres per person. If, as predicted, the US's population grows by a further 100 million people by 2100, there will still be plenty of space for everyone.

Urban areas make up only 3.7 percent of the land area in the Lower 48, just under 70 million acres in total. However, this grows by around one million acres, or a Houston, every year. This urban space is quadruple what it was at the end of World War II. In the contiguous 48 states, there are 654 million acres of pasture (34.6 percent of the total landmass), 392 million acres of cropland (20.7 percent), and 539 million acres of forest (28.5 percent). Plenty of space to grow into. For those who like their percentages to sum to 100 percent, there is 12.5 percent for "miscellaneous" and "special use." These two categories include a range of features: America has 22 Waleses of national parks, state parks & wilderness areas and almost half of a Wales each of golf courses and airports.

Montana is home to seven Native American reservations, and Native Americans make up about 7 percent of Montana's population. Unlike North Dakota, however, most live off-reservation in the cities here.

Native Americans were once themselves immigrants to America, the last continent to be populated with humans. Until a few years ago, historians and archeologists believed that the so-called Clovis people were the first to come to America about 12,600 years ago from Asia over an ice bridge between Russia and Alaska. However, historians now agree that multiple waves of First People migrated to America between 15,000 and 22,000 years ago, and they continued to do so until about 10,000 years ago when the bridge was destroyed. Archeologists have uncovered human evidence in the Americas from around 15,000 years ago, including fossilized human feces in Oregon, stone tools in Florida, and other human evidence in southern Chile.

A recent DNA analysis of the remains found in Montana of a native boy from around 13,000 years ago showed that this boy's ancestors came from Siberia and Germany. Further genetic analysis shows that 80 percent of all native peoples in the Americas today are descended from this southern Montana boy's lineage.

Pre-European colonization, estimates vary as to how many Native Americans there were across the whole of Turtle Island, which is the name for North America used by many Native Americans in line with a common creation story. Perhaps the number four million is the most agreed upon number, almost double the likely number today. Some tribes had loose alliances with each other, but many were in a semi-permanent state of warfare.

On first contact with the European colonizers, most First People lived in subsistence economies as hunter-gatherers. In the early days of contact, there was what is now called a Columbian Exchange. Here, First People traded all sorts of commodities and services with the colonists. Unfortunately, the other trade that happened on contact was an exchange of the smallpox virus. The Europeans had developed some immunity to this virus through living near animals, but it tore through native communities, killing an estimated 80 percent of all Native Americans in the first hundred years. Most were accidental, but – in an early example of biological warfare – some were spread deliberately by the British Army via smallpox-infected blankets. By 1890, Native American numbers had declined further to less than one-quarter of a million.

When do you think that Native Americans had the right to vote? I'll put in one further sentence to give you time to think about it. Actually, it's not a straightforward answer, but it was as late as 1969 for many. Some Cherokee were the first to be recognized as US citizens in 1817, but only if they renounced tribal membership. The Civil Rights Act of 1866 and the ensuing Fifteenth Amendment, which granted all male citizens the right to vote regardless of race, should have enfranchised Native Americans. However, many parts of government interpreted the law so that it did not apply to Native Americans. President Calvin Coolidge signed legislation in 1924 that conferred unconditional US citizenship to every Native American and safeguarded them against unfair land purchases. At this point, most Native Americans again should have had the right to vote. However, many states continued to deny votes to Native Americans until all loopholes were finally closed in the 1968 Indian Civil Rights Act.

Incidentally, Coolidge is an interesting fellow. Born on the fourth of July, he was sworn in as president by his father, a notary public, when they learned about President Harding's death. He had a reputation for being taciturn. It was once reported that a woman seated next to him had told him that she made a bet that she could get him to say more than two words at dinner. Silent Cal is alleged to have said, "you lose," and then didn't speak to her for the rest of the evening. He was silent to the end; his last will and testament was just twenty-three words long.

According to the 2010 census, nearly three million people self-identified as Native American, and a further two million said they were a mix including Native American.

Some believe this is likely to be an overestimate, with the actual number of Native Americans more likely to be around two and a half million, about 0.8 percent of the total US population. Approximately 1.9 million people are tribal members, and some tribes, which require more robust proof of Native American ancestry than self-identification, are dis-enrolling those they think do not qualify.

There is some evidence that Native Americans are beginning to grow more prosperous, albeit from a low base. In the 1990s, income levels rose by a third, and those in poverty fell by 7 percent. Wealth has increased further since then. The latest figures suggest that Native American median household income is more or less on a par with African Americans, both of which are about 40 percent less than white households. If you travel to America, one worthwhile thing to do is to contact the various Native American communities. We have often found that the simple act of listening allows you to improve your understanding of their perspective.

We were still driving through the endless corn and wheat fields in eastern Montana, punctuated with the occasional trio of oil derricks. Small towns of five hundred people appeared every hundred miles and even smaller encampments every fifty miles. We decided to be prudent and fill up with gas when we reached half tank. We stopped for food in one forlorn town, but there were no open restaurants. We ate a wrap of eggs and cheese from our picnic box instead. The motel there looked as if it had never seen a better day.

Many towns boasted mini-casinos. They were typically attached to gas stations and run by Native Americans. God knows why anybody would choose to spend time in these sad little places. I don't understand why people go to Las Vegas, let alone some pokey small back room with some flashing slot machines.

We had driven for more than two thousand miles and not seen a single member of law enforcement. When we did see one, it was only a sheriff. Sheriffs are usually elected officials responsible for the county jail, court safety, and jurisdiction for enforcing laws in the county. This means that they transport prisoners, run crime labs, and ensure taxes are collected. Most importantly, they rarely stop you for speeding.

We had seen many meth murals throughout our trip across America. These large artworks were painted on walls, buses, or grain silos and held prominent positions by the side of the road, imploring people not to use methamphetamine products. These murals were especially notable in Montana. Most were part of an initiative from the Montana Meth Project, a foundation started by billionaire Tom Siebel to reduce the use of crystal meth, the smokable form of the drug. Initially, the foundation ran ads throughout the state, warning teenagers against crystal meth use. As with most of these types of public-good ads, success was limited. The foundation then held "Paint the State" competitions in 2006 and 2010, where teenagers created artworks sporting anti-meth messages that were highly visible to the public. This initiative started in Montana but spread into neighboring states and a couple of states in the South. These artworks often used the Montana Meth Project motto "Not Even Once."

Methamphetamine is one of a long line of drugs that have blighted US communities. As we have seen in Breaking Bad, meth is manufactured in hidden labs by cooking amphetamines with other chemicals. Meth costs about $5-10 a hit and is highly addictive; some report addiction from the first dose. It was particularly devastating in Montana. Half of all adults in Montana jails were arrested for crimes linked to meth, and more than half of children in foster care were there due to their parents' meth addiction.

The Montana Meth Project reported a 60 percent decline in meth use in Montana, Idaho, and Arizona in the last decade. However, meth use was on the rise in other states. In any case, the illegal narcotics industry quickly moves to other drugs if one of its products declines. Now, the received wisdom is that you have to tackle all drug addictions together, rather than focus solely on one drug.

In the latest decade, opioid addiction has dominated the narcotics news agenda. This opioid epidemic is a combination of legal prescription, heroin, and synthetic opioids. Pharmaceutical companies initially assured the medical community that their legal opioid products were not addictive, and doctors widely prescribed these legal products.

Opioid prescriptions peaked at 255 million in 2012, or 81 prescriptions per 100 people. While this fell by about a third by 2018, more than one in ten US counties dispensed more opioid prescriptions than they had people. This opioid epidemic has hit white, rural communities especially hard.

Late in the evening, we finally arrived exhausted in Great Falls, which takes its name from five consecutive waterfalls on the Missouri River that the Lewis and Clark Expedition had to portage around in 1805. It took them a month to take their boats in and out of the river at this stretch. Lewis and Clark had to leave their largest vessel at the upper camp and build two smaller canoes further downriver. Today, these cascades power hydroelectric dams.

Great Falls is also known for the Mariana UFO Incident. Nick Mariana, the general manager for the Great Falls minor league baseball team in 1950, captured on film two silver spheres that spun above the stadium. It was the first time anyone had captured a UFO on film. Mariana sent the film to the US Air Force for investigation, who returned the film minus the most explicit images in the first 35 frames. Multiple conspiracy theories abound on this incident, and no natural explanation has been confirmed for these objects. In a nice touch, more than fifty years later, the baseball team's logo was changed to a green alien on a flying saucer.

We stayed the night at a riverside hotel on the mighty twenty-five-hundred-mile Missouri river, which in St Louis will join with the Mississippi River. A few years earlier, we had visited Memphis. On an island in the middle of the Mississippi, they had a scaled model (30 inches to a mile) of the Mississippi River's lower thousand miles. Lorna got a little tired from walking the length of this scaled model.

Montana had taken an initial hard line on Covid and, until just before we arrived, had a mandatory two-week quarantine for anyone entering from out of state. Like North Dakota, mask-wearing was practically non-existent in Great Falls. Nothing tags you as not being from around here as wearing a mask when everyone else is naked from the neck up.

In places where mask-wearing is commonplace, you did come across people who refused to wear a mask in a public place. These non-mask wearers tend to be middle-aged men of all ethnicities and they sport their facial nakedness proudly. This act of defiance isn't new. In 1918 and 1919, during the Spanish Flu epidemic, it was compulsory in many cities to wear a mask. The penalty for not wearing a mask was between $5 and $10, or up to 10 days in jail. In one day in San Francisco, a thousand people were arrested and fined or jailed. Prisons became so full that there was standing room only. When sentenced to five days of jail time, one San Francisco railway worker, Frank Cocciniglia, told the judge, "That suits me. I won't have to wear a mask there." For some, masks became a political symbol of government overreach. The Anti-Mask League was set up during the second wave, mainly by women. They argued that there was a lack of scientific evidence for the mask and that it was unconstitutional to force them to wear one.

The restaurants were not yet open for dine-in, but we bought takeout from a nearby brewery. We had a surprisingly rare experience in the USA of eating our meal by the side of a river or lake. Many rivers and large lakes in the USA are administered by the Corps of Engineers, and commercial activity is often limited. We enjoyed watching another traveling family play first football and then nerf guns with their boys.

Small breweries have exploded in the USA in the past decade, rising from about 1,500 to 8,500 in number. Montana has the third-highest number of breweries per capita, with a brewery for each eight thousand people. Since you ask, Bernie Sanders' Vermont is thirstiest in both beer consumed and the number of breweries per capita.

The next day, we visited the Lewis and Clark Interpretative Centre, situated on the banks of the Missouri River. As we had seen previously, amateur historians have done extraordinary work in documenting history. Nowhere was more so than in this museum. It has to be said that the story of Lewis and Clark's journey is one of America's great stories.

At the beginning of the nineteenth century, shortly after the sale of Louisiana by a desperate Napoleon, United States began to think seriously about the prospect of controlling all of North America from sea to shining sea. Jefferson's hope was that a route could be found that used the Missouri and Columbia Rivers to the Pacific Ocean. Jefferson funded an expedition ostensibly to explore this wilderness, document its flora and fauna, and map the new territory with the aim of finding a route through to the Pacific Ocean. However, the reality is that he wanted the USA to establish trade with natives and document their presence in the new region before European nations could lay claim to the land.

This territory was fairly unknown to the USA at the time. Jefferson's expectation was that the expedition would find woolly mammoths prowling the countryside, six times the size of elephants, and come across ten-foot Megalonyx lions.

Jefferson chose his private secretary, twenty-eight-year-old Captain Meriwether Lewis, whom he had known as a boy, to lead the Corps of Discovery expedition. Lewis insisted that his friend, Lieutenant William Clark, come as joint leader. Lewis was something of an outdoorsman who had a small amount of expertise in science and some familiarity with Native Americans. Lewis was a quick learner, though. He was taught to navigate, educated on basic medical skills, and given access to Jefferson's own library, which had the largest number of books on the North American continent. Clark was much more adventurous. He came from a military family and had served with distinction in militias and with the US Army in the Northwest Indian Wars.

There were forty-three others in the expedition, mostly members of the US army, plus Lewis's black Newfoundland dog, Seaman. Lewis and Clark hired Toussaint Charbonneau, a French Canadian fur trader, and his two wives as translators. These two young women – the Otter Woman and the more celebrated Sacagawea – were either bought by Charbonneau or won in a gambling game, depending on which source you believe. It seems that the Otter Woman did not go on the expedition, as she was never again mentioned in the thirteen volumes of journals. These journals were ten times the length of this book and contained more than one million words, most of which were misspelled. The fifteen-year-old Shoshone-speaking Sacagawea was a vital member of the expedition. She was an accomplished linguist, born a Shoshone but kidnapped at eleven by another tribe. The expedition's numbers grew by one when Sacagawea gave birth to a boy on the journey. She was the ultimate working mother. A young Indian woman with her baby was apparently instrumental in convincing Native American tribes that the expedition came in peace. After all, which attacking army would bring a baby with them?

I don't want to be a plot spoiler here, but all but one of the party completed the three-year journey. Sergeant Charles Floyd died from appendicitis, untreatable then, and was buried in a bluff now named after him in modern-day Iowa. Lewis and Clark were the expedition's doctors, and they were busier than modern-day Baghdad brickies. The journals are full of treatments that they administered. Both the semi-trained Lewis and the amateur Clark cared for all the people in their party as well as many Native Americans they met. All members of the party had malaria as well as constant "running of the bowels."

One-third of the expedition's budget was spent on mosquito protection. All members of the party smeared themselves daily with pig's lard to ward off mosquitos. They also ate their food in the campfire smoke to minimize the amount of mosquitoes they would consume. Despite these precautions, mosquitos plagued their journey. In the journal, Lewis recorded that "the mosquitoes continue to infest us in such manner that we can scarcely exist...My dog even howls with the torture he experiences from them" (spelling and grammar corrected).

The care given by Lewis and Clark was probably as good as most available in America at the time. Unfortunately, this included treatments that did more harm than good. Bloodletting was common in the early nineteenth century and used for all sorts of ailments. When Sacagawea gave birth, they both let some of her blood as well as administered rattlesnake venom. Miraculously, she survived. They also performed surgery on Seaman's leg when an artery was severed by a beaver bite.

In 1804, the expedition started in St Louis, a village at the time, went north on the Missouri River and then west through Sioux Territory. They traveled together to what is today the border of North Dakota and Montana, where they spent the first winter. The first part of their journey was sixteen hundred miles, mostly along rivers.

Lewis and Clark made contact with about seventy Native American tribes along the way, many of which helped them. Communication was often challenging. At one meeting, Lewis's English was translated into French by one translator; from French into Minitari by a second translator; from Minitari to Shoshone by a third translator; and from Shoshone into Nez Percé by a fourth. It was a formalized game of Chinese Whispers. Gifts of medals, household goods, and whiskey were offered, and their passage was permitted. The silver Peace Medals ranged in size from two to six inches in diameter and bore the head of President Thomas Jefferson on one side, and the words Peace and Friendship, with a native and Caucasian hand clasped together, on the other side. These medals still turn up on the US version of Antiques Roadshow from time to time.

The expedition would not have survived its first winter in North Dakota without Native American help. The Sioux tribe was much less friendly towards them, however; Clark described them as the "vilest miscreants of the savage race." However, the expedition feared Grizzly bears more. In a rare passage of mostly accurate spelling, Lewis commented that he would "reather fight two Indians than one bear."

At the time, the international discovery doctrine, confirmed later by the US Supreme Court in 1823, said that a colonial power could claim ownership of land if colonial explorers traveled to and occupied that land. It ignored any native settlements or history. This expedition was careful to take the legal steps needed to claim title to each of these indigenous nations' lands under this doctrine of discovery.

Their most significant underestimation was reflected in how they traveled between the eastbound Missouri River and the westbound Columbia River. From an earlier semi-documented journey, they had assumed that they would be able to carry their boats between the two great rivers. Unfortunately, these rivers are many hundred miles apart, and this previous expedition had failed to mention the need to cross the Rocky Mountains.

York, Clark's boyhood African slave, was a hit with the Native American tribes who had never seen a black-skinned person before. York was tall and muscular, and the natives treated him as a superhuman. He was immensely popular with women. Men allegedly would encourage one of their wives to sleep with him, and most mornings, he would emerge from a woman's tent.

Many Native American tribes, even the matrilineal ones, had the custom to offer their women as temporary gifts. It's said that they believed that spiritual power passed between people during sex. The members of the expedition were sufficiently culturally sensitive to accept these offerings. Still, most men contracted STDs as condom recipes were not available for another forty years in the USA. Mercury was used in the treatment of syphilis until there was frothing at the mouth, the sign of mercury poisoning. Ultimately, the expedition ran out of STD medications by their journey's end. An interesting aside is that, as mercury doesn't decompose or synthesize, archeologists have been able to trace the exact route of the Lewis and Clark expedition through the trail of mercury remaining in the soil from the men's latrines.

The expedition ran out of supplies by the end of the journey, partly because they had traded so many of their assets for sex with native prostitutes along the journey. They were reduced to eating candles to survive. All food either had to be traded with natives or hunted. One of Corps of Discovery's favorite foods was dog, of which they devoured more than two hundred. Fortunately, this did not include Seaman. Seaman was an integral part of the expedition team. He acted as a watchdog by night, warning of passing grizzlies, bison, or Native Americans. By day, he was a catcher extraordinaire of squirrel, goose, deer, and beaver.

The expedition finally hit the Pacific Ocean towards the end of November 1805 after four thousand miles and more than five hundred days of travel.

The return trip was more challenging. Seaman was dognapped by Native Americans and then rescued. The expedition split into two parties to explore different routes, on which they both had problems with separate Native American tribes. When they reunited, one of Clark's party mistook Lewis for an elk, shooting him in the thigh.

Lewis fell into depression after the expedition ended. Although they had received a heroes' welcome initially, their expedition had been quickly forgotten thereafter. Their journals were unpublished for almost a hundred years, and it wasn't until two expositions in the early twentieth century that their story was retold. Unfortunately, neither author was a particularly good speller. They spelled Sioux in more than thirty different ways, sometimes on the same line in the same sentence. Their expedition gained fame in the twentieth century, and Lewis and Clark became America's most famous explorers, probably only eclipsed by the Apollo 11 expedition in 1969.

Lewis took his life in a tavern in 1809. He shot himself initially, but not expertly. He then reshot himself, this time removing most of his head. Unfortunately, this also did not end his life. At this point, Lewis seemed to change his mind about suicide, and he yelled at the innkeeper to heal his wounds. The innkeeper ignored his cries. Lewis drifted into unconsciousness overnight and, when he came to, found that he had cut himself from head to foot. He died later that day.

Clark took custody of Sacagawea's children after her death in 1812. It is said that there are more statues in the USA to Sacagawea than any other woman. Her legacy is a paradox. She is celebrated for the success of the expedition, which ultimately destroyed Native American cultures. Clark became governor of the Missouri Territory in 1813 and eventually freed his slave, York.

I recently read that Tom Hanks and Brad Pitt will produce a mini-series of the expedition. They certainly have a great story. But why is this story important for Americans? At its heart, their journey is a story about pioneering explorers. At the beginning of the nineteenth century, 95 percent of all US citizens lived within fifty miles of the East Coast. By the end of the century, the USA would control the whole continent from East to West Coast. Therefore, the nineteenth century's main story is how pioneers claimed the rest of the North American continent, and Lewis and Clark are an early part of this story.

Lewis and Clark were forgotten for most of the nineteenth century. At best, they were a footnote in history, and many history books did not even accord that accolade. Twentieth-century Americans were interested in hearing about the pioneers' experience, and Lewis and Clark were indeed brave adventurers. Portland organized a Lewis and Clark Exposition to mark the hundredth anniversary of their arrival in Oregon. This exposition attracted exhibits from twenty-one countries and most other states. It contributed to a massive 70 percent growth in Portland's population five years after the event.

If you would like to trace the expedition's route, you can. The Lewis and Clark National Historic Trail, which runs past the Grand Rapids interpretative center, starts in Illinois and ends on the Oregon coast. If you feel so inclined, you too can walk the thirty-seven-hundred-mile-long national park's trail.

We could have stayed at the museum all day but had to leave Central Montana for the next national park.

Chapter 13 – Glacier's Continental Divide

In much of the Land of the Free, land is almost free. The house price is principally just the value of the house structure itself. In the UK, we get used to house prices rising every decade, and this rise in house values reflects mainly the increase in the value of the land on which it sits. In the USA, the tax code explicitly provides for the depreciation of your declining property asset. For those with a penchant for detail, this is 3.636% per year over a 27.5 year period. The older your house is, the less it is worth until it gets so outdated that your home is worthless.

Mobile homes, or manufactured homes as the industry that fabricates them prefer them to be called, are popular in the USA. Around 20 million Americans live in these homes, and they make up more than 6 percent of the US housing stock. These homes are not mobile in the strict sense of the word, and four out of five manufactured homes never move after the first installation. You can't take them down to the corner shop to buy a newspaper, but you can move them in theory. On US roads, you get stuck from time to time behind a home being relocated from one town to another.

Warren Buffett, who knows a few things about making money, owns the largest mobile home manufacturer and the two biggest manufactured home lenders. You can also buy thirty-seven different modular house types on Amazon, though none yet through Amazon Prime.

The lifespan and energy efficiency of manufactured housing is now comparable to other housing, though it does lose its value more quickly. And if you have seen those pictures of a trailer park after a hurricane has hit it, you may be pleased to learn that new manufactured homes, like site-built homes, are now built to withstand winds of up to 110 mph.

You may think that most mobile homes are situated in trailer parks. The truth is that two-thirds are on private land. These were the type of homes we saw everywhere as we drove north through Montana. Of the minority located in mobile home communities, these vary a lot. Some are retirement communities with amenities like swimming pools, while others do indeed house "trailer trash." A specialist need is for sex offenders, who have severe restrictions placed by most states on where they can live. Crime in these parks is almost zero, as most criminals don't want to go anywhere near these neighborhoods. These specialist communities are, at face value, a good investment opportunity as there is almost no resident churn as these sex offenders have nowhere else to live. In making this statement, I should point out that I am not a financial advisor; investments can go down as well as up; this investment opportunity may not be suitable for all investors. If you have any doubts, you should seek advice from an independent financial advisor.

The great advantage of manufactured homes is their cost. Mobile-home residents spend just under half as much on their homes as non-mobile-home residents in the same metro district. You might be able to pick up a secondhand two-bedroom, two-bathroom mobile home for $10,000, though it will cost you at least $5,000 to move it. The average new manufactured home of the same spec will cost $50,000 but will be delivered free.

Almost three-quarters of mobile homeowners buy or rent land for a small amount of money and then install their mobile home onto this land and plug in the utilities. In many American towns, the majority of homes are mobile. These homes are modular and typically ranch-style. Manufactured houses are most popular in the Southern States, such as South Carolina, where one in five homes is manufactured, but they are also popular in Montana, which is why we saw so many that day.

I suppose manufactured homes and prefabricated homes are a niche style of US architecture. The first, from the Outer Banks of North Carolina, dates back to about 1870. However, manufactured homes took hold in the Baby Boom era after World War II, when soldiers returned home requiring cheap housing quickly. The traditional role of architecture is to meet local community needs appropriate for the environment. In these post-war times, the needs were both low budget and quick construction time. Over time, these pre-constructed homes have gotten bigger and cheaper.

The history of architecture in post-colonial America was bifurcated. On the East Coast, early-immigrant house builders used materials of wood and brick that were available to them and attempted to construct buildings with which they were familiar. The British-influenced terraced housing in Charleston, for example, would not look out of place in Kensington. In Spanish Florida and southwest America, homes were usually constructed from adobe, a red clay brick.

After the American Revolution, some Founding Fathers attempted to introduce a neo-classical style to important buildings. These would sport columns, friezes, and pediments. You can see this influence in many old universities and some plantation houses. Jefferson, a keen amateur architect, even tried to introduce Palladian architecture into the East Coast. As an aside, President Kennedy once hosted Nobel Prize winners at the White House State Dining Room and remarked, "I think this is the most extraordinary collection of talent, of human knowledge, that has ever been gathered together at the White House, with the possible exception of when Thomas Jefferson dined alone."

In general, though, for most of the nineteenth century and the early part of the twentieth century, America followed the European fashions for architecture. For example, the old parts of San Francisco have many Victorian houses because that architecture style was fashionable in Britain in the second half of the nineteenth century. As American industrialists became more affluent in the Gilded Age around the turn of the twentieth century, they had the money to build homes of every imaginable European style.

The first American-originated architecture was Modernist Architecture from around 1925. Modernist architecture emphasized functional design, used new technologies and materials, and rejected all previous architectural styles. These modern glass, steel, and concrete materials were molded into balanced, non-ornate, and not necessarily symmetrical buildings. The Modernist style was created *intra alia* by European-immigrant refugees Ludwig Mies Van Der Rohe and Walter Gropius. However, it was developed further by natural-born Americans Frank Lloyd Wright and Philip Johnson. This was the architecture used on many corporate skyscrapers in Chicago and New York.

This American architecture morphed over time. Frank Lloyd Wright moved away from functionalist design to create breathtaking buildings like the Guggenheim Museum and develop the prairie style of architecture. Philip Johnson, with others, formed the New Formalism style. Frank Gehry and other modernist architects developed the architecture into Post-Modernism and Deconstructionism. Western Architecture in twentieth-century America mostly belonged to American architects.

Other art forms seemed to follow a similar pattern. In the eighteenth and early nineteenth century, the art form was reliant on the old world. The War of 1812 gave Americans more confidence to start creating their own art forms, but essentially the global trend continued to be driven out of Europe. The twentieth century saw America drive innovation, and ultimately, in most cases, saw America dominate that art form.

British-influenced theater dominated with classics and vaudeville until the early twentieth century. However, Leonard Bernstein, George and Ira Gershwin, Rogers & his troubadour Hammerstein, and Stephen Sondheim pioneered musicals in the twentieth century that still dominate Broadway and the West End today. Post-World War II, other American playwrights such as Albee, Miller, O'Neill, Shepard, Simon, and Williams projected their American view of the world.

American literature in the nineteenth century showcased the diverse talents of Dickinson, Emerson, Hawthorne, Irving, James, Melville, Poe, Thoreau, Twain, and Whitman. However, the twentieth century saw US authors produce their own form of succinct literature. Capote, Faulkner, Fitzgerald, Hemingway, Lee, Morrison, Nabokov, Roth, Salinger, Steinbeck, and Updike formed the bulk of the English literature that I studied at school. The USA won eleven Nobel Literature prizes between 1930 and 1993, far more than any other nation.

Nineteenth-century American Art had almost no impact on the art community globally. However, some significant US-born artists – Cassatt, Whistler, and Sargent, to name three – painted mainly in Europe as part of European art movements. Some American Impressionists also tried to paint the vistas of American landscapes. Unfortunately, these Impressionists were inferior in technique to their European cousins and copied a European idiom that was inappropriate for American landscapes with their different colors and cultures. This is not to say that this period's American art is valueless; it is useful as a social document. Everyday nineteenth-century American genre art provides a fascinating historical record of the immigrant, Native American, or pioneer's life. The other feature of nineteenth-century art in America is that, as the USA became wealthier, significant European artworks were imported into the USA, much of which forms the basis of American art collections today.

As the USA became more confident in its sovereign identity and branched upwards on Maslow's hierarchy of needs, American art became more adventurous and innovative. Post-World War I, American artists, such as Hopper and Rockwell, rejected the trend towards abstract art but made little impact globally.

However, post-World War II, American artists such as Pollock, Rothko, and Newman introduced the hugely influential Abstract Expressionism. This was abstract because it did not represent any recognizable subject, and expressionist because it reflected a state of mind. This new art form focused instead on rhythm, movement, color, shape, and form. Somewhat implausibly, the CIA used this art movement as a weapon in the Cold War. The USA needed to show the world America's superiority in creativity and freedom in art and contrast it with the rigid and confined structure of Socialist Realism Soviet art. From 1950, the CIA funded art magazines and touring exhibitions throughout Europe. This was done clandestinely, without the knowledge of any of the artists or indeed of those in power with traditionalist art tastes like McCarthy or Truman.

The Abstract Expressionism movement, in turn, later spawned the Post Modernism, Neo-Dadaism, and Pop Art movements. Without a doubt, America dominated the second half of twentieth-century art.

Although the vast majority of Americans dress in casual attire, even fashion has seen American designers such as Ford, Karan, and Lauren become household brand names worldwide. For now, the USA remains the highest value apparel market in the world, though US companies are drawn mainly to the high-value parts of the industry such as supply chain, research and development, and design.

For all of these art forms, America represents the most lucrative individual market and the source of many of its key practitioners.

As we drove through Montana, we saw signs for rodeos. Almost all rodeos had been canceled in Georgia, but some still appeared to be taking place in Montana. Daughter #1 is horse mad, so this wouldn't have been our first rodeo. Rodeos are fascinating sporting events from a cultural perspective. They are attended almost exclusively by white, conservative, country folk, a group with whom I do not usually hang out. They are also more of a way of life rather than a sport. They are one sport that has not been mollycoddled in any way, with no helmets or body protectors.

A familiar shout at a rodeo is "Ride him, Cowboy, High, Wide, and Handsome," from which this book's title is taken. It is an American phrase, meaning both "expansive and impressive" and "in a carefree, stylish manner." High, Wide, and Handsome is also a term applied to the American West generally and Montana specifically to describe the country's nature. Incidentally, this almost wasn't the book's title. When we tested the book covers, we had High Wide & Handsome without commas, the convention for titles. Some British people were incensed by the lack of a comma between "High" and "Wide," while Americans thought there should be two commas as in the Oxford-style. I toyed for a while about having the title *High, Wide(,) and Handsome* (sic) before accepting that this was just too subtle.

Rodeos in the West are a little different from those in the South. Both showcase the bravery of the cowboys and cowgirls, but the Southern rodeos add in more significant dollops of religion, family values, and Republican politics. The typical Southern rodeo is jingoistic. The announcer – who has probably never traveled out of state, let alone out of country – extols that America is the greatest country in the world. In this community without political correctness, the Confederate flag is flown alongside the US flag, and a white woman is painted and dressed as a Red Indian.

More unusually for US sporting events, Georgia rodeos have a pronounced religious tone. The announcer tells us that America has turned into a heathen country and that only faith in Jesus and a return to traditional values will save the USA. The crowd cheer in substantial agreement. The rodeo knows its audience.

The rodeo is similar to a circus, and, indeed, one of the two main comperes is dressed in a clown outfit. Unlike most circuses, however, the rodeo is entertaining. Constant good-natured-Democrat bashing ensues, including this old joke:

> Barack Obama, Joe Biden, and Hilary Clinton were stranded on a desert island. Who was saved? America.

At one rodeo we attended, there was a pre-show act, an Elvis impersonator so bad that I wondered whether he was supposed to be Presley or Costello. You might guess that the music would be mostly country, but instead, a broad mix is selected to entertain the crowd, including Black R&B and the UK's own Slade.

And, of course, there is always the horse riding itself. These men and women are courageous and fantastically skilled. Nothing would persuade me to jump onto an already bucking steer or deliberately distract the bull to prevent it from goring the fallen rider. The competitors ride unbroken horses and bulls, lasso and bundle calves, and race around barrels. I can't imagine an animal charity in the world that would approve, but it is impossible not to marvel at the skill and bravery.

Daughter #1 used to say that she would marry a cowboy when she was older. I think she could do worse, and, indeed, has done worse in some of her choice of boyfriends. Before I came to live in America, I was traveling on business with a colleague when a man in a pickup truck changed lanes without signaling and crashed into my rental car. He immediately admitted responsibility and, while we waited for the police (a requirement in the US after an accident), the cowboy told us his life story. He had been a professional rodeo rider for many years but had broken his back after an unexpected buck and been confined to bed for almost two years. When he recovered, he returned to rodeo. Was he as stupid as an Idaho potato? Maybe. Brave? Certainly. However, it was my privilege to spend thirty minutes talking to this man who was so unlike me in almost every way.

> I will leave you with one other joke I once heard at a rodeo:
> Why is it so hard for the police to solve a redneck murder? Because there are no dental records and all the DNA matches.

Our destination was Glacier National Park, in the north of Montana. It is one of the most celebrated parks in the system and is the tenth most visited park receiving more than three million visitors a year, almost all between June and September. There is a Canadian national park on the other side of the border, Waterton Lakes National Park. Together they form the Waterton-Glacier International Peace Park.

The warlike Blackfeet tribes themselves only arrived in the region relatively recently, probably in the latter part of the eighteenth century. They captured a raft of land covering large parts of Montana, North Dakota, and southern Canada. The Blackfeet were forced in 1895 to sell the Glacier land to the US Federal Government for $1.5 million due, in part, to the decline of bison on its territory. As part of the deal, the three Blackfeet tribes were permitted to continue to use the Glacier land for hunting as long as it remained public land. However, when the ceded land was given to the National Park System in 1914, the land technically was no longer public. This meant that hunting was now illegal in the park, which caused conflict with the Blackfeet, who believed that the US Government has reneged on yet another promise. The present-day Blackfeet Reservation starts at the east of the park, and the tribe had used Covid as an excuse to restrict access through their remaining territory, forcing the closure of the eastern entrance to the park. Incidentally, the Blackfeet Reservation holds the world record for the biggest change in temperature on consecutive days, a staggering 100°F (56°C) difference when temperatures fell from 44°F to -56°F overnight.

The Continental Divide partitions the Park in two. This means that precipitation on the west side of the park will eventually find its way into the Pacific Ocean, and that precipitation on the east side will ultimately reach the Atlantic. This also affects the weather in the park, and the National Weather Service issues separate forecasts for each half of the park.

One of the three great American hikes, the 3,100-mile Continental Divide Scenic Trail, runs through Glacier Park down the middle of the country from Waterton to Mexico. It is less famous and apparently less clearly emblazoned than its sister trails of the 2,650-mile Pacific Crest Trail on the West Coast and the 2,184-mile Appalachian Trail on the East Coast. All three routes are for the dedicated only. Even the fittest people take most of the summer to complete each trail. I've hiked a few sections of the Appalachian Trail, and they are very hilly indeed. A few thousand walkers attempt to thru-hike each of the trails every year. The trails also showcase how much of America remains in wilderness; you can habitually walk for a week or more without seeing either a road or a house.

It had snowed on the way to the park, but this snow had turned to pouring rain on arrival at the park entrance. All private watercraft had to be inspected by park rangers for invasive species, so we had to unpack our kayak in the driving, cold rain. This park receives so much snow that many roads are not cleared until July at the earliest. Even in August, it isn't unusual to get a foot of snow. With up to eighty vertical feet of winter snow to clear, the most advanced snowplows can only clear around five hundred horizontal feet of road per day. Such is the weight of this snow that every road guardrail is destroyed each year and has to be replaced by new barriers. We drove along the fifty-three-mile "Going to the Sun Highway," or at least as far as the snowplow allowed. In latish-June of 2020, this was fewer than ten miles of the whole road. We also took a couple of short hikes to two magnificent frosty-blue waterfalls. You will probably recall the road if you have seen the movie Forrest Gump, where he describes running alongside the mountain lake as like two skies on top of each other.

We stayed in the Swiss-style Lake McDonald Lodge, built in 1914, and one of the many national park properties once owned by the Great Northern Railway Company to attract their customers to the park. The original front entrance faced the lake to receive the first visitors who arrived via steamship. At $400 per night, it was the most expensive hotel room we had ever paid for, even though it had no TV, Wi-Fi, air conditioning, or elevator. Our room did have a panoramic view of the nine-mile-long Lake McDonald, which had been carved out of the landscape by ancient glaciers. It also had a spectacular entry hall, decorated with stuffed animal heads. Some brave fellow guests – of Scandinavian origin probably – swum in the 45°F crystal clear lake outside the lodge. We noticed that the park's clientele came from all over the USA. Out of the twenty-five cars in one section of the car park, we counted tags from twenty-five separate states.

Within the next decade, Glacier National Park may need a new name. In the mid-nineteenth century, the park boasted 150 glaciers over twenty-five acres in surface area. Only 25 active glaciers remain today, and scientists estimate that all active glaciers may disappear by 2030 if the climate continues to warm. Unfortunately, these are just a small part of the world's six trillion tons of mountain glacier that have been lost since 1994.

Lorna, that modern-day Sacagawea, had had somewhat-recent surgery on one of her ankles, and that day did not trust her ankle to take the strenuous hike that I had planned. I, therefore, took this walk alone in contravention of the park guidance. The trail was only eight-miles long but had a two-thousand-foot change in elevation.

The park also had multiple signs warning you of bears. The USA has two main types of bears: the Black Bear and the Grizzly (or the Brown Bear). Bear attacks are relatively rare, but both bears are hazardous to you and require different precautions. If you are attacked by a black bear, you must try to escape to a secure place. It is unlikely that you will outrun a bear; they run more than twice as fast as humans and can outrun a racehorse over a short distance. If escape is impossible, you should fight back, aiming kicks and punches on the bear's face. You should never climb a tree. Black bears are excellent climbers and are more courageous in a tree. Indeed, they often kill other bears by throwing them out of trees.

If you are attacked by a grizzly bear, the advice is that you should climb a tree. If this is impossible and you are already in contact with the bear, the best advice is to play dead. You should lay flat on your stomach with hands clasped behind your neck and legs spread out, so it's harder for the bear to turn you over. I applaud the people who, having been attacked and presumably injured by a brown bear, have the presence of mind to do this.

Now here is the thing. Bear identification is not straightforward; black bears aren't necessarily black and brown ones, not brown. Black bears can be black, dark brown, brown, light brown, or even white. Brown bears range similarly in color, from black to blond. Grizzlies are usually bigger than black bears, but not always so. More importantly, these two types of bears are rarely seen together, making comparisons difficult. If you are wrestling with a black bear, you may not necessarily have the presence of mind to conclude that this bear seems a wee bit smaller than others you may have come across in the past. The bear which is crushing you will always likely be seen as rather large.

To be serious for a New York minute, the best differentiator is that grizzly bears have a slight hump in their shoulders and are the owners of a more prominent snout. The black bear has a straighter facial profile and has its eyes set further apart.

Unfortunately, I saw no bears on my hike. I did spend a joyful twenty minutes in the company of a young elk feeding on forest foods. The youngster didn't seem to be bothered by my presence at his dinner table.

Two weeks after our Glacier visit, a woman on a trail run with friends collided with a grizzly bear picking huckleberries, and they tumbled off the path together. Both parties were described as surprised. The thirty-year-old woman managed to escape and report the attack to park rangers.

There are semi-regular bear sightings in Georgia, even in suburban neighborhoods like ours. The black bears come from the countless forests in northern Georgia, looking for food and maybe some excitement. Georgia Department of National Resources find and tranquilize the bear and return it to another nearby forest.

The walk that day was spectacular. It was mainly wooded, but with regular streams, rivers, and the occasional lake-filled vista of Glacier National Park. This hike's destination was a spectacular large mountain-top lake. The lake was translucent, perhaps one of the best sights I had ever seen. It was only one of more than seven hundred lakes in the park.

It was at this point – that is to say, the furthest point away from the lodge – that I noticed that the back of my heels ached. The temporary walking shoes had worn away all of the skin at the back of my ankles. My socks were completely red. Although the return journey was mostly downhill, every step downward was agony as the back of my shoe rubbed against my raw flesh with each fresh step. Lorna's face registered a look of horror when she saw my feet. Thankfully, the park shop had some rudimentary plasters.

Contrary to some public perception, Montana is not filled solely with survivalists and domestic terrorists. It does, however, attract many bohemians and eccentrics who choose to live their life more naturally.

Montana is one of only six states where more than half of its citizens own a gun. This might surprise you, as you probably know that there are more guns in the USA than people. Americans own 40 percent of the world's guns in private ownership but represent only 4 percent of the global population. However, in the USA as a whole, only 30 percent of adults own a gun, and a further 11 percent live with someone who owns a gun. Most gun owners like to have multiple firearms; two-thirds of gun owners own more than one gun, and 30 percent of gun owners have five guns or more.

Most Americans have shot a gun, though. Every town will have a shooting range, where you can practice marksmanship with your own weapon or rent a firearm for the afternoon. When we have overseas guests, it is a popular activity for many. It is most certainly an enjoyable people-watching activity.

While some people own guns for hunting purposes, most gun owners say they have a weapon for their own protection. The perception from the vast majority of Americans is that crime rises year on year. This perception is probably gained from the media and some politicians highlighting the genuine issues in a couple of outlier cities. However, the statistics – no matter whether FBI or from victims themselves – tell a different story. Both violent crime and property crime have fallen by more than half in the last twenty-five years. The majority of US neighborhoods are almost entirely safe.

Many local newspapers will print or post online all the felony arrests in their jurisdictions. In many districts, it is incredible how few occur in any week. Despite or maybe because of their high incarceration rate, Americans are fundamentally law-abiding. Some counties produce a monthly newspaper from the police blotter with pictures of each person arrested. While these newspapers come with a warning that a warrant is merely an accusation of a crime and that accused people are innocent until proven guilty, it is a fun – but potentially discriminatory – game to go through the list of pictures and guess guilt based on the photo alone.

Another great game to play is to look up all your friends and neighbors on the court's online databases, which go back decades. All non-juvenile court hearings are public record, and, as you probably know, America is a stickler for granting public access to matters that are of public record. Almost all court documents are there: divorce details, each traffic offense, every complaint made by them or made against them, and any criminal charges taken against them. Seemingly upstanding community members transform before your eyes as you find out the details of their experience with the law.

While violent crime is more common in the USA, presumably due to high gun ownership rates, total crime per capita is three times higher in the UK than in the USA. We once met a Chinese teacher from Shanghai on an Amazon rainforest trip in Ecuador. She told us that she was too frightened to travel to the USA because her perception was that it was the most dangerous place on earth. No amount of us presenting alternative facts would persuade her otherwise.

Almost two-thirds of gun deaths are suicides, and the highest suicide rate is in, yes, Montana. Of those who try to commit suicide by firearm, 97 percent are successful, compared with success by only one in twenty who cut themselves and an ever-so-slightly-higher proportion who poison themselves. It is self-evident, therefore, that a reduction in guns would reduce suicide.

The economist and creative-cities expert Richard Florida analyzed the correlation between gun deaths and various social indicators. The primary positive correlation for non-suicide gun deaths, both accidental and deliberate, is with poverty. Larger populations, greater stress, more immigration, and higher incidence of mental illness were not correlated with increased gun deaths. It won't be surprising to you – but he proved it anyway – that the states with most guns have most gun deaths, nor is it any surprise that states with tighter gun control laws also have fewer gun-related deaths.

Our first exposure to guns in America was the Sandy Hook Elementary School massacre, which took place a few months after moving here. In just over four minutes, a twenty-year-old misfit killed twenty children and six teachers at a Connecticut school, having earlier killed his mother. He fired a hundred and forty-six bullets during this period. There were calls for a ban on the sale of semi-automatic firearms and magazines with more than ten bullets. Ultimately, the proposed federal legislation was defeated. Three states – New York, Connecticut, and Maryland – introduced more restrictive gun laws. Ten states passed laws that relaxed gun restrictions.

I once asked Daughter #2 whether there was anything she could be in the USA that she couldn't be in the UK. She gave the succinct answer, "shot at school."

We were concerned about our children's safety at school and learned that they had regular school-shooting training. According to my daughters, the action students needed to take was to lock the classroom door, turn off the lights, and stay silent out of sight of any unauthorized person. Teachers also cowered on the floor under desks with the children, but one or two lacrosse teachers fetched their lacrosse stick ready to tackle the incoming shooter with their unequal weapon. Both daughters saw the training as a little pointless. As Daughter #2 said, it's not as if they will see a closed door and think that everyone has gone home for the day. Of course, most school shooters were students who had attended this training themselves. Both daughters told me – in the event of a real shooter – their plan would be to flee from the building as soon as possible.

It is shocking for most first-generation immigrants when you first see someone carrying a gun in public, what they call "open carry" here. What would shock us more is that nineteen million people have "concealed carry" permits. As one recent immigrant told me, though, she always lets another car out of a side road or has learned to ignore all bad driving as you just never know if the other driver has a gun. Another immigrant told me that she was shocked when she went on a first date with someone and found a handgun in his car's center console.

I read a local news article this morning about a drunk man who had knocked repeatedly on the wrong house's door in the next town along from us. He had been shot in the shoulder through the door by the homeowner. The article's final sentence did not surprise me, but it will likely appall you and aggravate Tony Martin. "The injured man was…charged with a count of misdemeanor criminal trespass. The homeowner does not face any charges." This news story was not in any way shocking because it happened in my neighboring town of Kennesaw. In the USA, it's not only the country, the state, and the county that can make laws, the city you live in can create laws, too, provided the law is consistent with the American and relevant State Constitution. In 1982, Kennesaw made it compulsory for every head of household – whatever one of those is – to maintain a firearm and ammunition. In case you think this a bad law, this statute has exemptions for people with mental disabilities, paupers, people convicted of felonies, and conscientious objectors.

Now here's the thing about the Second Amendment, the right to bear arms. It's still popular; in fact, it is more popular than ever. While increasing popular support exists for more stringent gun sales regulation, notably restrictions on purchases from people with mental illnesses and background checks for gun-show sales, there is low support for a total ban on guns. The country was set up on the assumption that you could not trust any government, and having the right to own guns seems to be an essential part of ensuring you can protect your family. Despite their different political leanings, my own children are both supportive of the Second Amendment. They believe it is instrumental in preventing future tyrannies. One of Daughter #1's roommates, Room Mate #2, has a gun for their apartment. I would like to suggest that they consider locking their apartment from time to time as a better initial precautionary measure.

Will gun laws change in America? Some people, including former Supreme Court Judge John Stevens, argue that the Second Amendment should be amended to clarify that the right to keep and bear arms is only relevant when serving in a well-regulated militia. In my view, this is a pipe dream. As we explored earlier, it is complicated to change the Constitution. Both the House of Representatives and the Senate would require two-thirds majorities, and two-thirds of the states would also need to agree. My perspective is that too much popular support for guns exists, and therefore I don't see this change in my lifetime or that of my children. Will there be tighter state gun control laws? Probably, it's what most people want. Ultimately, however, it is a very odd society that allows almost everyone to have a gun but decrees that you can't buy a Kinder Egg because the toy inside might be harmful.

The year after Sandy Hook, our next-door neighbor shot his wife dead on a Sunday morning as she dressed for church. Lorna heard the scream while in the bathroom and thought at first that it was perhaps a cry from a wounded animal. A few minutes later, I looked out over our front lawn from my study and saw a dozen policemen with guns and flak jackets in the act of a raid on the house next to us.

There were many news trucks outside our house for many hours, desperate for interviews with the neighbors until the inevitable next tragedy dragged them elsewhere. I asked the detective who interviewed us what we should do about the news trucks. He reminded me of something that I had temporarily forgotten; we lived in a free country, and we could do what we wanted to do. We ignored the regular knocks at the door from the media.

The pastor at her funeral service later that week declared that it was a great day. He claimed that our neighbor had met her maker much earlier than she could have envisaged.

We knew both neighbors well. She was a mainstay in her church and had a two-hour-daily commute in a job that she only did to provide her husband with healthcare. He was disabled; it took him about thirty minutes to shuffle to the postbox on his front lawn to collect the mail. He had also been given six months to live by doctors. One neighbor went to visit him in jail but returned disappointed when he had not repented his sins. The husband would shortly be released from jail to live with his sister after his lawyer said that he was a victim of Agent Orange from when he served in the Military. Ultimately, he was too sick to be tried, and he died within the year.

Another bizarre aspect of this case was what happened in the legal system. The husband had sold the house at about half its market value to his defense lawyer within a few days of the shooting. He needed the money for his legal bills. The lawyer, in turn, had sold it on later that week at a much higher amount. Her children, they had both been married previously, were grieving and were too slow to prevent the house sale. Many years later, Lorna served as a witness in the case to decide whether his or her family should receive the remaining proceeds of the estate. Fortunately, some justice did prevail.

We are not that unusual in knowing someone who has been shot; almost half of all Americans do. About a hundred thousand Americans are shot and injured every year.

In line with other countries in the world, a growing distrust of institutions has taken hold. Those excellent people at Pew Research have looked into Americans' trust in each other and found that it has fallen continuously since the 1960s. The poll shows that two-thirds of respondents have low trust in other Americans. Those who trust least are likely to be younger, non-white, less educated, and lower earning. Democrats trust much more than Republicans, though both groups have a high desire to trust more.

Gallup also regularly measures Americans' trust in fourteen institutions, and only one in three now has at least quite a lot of faith in these fourteen institutions. This is ten percentage points lower than two decades ago. Two-thirds of Americans believe – probably correctly – that this lack of trust makes it impossible to solve some of America's challenges.

Politicians are seen as less trustworthy than a lawyer on a billboard. Only 4 percent of Americans think that Congress members are trustworthy all or most of the time, but this may be just the congressmen, senators, and their families responding positively.

Trust in other things has also dropped. Organized religion is trusted by only 41 percent compared with 65 percent when the question was first asked in 1973. There is a similar level of trust for leaders of Technology companies and journalists. Only one in five trust the federal government most of the time. The medical system is trusted by only two out of five, compared with four out of five from 1973. Military leaders and public school principals are the most trusted and have levels of trust substantially above 50 percent.

This lessening trust in institutions is causing issues for Covid management. For example, on contact tracing, those individual states that run contact tracing struggle to contact people who have tested positive. In Miami and Maryland, three-quarters of those with positive tests never answer their phone to contact tracers, and half of those spoken to in Houston, New Jersey, and California refuse to co-operate when contacted. I can fully understand why people don't trust those who phone them up, claiming to be contact tracers. Lorna and I receive so many phone calls from people pretending to be something they are not that we disregard any call not made by somebody we already know.

Before we move onto the next related topic, let's have a joke:

Three conspiracy theorists walk into a bar. You can't tell me that's not suspicious.

Conspiracy theories are often thought of as very American, but I guess they are a worldwide phenomenon. The last one I heard was a month ago at the community swimming pool when talking to an affable British guy. We had talked for about an hour on a range of subjects, and he seemed pretty sensible. As usual in these times, we eventually moved onto the subject of Covid. He told me that he had written a book with his father about biological warfare and that he was pretty confident that Covid was the first of two infections designed by Russia sent to soften us up before the next more powerful virus.

The definition of a conspiracy theory is something that explains an event or set of circumstances to be the result of a secret plot, generally carried out by a powerful set of conspirators. It is habitually unprovable, and people who hold these beliefs rarely reduce their credence in them even as contrary evidence becomes known.

A couple of conspiracy theories have indeed turned out to be true. Both the Iran-Contra scandal and Watergate were conspiracy theories for a while before they were later confirmed. With so many theories out there, wouldn't it be suspicious if none were true? Some believers seem to argue that because a couple have turned out to be accurate, others are also true.

There is a perception that conspiracy theories are more common now than in the past. This doesn't appear to be accurate, at least until 2010. An analysis of more than one hundred thousand letters sent to the New York Times and the Chicago Tribune between 1890 and 2010 showed that the percentage of letters that promoted some unproven conspiracy theory slowly declined between 1890 and 1960s, where it has remained steady since. It's unclear what has happened since 2010 because fewer people now write to newspapers. However, the internet's rise now makes it less effort to propagate unproven theories, so their incidence may increase.

The University of Chicago calculates that approximately half the American population believes at least one conspiracy theory. However, once you believe one unproven theory, you are more open to others. Belief in any individual conspiracy theories tends to max out at around 25 percent, and usually a lot less than this.

Conspiracy Theories in politics are by no means new. In the 1790s, some Federalists believed that Jeffersonians were under the Bavarian Illuminati's control, and there was an international conspiracy to defeat Christianity. In response, some Jeffersonians believed that Federalists planned to return the USA to the King's rule.

Academics from reputable universities have concluded that Republicans and Democrats appear to be more or less equally susceptible to conspiracy theories, but not typically the same ones. Universities from other countries have found that the extremes of both the right and left, as well as all the shades in the middle, seem to be equally gullible. Victims of conspiracy theories are also just as likely to propagate conspiracy theories on others. Recent claims from Hilary Clinton, for example, that Russia had groomed fellow Democrat Tulsi Gabbard for the presidency were found to be ungrounded.

There is no particular strong relationship either with intelligence. Some believers can be smart, while others are also quite stupid. Plenty of people with postgraduate degrees believe in conspiracy theories, but generally, the more formal education you have, the less likely you are to believe in them.

A key question is, why do people believe in conspiracy theories? Academics agree on the causes. First, psychologists from Universities in Vienna, Kent, Delaware, and Union College find that people turn to conspiracy theories when they feel powerless. For example, when they are scared, vulnerable, or feel a lack of control. As the world becomes more complex, this feeling of powerlessness and anxiety will likely increase. Second, conspiracy theory advocates have a higher sense of disgruntlement and tend to regard the world as an inherently dangerous place. They are more likely to feel discriminated against, excluded from society and insecure in their jobs. It also allows the believer to present himself – and it is more often a him than a her – as the smart person in the room, rather than one of the brainwashed herd. A conspiracy theory typically divides the world neatly between the forces of good and the forces of evil. All evil can be explained by a small number of harmful agents to which the believer has no relation. Third, believers are more likely to connect the dots between variables, even if no connections exist. They easily infer meaning and motive, and they don't like uncertainty or unexplained things. Daughter #2 has a fourth, more cynical cause. She is a subscriber to Juvenal's bread and circuses theory, in which those in power offer extravagant entertainment as a way to divert the attention of their citizens.

Conspiracy theories tend to assume that the bad guys are unusually competent. Their plans are always executed with unerring accuracy, and those involved in the deception always keep their secret. This assumption always comes as a surprise to anyone who has managed any complex project.

Conspiracy theories are not new or certainly not confined to the USA. Pretty much every aircraft that has crashed anywhere in the world has generated an alternative theory of foul play that deviates from official findings. One-third of all notable deaths or disappearances since Nero has an alternative ending where the person is not dead but rather hiding and waiting to return to power again. Hitler, Elvis, and Lucan are good examples of this. Another third were actually secretly murdered, for example, Chaucer, Mozart, and at least two Lees. The final third was killed by someone other than their identified killer: John Lennon was murdered by the author, Stephen King, and more than one thousand books have been written on JFK's assassination. Some people who appear to be alive are, in fact, dead, including Paul McCartney, Avril Lavigne, Eminem, and Melania. Stevie Wonder isn't blind, and JK Rowling is only an actress. Any number of people were Jack the Ripper, from Lewis Carroll to members of the royal family. Alien visitations are routinely covered up by governments. Every religious group is engaged in plots to ensure their religion is victorious.

Every secret society, including ones that don't exist, have masterminded complex events. Katy Perry is a grown-up JonBenét Ramsey. Every unfortunate event is carried out by the victim as a false-flag operation. Shakespeare did not write his works, and Emily Bronte did not pen Wuthering Heights. Medicines are designed to hurt humans, and medical agencies routinely suppress natural cures. Every disease is created by a man in a white coat. Fluoridation is a way to dispose of industrial waste. Vaccinations are evil. The earth is flat. Governments control the weather via cloud technology. Americans did not land on the moon, and Stanley Kubrick directed the moon landing shots. Ronaldo, the fat one, not the smug one, was drugged before the 1998 World Cup Final. Jeffrey Epstein did not commit suicide; OK, I've found one that I might believe.

You can be pretty sure that any new sizeable event will have a conspiracy theory attached to it. In writing the previous paragraph, I also started thinking that it might be quite fun to invent a conspiracy theory of my own. The more absurd, the better. A substantial minority of readers will likely be predisposed to wanting it to be true, and I don't want to let this reader down.

The person pretending to be Elon Musk following his death in a Tesla automated driving experiment – in conjunction with the Illuminati – has created the Covid virus as a way to drum up interest for his future Mars shuttle business. Do I have any believers?

Covid, of course, is and will be no exception for conspiracy theories. A surprisingly high 29 percent of Americans believe that the COVID-SARS-2 virus was made in a laboratory, 23 percent intentionally and 6 percent by accident. One in four Americans believes that the media does not tell the truth about the virus and prefer to get their information from Dave on Facebook. One in eight young people thinks that this is a plot by Bill Gates to set up a new world order. Incidentally, old people actually like Mr. Gates and don't have any truck with this theory.

In case you think this is a US phenomenon, some British people believe that 5G has caused the virus. As of June 2020, there were ninety arson attacks against mobile infrastructure and two hundred documented incidents of abuse against telecom engineers. Believers of this conspiracy theory saw a correlation in the timing of new 5G networks and the Covid epidemic and – despite warnings that correlation does not imply causation – chose to believe that one causes the other. When it is pointed out that the countries that developed 5G networks much earlier had no Covid infections until recently and that other countries with no 5G networks have plenty of Covid infections, the believers shrug their shoulders, quote their own statistics, claim that they are not the gullible ones, and continue to say that they are the only ones who have done their homework. In case smug people from Netherlands, Ireland, Belgium, Italy, Cyprus, and Sweden are reading, you had 5G network arson attacks, too.

This is all a bit too serious, so time for a joke before the next chapter.

Did you hear about the epidemiologist, the accident and emergency doctor, and the contact tracer who went into the bar? Of course not, because they all know better.

Chapter 14 – Into Washington State

I drove west out of northern Montana towards that thin strip of northern Idaho near Canada. Wherever I looked, endless vistas of leviathan lakes and monumental mountains filled my landscape. However, like with an iceberg, I knew that I saw only a tiny proportion of what was on offer from near the traveled road.

We bought huckleberries from a roadside stand. We had eaten them the previous evening as a jus but didn't know what they were other than Finn's epithet. They taste a bit like blueberries but are a shade tarter. You can pick huckleberries in the wild like you can blackberries in the UK, but take care; they are the favorite foods of grizzly bears.

The weather was glorious, and Lorna did not critique my driving too frequently. She took pictures continuously through the insect-impregnated windshield. No amount of cleaning this window would create a genuinely see-through barrier.

We had just four hundred and fifty miles to drive over the next two days before our next national park, so I should have been in no hurry. However, for the first time in almost a couple of thousand miles, I took an interstate road on Montana's long descent. I resisted the temptation to take one of the many emergency runoff roads just to see what it would be like. If you are ever going to do this, though, a rental car is a perfect vehicle. Shortly after we entered Idaho, I saw from the road an interesting town below. I doubled back, and we decided to take our lunch there.

Wallace is an old silver town, self-proclaimed as the silver capital of the world. Gold was discovered by several prospectors from 1859, some of whom attempted to keep their discovery quiet. The year 1882 saw a stampede of mining camps in the region. Experienced miners soon discovered that the amount of gold was dwarfed by the availability of silver. By 1884, Civil-War-veteran Colonel William Wallace had started a township and built a grocery store, fences, and roads. Within a year, the town added a hotel, brothel, general store, and sawmill. As more miners came to the region, the city expanded. By 1887, it had a school, brewery, and even a railway.

While we are talking about miners, this reminds me of an old joke.

What do you get when you throw a piano down a mine shaft? A flat miner.

Wallace was not always a peaceful place. In 1892, when railroads increased their freight pricing, mining owners sought to cut costs by reducing miners' wages. The miners responded by striking, so owners attempted to replace them. One Wallace mine was destroyed in the local conflict, and three men died from each side. A dozen replacement miners were also attacked and killed by an armed mob. At that time, mine owners retained private agents from Pinkerton to infiltrate unions, integrate themselves with miners, and provide intelligence on union activities. The Anti-Pinkerton Act of 1893 prevented government agencies from hiring Pinkerton, but this law did not apply to private companies. Individuals suspected of being Pinkerton agents mysteriously disappeared, never to be seen again. In 1899, one mining company refused to recognize the miners' union. A thousand men attacked and destroyed the company's mill. Martial law was again enforced, and a thousand men were rounded up into a bullpen prison.

Employment in the USA is "At Will" in all states except Montana. This means that an employer can fire an employee for any reason, other than discrimination, without warning, and an employee can leave an employer immediately, too. This means that the employee's certainty of employment can be low, but it also means that companies are more inclined to hire new employees. Therefore, it may not surprise you to learn that Americans have a net positive view of unions. Despite this, union membership has declined from 35 percent in the 1950s to just above 10 percent today.

Mining continued more peacefully in Wallace in the twentieth century. From 1955, Congress passed a series of acts of legislation around air pollution. Wallace, whose unfettered mining development had caused terrible pollution over the previous decades, saw most mines close in the next twenty-five years.

The town has been saved from ghosting due to its proximity to the interstate that it once resisted. Hundreds of similar towns weren't so favored by their positioning. In the nineteenth century, frontier towns came and went. If the economic reason for a town's existence disappeared, so would the people and eventually the town. Ghost towns in America are common; Texas alone has more than five hundred. Residents of a new settlement didn't know if their village would become a big city or disappear into the ether. The village of Fort Dearborn went from a few hundred to more than a million people in just sixty years in the nineteenth century. It's called Chicago now, of course.

The town of Wallace had its heyday in the late nineteenth and early twentieth centuries. The long decline of mining has slashed the town's population by more than three-quarters to around seven hundred people today, but it is now eking out a living through people like us stopping for lunch, or maybe the night. Dante's Peak was filmed here, and Wallace has a traditional Main Street downtown set against the nearby towering mountains.

We took our lunch outside at the Blackboard Cafe on a street corner that overlooked the old cowboy town. The streets were wide, and you could see vestiges of old saloons, brothels, and a masonic hall that once serviced a mining population. A brothel museum showcases the ladies' work, which was encouraged and regulated here until the last mine's closure in 1981 and the final police raid of 1988. The restaurant was an eclectic place that was divided into three sections. The first was a trendy cafe; the second a clothes shop that sold outdoor attire; and the third a book shop that offered iconic travel books, all of which were placed on their individual shelf like a connoisseur might house his porcelain collection.

It seemed to be compulsory to have a dog here. Men with peculiar facial hair descended from their oversized trucks, walked around to open the passenger door of their waiting spouses, and finally retrieved their dogs from the cargo bed. We liked the place. For the first time, we felt a bit of a West Coast vibe. Young people with long hair on modes of transport we couldn't name cruised the streets.

It was in this town, as I was people-watching, that I decided to write this book. I wanted to better understand America and explain my take on America to other people with a similar interest. Here in the Idaho sunshine, America seemed both perfect and quite unlike the media's typical stereotype. I regretted that I hadn't taken notes from the earlier part of the journey, but, at that point, I hadn't wanted to write a book.

Idaho was recently ranked as the dumbest state in America. The algorithm modeled college and advanced degrees, high school graduation rates, and test scores to rank-order each of the fifty states plus Washington DC. New Jersey was ranked the smartest state, which may explain why it has so many millionaires. Here in the bookshop of the small town of Wallace, it was not possible to see this lack of educational achievement in Idaho.

We explored the lake town of Coeur d'Alene. We pronounced it as the French would lion heart but realized that the locals called it core de lane or CDA. As was typical of all the states since Michigan, the lake was huge. Most of it was underdeveloped, but the best bits near the town were reserved for residential living. We couldn't find accommodation on the lake and were now so spoiled that highway hotels were unacceptable.

I drove on to Spokane in Washington State. We had shunned cities hitherto, but we found a cheap hotel with views over the river, so we decided to risk it. I asked the receptionist what she would recommend doing in Spo-Cane. She had a puzzled look on the part of her face not covered by a mask before she realized I had spoken about her home town of Spo-Can.

You would never have guessed that Spokane is exactly the USA's hundredth largest city, as the parks, streets, and massive car lots were almost deserted. I imagine that the downtown offices were now closed, and accordingly, activity in the rest of central Spokane had declined to almost nothing.

I believe the city had experienced some difficult times in the 1970s, but it had cleaned itself up for a new Millennium. This development's centerpiece was the large park set on an island in the middle of the Spokane River. It was a pity that so few were enjoying its charms. We selected one of the best restaurants in town and took one of the few outside tables. Like elsewhere, it looked like restaurants here were scrambling to survive through enhanced collection services and outside eating. According to our waitress, after decades of resistance, Spokane authorities had allowed businesses to utilize the sidewalks outside their premises.

There was a complete absence of dating couples in Spokane. We wondered what had happened to dating during the Covid epidemic. As we had met each other when we were fifteen, neither of us had any great dating expertise, and the conversation didn't last too long. Therefore, for this next section on the culture of dating and sex in America, I have depended on the experience of other foreigners in the US and the meager data that is available.

America has a reputation for being somewhat prudish. Many people blame the Puritans for this attitude. However, this would be unfair. The Puritans were indeed enormously unforgiving for those who transgressed their society's norms. Many transgressions, including adultery and masturbation, could, in theory, lead to death. However, the Puritans were surprisingly frank on sexual matters, discussing them as naturally as they would the food they were eating. Books written at that time later had to be heavily edited for future, more prudish, generations. In marital matters, it was commonplace to "try before you buy," or bundling as it was then known. If you got pregnant, you had to marry. But if not, you could bundle some more with a different partner. Marriage data in the 1770s showed that half of New England brides were pregnant at the time of marriage. Further down the coast, 94 percent of those harlot brides in Appalachia had a bun in their oven.

It was, of course, the British who introduced prudery into the USA in the nineteenth century. Contrary to popular belief again, this started pre-Victorian era. By 1807, Dr. Thomas Bowdler and his spinster sister Harriet Bowdler decided to re-write Shakespeare's works to exclude the naughty bits so that the stories could be safely read to children. Many things were bowdlerized, with many suspect sections omitted from the plays altogether. The Bowdlers made numerous language changes too. In Othello, for example, "your daughter and the Moor are now making the beast with two backs" becomes the more widely interpretable "Your daughter and the Moor are now together." Problematic words were found and replaced; for instance, God is interchanged by Heaven. Plots were also altered – and plot spoiler ahead – Ophelia no longer commits suicide; she merely accidentally drowns.

By the Victorian age, sexual ignorance was rife in both the UK and the USA. The American novelist, Edith Wharton, asked her mother on the evening before her wedding what she should expect from her wedding night. Her mother replied that her daughter should have noticed the differences between men and women in statues and promptly left the room. This was remarkably similar to my father's advice the evening before I went to boarding school.

By 1873, prudery in the USA had scaled greater heights. Anti-vice activist and Post Office employee, Anthony Comstock, persuaded Congress to pass the Comstock Law, which made it illegal for anyone to deliver lewd material by US Mail or indeed any other mode of transport. Had Congress spent more than the ten minutes they did spend on this debate, they might have noticed that lewd behavior was not defined in the bill. Comstock's response was that he would know improper conduct when he saw it. Comstock was appointed the special agent of the Post Office to enforce this law, which he did by bullying other people for the next few decades. By the end of the century, he had destroyed fifteen tons of titillating books and four million dodgy pictures. By 1915, he boasted that he had been responsible for four thousand arrests.

There were many state laws too. These were also short on definition of what they were banning. Self-pollution was banned in Indiana until 1955. As the botanist but more celebrated sexologist Alfred Kinsey said in 1948, according to law, 85 percent of people in Indiana should be in prison.

After a stream of Hollywood scandals in the early 1920s, thirty-seven states passed more than a hundred laws in 1921 designed to censor motion pictures. As these laws were independently drafted, countless anomalies arose. This form of censorship was also extremely inefficient as each film had to be doctored separately in accordance with the state in which it was showing. The movie moguls insisted that something be done, and they set up a trade association to blunt the censors' blue pencil. They installed Postmaster General Will Hays to run this organization. Initially, Hays persuaded states to relax their censorship regimes. He introduced a morality clause for actors' contracts and, in an example of self-regulation, persuaded the studios to reduce their movies' sex content. As the 20s progressed, however, the movie companies returned to producing more risky films.

In the early 1930s, Hays produced a new set of guidelines. The inaptly named Colonel Joy and his team reviewed every film and predicted which scenes were likely to be censored by individual states. As their predictions were invariably correct, the filmmakers began to trust them. By 1932, an uneasy truce prevailed; the filmmakers wanted to produce money-making films but did not want to incur state censors' wrath. However, in 1933, the almost bankrupt Paramount released a film version of the Broadway play *Diamond Lil* written by Mae West. *She Done Him Wrong* is a mild sex comedy, famous now for the first use of the line "Why don't you come up sometime and see me?" Colonel Joy's successor, Dr. James Wingate, begged Paramount to reconsider parts of the film. Paramount released the film largely intact to great financial success. However, the Catholic Church opposed this movie and, in the guise of the League of Decency, began a rating system of their own: A – morally acceptable; B – morally unacceptable; C – condemned.

The mostly Jewish movie moguls were terrified of uncontrollable, religious-based censorship and handed Hays more control. Hays and his new henchmen, Breen and Shurlock, insisted on reading every script of forthcoming films and watched every "finished" movie. Filmmakers were given advice on how their movies could fall within guidelines. If the filmmaker did not heed this advice, the film did not receive approval. No major movie between 1934 and 1958 was shown without this seal of approval.

On sex, the guidelines were numerous. The sanctity of the institution of marriage always had to be upheld, and adultery could never be justified or presented attractively. Scenes of passion, including lustful embraces between married people, were banned. Sexual perversion, which was undefined, was forbidden. As before, no white slavery, miscegenation, sex hygiene, or childbirth was permitted. Religious ministers, too, continued to be protected. If you see one in a film from this period, you can be reassured that they aren't either the villain or a comic character.

Prudery continues today. There is little nudity on American beaches, and those where clothing is optional are often pay-to-enter and can be fully listed in a short article on USA's nudist beaches. The average American eighteen-year-old will have viewed sixteen thousand murders and two hundred thousand other acts of violence on TV. Still, woe betides a wardrobe malfunction, which grants little Johnny a micro-second of an uncovered nipple.

In the town we live in, somebody had the temerity to open an erotic store in a self-contained strip mall before we embarked on our cross-US trip in June 2020. Incidentally and ironically, it was located in one of the many Mattress Store locations we used to have. This store, inappropriately named Tokyo Valentino, as you will read shortly, caused a lot of excitement on local social media. And I mean a lot; each post generated hundreds of comments, predominantly negative. It seemed that most people feared that our middle-class town would turn into 1970s Harlem and that children in an elementary school almost a mile away would be scarred for life. In July, the local town council wanted to revoke the business license for violating the amount of sexual paraphernalia allowed but soon realized that they did not have the necessary legal backing. "I know what it is when I see it" was no longer sufficient grounds for shuttering a shop, so the town council had to create a new code that would help them define a sex shop. In September, the town council passed a new ordinance that identified a sex shop as one which stocked more than a hundred sexual devices or a store that devoted more than five hundred square feet to sex items. No sex shop could be located within fifteen hundred feet of a school, church, government building, park, hospital, prison, library, or residential area, nor five hundred feet from any place which sells alcohol. As our residential community is chock-a-block with churches, schools, and hospitals, this would make no location possible for a sex shop.

Surprisingly, there is little academic material that compares sex globally, and that which exists is old, incomplete, non-comparable, or uses dubious sampling techniques. Durex, the prophylactic maker, carried out an international survey about a decade ago. They found that 53% of Americans said they had sex weekly, many of them weakly too, no doubt. This was about the same as the British (55%), but well behind the amorous French (71%), the missionary position-loving Germans (68%), and the randy

Greeks (87%). These countries are well ahead of the frigid Japanese (34%), who now have sex shops named after them. The average age of losing one's virginity in America is 18.7, more or less the same as 18.5 for Europe. Young American women may wear abstinence rings at high schools, and one-third of Americans may say sex before marriage is immoral. Still, the Guttmacher Institute found that 95% of men and women have sex before marriage and that this percentage has been similar since the 1950s.

My single ex-pat friends tell me that dating in the USA is much more casual than in their home country. Although most now meet via an app, the first date is customarily casual. Dating is low commitment at first, with people dating multiple people simultaneously for fun with no obligation. I remember listening to stories about dating in New York when I was in my twenties and thinking that it sounded glamorous compared to the more committed culture in the UK. Apparently, the UK has now followed the USA model of low commitment but with a much heavier reliance on alcohol.

A 2019 Pew Research Center Survey surveyed Americans about their experience of dating. Nearly half of Americans think dating is more challenging than ten years ago, with only one in five – probably the good-looking ones – saying that it's easier. Two-thirds of single people say that their dating life isn't going too well or isn't going well at all.

My daughters have educated me on the complicated steps of modern US dating. The first stage is flirting, which is what it has always been. The second stage is called "Talking To," also called "hooking up." This is decidedly not exclusive and may or may not involve sex. Americans often are talking to multiple potentials simultaneously or at least on different days of the week. The third stage is called "dating"; this is more exclusive, and Daughter #2 describes it as the final interview before you get the job.

If dating is different, so is friendship. The vast majority of first-generation immigrants told me that, while it was easy to make superficial acquaintances, it was tough to make American friends in the USA. Consequently, most of their close friends were fellow-immigrants. Many people I interviewed thought that the lack of American friends was because Americans defined friendship differently from what they were used to. They believe that most Americans are satisfied with many situational friends that they are friendly with, rather than a few close friends in whom they will confide. Foreigners present more risk, and thus it takes longer to earn their friendship.

Indeed, Americans are charitable towards people that they do not know well. If you break a leg, you won't have to cook for the next two months. If you move into a neighborhood, you will likely receive welcome baskets. Your new neighbors will tell you that you must come over to their house, but the invitation will never come. It's undoubtedly counter-cultural to drop in on someone without an invitation.

When we arrived in America, I asked two fellow first-generation immigrants who had been here for decades whether they had any American friends. They just laughed and said that they had long given up hope of making any American friends. I disagree with this perspective. It only takes much longer for an acquaintance to develop into a friendship. It is also easier to establish friendships if you are at school or college, at church, or through your children.

One final niche area of friendship that arose from my interviews are those first-generation black immigrants. Most told me that they couldn't be accepted into African American friendship groups. They believed that this group did not see them as black, but rather as British. The differences in their vocabulary and vernacular were too much of a barrier.

Social class in America is different from that in the UK. We British are experts at delineating someone's class immediately on meeting them. Lorna can tell instantly just from their clothes and shoes, the subtle tones of their vowels, and some mannerisms. I can too, but I prefer to choose not to.

In the USA, class is less important, but it is not absent. Two broad mechanisms in the USA exist for measuring class. The first and most common is simply by income, and the second – more like that of the UK – a combination of income, wealth, education, occupation, and social groups. When we were in our twenties, we swapped houses for a month with an older couple in Grand Junction, Colorado. We felt it a bit of an unequal trade at the time. They stayed in our South London apartment while we resided in their spacious ranch home in western Colorado. They used our Toyota Corolla while we got to drive both their pickup truck and camper van. I remember meeting many of their friends, who seemed to be stratified by income, not traditional British Class. They had friends who were truck drivers, waste disposal experts, teachers, and managers. Even in our twenties, most of our UK friends were fellow professionals. Another example of this stratification can be seen in your subdivision, which classifies your wealth in an obvious way. Homes in subdivisions are promoted as, for example, "From the 600s", meaning that each home is valued from at least $600,000. These homes will have slightly better status than those "From the 400s", but less than those "From the 900s".

When asked to self-identify, Americans categorize themselves into 3% Upper Class; 15% Upper Middle; 43% Middle Class; 30% Working Class and 8% Lower Class. This confirms the truism that the majority of America sees itself as middle class. Teams of US sociologists believe that the size of the middle class is inflated and that there should be around 27% in the lower-class category. It's the other way around in the UK, with 60% self-identifying as working class, even though only one in four does traditional manual work. Accordingly, election messages are different between the two countries. In the UK, the Labour Party traditionally appeals to the working class, while, in the US, their equivalent, the Democratic Party, unashamedly appeals to middle-class voters. Given citizens' self-categorization, both strategies make sense. What is also essential for America is that its working-class citizens have to see that it is possible to achieve middle-class status.

So, what explains this American desire to be middle class? One explanation is the American Dream. This is a social model where society is meritocratic and where class is achievement-based. Your class isn't determined by your birth but rather by your achievements.

We are often told that the USA is a classless society where upward mobility from the bottom is a cornerstone of the American Dream. While the American Dream is still in place and – perhaps just as importantly, while most people still believe that it's possible to succeed if you work hard enough – the American Dream is less prevalent than in previous generations. However, every person I spoke to knew people who had achieved the American Dream and, perhaps unlike the UK, were admired for their achievement.

Income mobility in America remains high compared with other developed countries, but lower than it was a few decades ago. In the 1970s, nine out of ten thirty-year-olds earned more than their parents did at the same age, adjusted for inflation. Today only half of thirty-year-olds make more than their parents.

For those that like proper data, the best measure for income mobility is probably intergenerational earnings elasticity (IGE), essentially the extent to which your father's income explains your income. The USA has seen a marked increase in IGE over recent decades, to a point where just under half of a person's wealth is now explained by their parent's wealth. Economists believe this increase is caused by the growing importance of advanced education on income generation and wealthy parents' willingness to spend money on their children's education. To move IGE downwards and maintain the American Dream, the potential solution must be to enable greater access to good quality and low-cost education for all.

With Great Gatsby in my thoughts, I ended the day by doing some laundry at the hotel. Masks get stinky quickly. Although we had brought a number with us, only paper cuts are worse than inadvertently putting on your partner's used mask.

Chapter 15 – A Stehekin Education

We took the three-hour drive to Chelan and stopped at every possible place of interest on the way. On the route we took, farms and grain silos were vast, but towns non-existent. At Lorna's instigation, we explored a farmers' cemetery and appreciated how few people had ever lived in this part of the country. A few years earlier, we had rented a houseboat on Lake Powell. One port from which you could rent the boat had warned that you needed to bring all groceries with you, as the nearest grocery store was three hours away. The road was burning hot, and Lorna was troubled by the fear that we did not have sufficient gas to reach our destination. The Washington scenery here was as good as anywhere we had been, and the drive into Chelan from the east along McNeil Canyon Road was especially magnificent.

The area is known for its fruit growing, and orchards stretched for as far as the eye could see. The farms proudly announced that they were members of the Chelan Fruit Cooperative, a three-hundred-member association that tried to get the best prices for its members' eight million boxes of cherries, apples, and pears.

We arrived early at Chelan, a resort town set at Lake Chelan's southern edge. Restaurants weren't yet open for dine-in, so, like everyone else, we ordered a pizza for lunch and ate it at picnic tables that overlooked the lake. The town center was filled with tourist businesses, only a few of which had re-opened. I bought food and beer at the supermarket for dinner, and we sneaked our way onto the beach at the fanciest resort in town. We watched as the emergency services successfully resuscitated a swimmer who had not quite managed to make it across the lake.

You've probably heard how expensive US health insurance is. It was not always this way; US healthcare costs have more than quadrupled since 1980 and are now about twice the cost of that in the average developed country. The second notable difference is that almost every other country's healthcare is paid from general taxation, whereas Americans have to pay their own healthcare costs. I have endeavored to be positive and optimistic about the US in this book. In most cases, this is easy because I do, indeed, feel upbeat. However, in the case of healthcare, I'm as hopeful as a Jehovah's Witness at a blood bank. Ultimately, US healthcare is of supreme quality, but it's far too wasteful. Furthermore, owing to the high expense and funding model, healthcare is also unequal and the largest cause of personal bankruptcy.

US health insurance policies vary greatly. Typically though – after you have paid for your monthly multiple-hundred-dollar health insurance policy – you must pay the first few thousand of your annual healthcare bills from your own pocket, called a *deductible.* Each time you use any service, you also need to pay a *copay* of up to $100. Most (56%) Americans are insured through private insurance via their employer, 20% are old people insured through government Medicare, and 14% are poor people insured through government Medicaid. This leaves just under 10% of the population who are uninsured.

Daughter #1 is a power user. She habitually burns through her personal deductible in the first month of the year. A few years ago, she had a relatively simple morning procedure that involved a general anesthetic. At 8 a.m., I took her to the specialist doctor, admiring his supercar on the way into the building. On reading the ten pages of small print, I noticed a clause on page nine that said that if the insurance company did not pay the full amount of the bill, I would be liable for any difference. I refused to sign this clause, and a billing specialist agreed to delete it. After a successful operation, our insurance company received a bill for $245,000 for the morning's work. Not surprisingly, our insurance company refused to pay for this obscene sum. Eventually, the two parties agreed that the insurance company would pay $40,000. Had I signed the papers un-amended, I may have been liable for the $200,000 difference.

Lorna – or as perhaps I should call her, Wife #1 – is not yet a power user of the system. However, she is an aging model that needs more and more repair work every year. On one of my many business trips away from the USA, she needed her appendix taken out. Just as she was about to go into surgery, she remembered to ask if the doctor was covered by our insurance, as some doctors are "in-network," while others are not. They said that it was too late to review that and, in any case, no one was else available to do the surgery. Thankfully, the doctor was in-network.

Ambulances are expensive, too, approximately $2,000 for each ride. On another business trip, my wife tripped over a blade of grass and broke her ankle in two places. No Uber would take her to the hospital, so she had to take this extortionately expensive taxi.

I would like to give you some advice. I know you didn't explicitly ask for it, but it is for your benefit. When you come to the USA for a vacation, please take out travel insurance. I know US travel insurance is expensive compared with any country you travel to. But, at least, any treatment you need won't bankrupt you.

Healthcare is a constant worry for Americans. You open each health bill with trepidation. The morning that I write this paragraph, we have just opened two invoices. On this occasion, it was good news. They had sent us only the copy of the invoice for the insurance company. We had already paid our share at the time of treatment.

With US healthcare so expensive, you would probably imagine that healthcare outcomes are the best in the world. Sadly not. The USA comes in thirty-seventh: life expectancy, infant mortality, diabetes outcomes, and safety during childbirth all score lower than for most other OECD countries.

The American health system is world-class in four areas. First, responsiveness. If you are sick, you can get an appointment more or less immediately at any hospital with more or less any doctor rather than take your place in, say, the UK's long appointment queue with its average wait times of about eighteen weeks. Second, pretty much all FDA-approved drugs are covered by US insurance. No NICE body determines whether a drug is cost-effective or not. I have never once seen a Facebook post raising money to send someone to the UK for treatment that isn't available in the USA. Third, America has a more positive attitude towards mental health. When I was growing up, there was something of a stereotype that most Americans saw a psychologist. This was stigmatized further at the time in the UK, as these mental health professionals were called shrinks. Just over nine out of ten Americans say that they would see a mental health professional if they experienced a problem. Almost half of Americans say that they or someone in their family has seen a mental health professional in the latest year. Fourth, US hospitals clearly have world-class expertise in one area of the medical industry: billing. You can guarantee that, as soon as you enter any hospital, the billing specialist will see you immediately on arrival and take your credit card details. I read recently about Duke University Hospital in North Carolina that had 900 hospital beds and 1,300 billing specialists.

Why is the US medical system so expensive? It's complicated because there are multiple reasons for the excessive costs. The first is the cost of administration. All those billing specialists and other administrators account for around 25 percent of all medical expenses. The second main additional cost is the fear of being sued and the cost of the doctors' malpractice insurance. This insurance isn't only expensive, but – worse from an overall cost basis – it also encourages each doctor to oversupply medical tests just in case. Even though the doctor can see you have a severed arm, s/he will make sure you have a whole raft of other tests on your throat, eyesight, and brain function just in case they have missed something. All these extra tests cost money. Third, specialist surgeons themselves are extraordinarily well paid. A basic surgeon will earn at least $200,000, but most specialists will start at $500,000.

Covid has necessitated a different healthcare model. As it is imperative for the country that people get tested, receive treatment, and are vaccinated, patients are not required to make a deductible payment or copayment. Covid treatment is free at the point of delivery, and this is a novel experience for most Americans.

Will American healthcare change in my lifetime? I am not optimistic. The vested interests are powerful. Like the UK Parliament, members of Congress are disproportionately composed of attorneys. These lawyers are unlikely to reduce the legal liability for doctors because it will affect their fellow attorneys' business. They are also unlikely to regulate healthcare salaries. Finally, the healthcare industry has a powerful lobby that will resist any reduction in private companies' profit levels.

The next morning, we made our way to North Cascades National Park. Stehekin lies at the top of fifty-five-mile-long Lake Chelan on the outskirts of the North Cascades National Park. Technically, Lake Chelan is a fjord in that it was created by glaciation. It also looks like a fjord in that it's long and thin. You can reach Stehekin by boat, seaplane, or nearest road plus a twenty-mile hike. We selected the three-hour express boat option, described by National Geographic as "a front-row seat as one of America's deepest lakes gradually undergoes a startling transformation from family playground into awe-inspiring wilderness." The journey was as promised by the fine people of National Geographic. Young people on jet skis surfed over the waves created by our boat while we admired the vineyards and houses on both sides of the lake. When the roads petered out, so did the houses. Glacier-topped mountains came into view, and the sides of the lake were uninhabited, save for the occasional cabin. If you wanted to be picked up from one of these remote cabins, you had to wave frantically until someone on the boat saw you.

National park rangers met us at the other end. This is one of the most lightly visited national parks; only thirty-eight thousand visit every year. Stehekin itself has a small full-time community of eighty to one hundred people. According to whom I asked, these estimates differed, but I did ask well over 10 percent of the population. Unlike some other communities we have visited on this trip, Lake Chelan has not frozen since 1893, and boats run all year round. The reason it doesn't freeze is that it is deep, the third deepest in the USA. You don't want to drop your water-resistant phone into this lake because, at its deepest point, your phone will fall 1,630 feet to the bottom, almost 500 meters. For those people who want to know the identity of America's deepest lake, you should carry on reading. For those who are impatient, it's Crater Lake in Oregon.

Like Loch Ness, Lake Chelan reputedly has its own monster. I will give you one sentence to guess its nickname. Yes, you are right; it's Shelly. Several old photographs exist of the beast. Some say that it resembles a dragon or winged alligator with the head of a serpent. I say that the photos also look a lot like one of those giant trees that has fallen into the lake.

Stehekin has a rudimentary twenty-two-mile road network, which, like on an island, doesn't connect to any other road networks. Residents have an old truck that they keep in Stehekin and another down-lake in Chelan. We saw one poor resident suffer a vehicle breakdown, contemplating an expensive barge trip down the lake to repair it.

Most visitors on the boat were day-trippers. A bus waited to take them for a quick trip to the bakery. The lodge we were staying in was just re-opening post-Covid as we arrived. It had the world's worst satellite Wi-Fi. If you tried hard enough for long enough, you might just be able to send one SMS. The community is changing as satellite gives some sort of internet connection to people whose only previous communication tool was the public CB radio. I can report that the boat we took had literally a whole truckload of Amazon, Walmart, and Zappos' parcels. One resident I spoke to said that one good thing about living here used to be that it was impossible to make any impulse purchases as you used to have to write your order down on a piece of paper and wait for someone to go down the lake and buy it for you. The internet had changed that.

We decided to take our canoe and nose around some cabins dotted around the bottom of the lake. Most houses seemed to belong to full-time residents, though some were also vacation homes.

What I have missed most about traveling in this Covid time is that it's much less easy to talk to others. People are understandably more cautious than usual and hidden behind masks. While canoeing, we saw one of our fellow boat travelers swimming in the lake. He invited us into their yard. Many Europeans have a negative view of Americans, supported by a cynical media portrayal that focuses on American society's outliers. My experience is that well-traveled Americans are amongst the most educated and interesting people you can meet. These two couples had walked both the Appalachian and Pacific Crest Trails, visited as many countries as we have, and one had even walked to the North Pole.

Stehekin is still a remote community. We rented bikes from a volunteer school teacher. These bikes had no locks, but, as he said, where would anyone take a stolen bike? He told us that he had not lost a bike in over thirty years. We cycled to some nearby waterfalls, which were more impressive than most others we have hiked to earlier in the trip. The short eight-mile ride through Stehekin had more activity than Chelan had the day before. There was an organic farm shop with its honor-based payments system, a vast picnic table built for giants, as well as the fabulous but pricey bakery with its meadow views. Lorna complained about the terrain we cycled through. Her perception was that they were huge mountains, while they were really just mild inclines.

Stehekin has a school. In fact, it has two schools: an old one, now a museum, and a brand new, larger school constructed in wood to accommodate the school's ten pupils up to the age of fourteen. The school has one teacher and eighteen volunteer teachers from the community. The school's newspaper, written by all ten children, documents the year. Each child writes about their rural life and the learning they have done during the year. They involve themselves in school-wide projects like designing a mural, participating in writers' workshops, and competing in knitting challenges. The school trips are literally field trips, which also study trees in detail. The school play this year was The Hobbit, and the whole community gathered to enjoy this production. The older children seem to be taught to lead and to nurture others. With so few children over a wide age range, it must be imperative that all the kids learn to get along with their friends. Reading their newspaper and seeing their community made it easy to understand how schooling might have functioned for the pioneers.

According to Washington State school data, the school has an impressive teacher to student ratio of six (old data), but a below-average diversity ratio of 0.00. We asked a resident with young infants whether he would send his children to the school. He said that it would depend on who the teacher was at that time.

Pre-1825, all schooling was homeschooling and focused on literacy, especially for boys. America planned for public education, but the two main parties disagreed about how this should be achieved. They agreed that students should be able to read the Bible and that schooling should, to an extent, homogenize America and equalize opportunity. However, the Whigs favored centralized control, while the Democrats favored local state control. We know that the Democrats won this argument, and – to this day – schooling is controlled by the state, which develops curriculum and other school policy.

The first Board of Education was formed in Massachusetts. They created six principles widely followed by other states: No ignorance, publically funded, all children, non-sectarian, free society, and professional teachers.

Our children's own experience of US public schools is positive. In significant part, this is because we chose to live in a school district with excellent schools. I suspect our children's experience was more or less on a par with a decent private school or exceptional state school in the UK. We have been impressed with the standard of teachers. In the main, they work extraordinarily hard and essentially are on duty from 8 a.m. to 10 p.m. We certainly don't begrudge them their two-month-long summer vacations. For many years before we lived in the USA, we said that we didn't want to live in America because our perception was the education would be too US-centric. This just hasn't been true from our experience.

The truth is that the quality of public education in the USA is uneven. Each of the fifty states has its own curriculum, and there are more than thirteen thousand separate school districts in the USA, each with its own leadership, management, and policies. The fifth-placed USA spends 17 percent more on average per pupil than the eleventh-placed UK, and both countries are well above the OECD average. Like most other countries, British and American teaching is dominated by women, representing 86 percent of teachers at primary level and 60 percent at secondary level. There is also a disparity in earnings; average teacher salaries in the USA are $55,700, compared with only $37,900 in England. Average elementary class sizes are different too: 21 in the USA compared with 27 in the UK. Average PISA scores – the international assessment of fifteen-year-olds for reading, math, and science – show that educational attainment is pretty similar in the USA, the UK, and most of the rest of Europe.

This averaging of scores hides a wide variance in attainment, however. US public education is funded by counties through property tax, which is based on your property value. The higher the property value, the more money the school system receives, though the district can ramp up or down its millage rate. Although schools in poor counties have their income supplemented by federal grants, this by no means eliminates the gap in outcomes. As we explored earlier, the USA has a highly democratic structure.

Every two years, our county regularly votes in favor of a voluntary increase in its sales tax. All additional tax receipts raised funds for specific capital projects for schools. As a result, schools in my county have superb facilities which compare favorably to the very best UK private schools. It's a democratic structure, but it's also slightly fixed. First, in our county, old people don't pay the school element of the property tax. Second, the ballot for increased funding is generally held on dates when the fewest people are likely to vote. That way, the school system can lobby their employees and parents to turn out to vote for more money.

I am impressed with the public education system in our school district. I appreciate that if I lived only ten miles away, I would not draw the same conclusions. However, I am writing about my experience in the USA, and others can write about theirs. The schools in our district are enormous, but they accommodate every ability within that school. By high school, children are streamed in every subject into four levels: special needs, on-level, accelerated, and university level courses. Theoretically, if you suck at math(s), you can still do advanced level courses in other subject areas. The reality is that clear differences exist in the educational content for dumb and smart kids. Both attend the same school, but their schooling is entirely different.

In case you think this is just our experience, the first-generation immigrants with children that I spoke to – whom I understand were not necessarily a random sample but did come from a wide range of school districts – were all very satisfied with their children's education. They were impressed with the teachers' commitment and professionalism; you could phone them day or night. They noted the high level of confidence instilled into the children, and they loved the school system's flexibility.

As mentioned earlier, the educational curriculum is set at the state rather than the federal level. In my state, most children receive twelve years of education on social studies, mainly history and geography. Some social studies courses are state-based, some are US-based, and some are global. Before I came to America, I had a view that Americans were ignorant about what was going on in the rest of the world based on what I saw on cable news networks. In reality, advanced-level high-school students in our school district study more about what is going on in the rest of the world than they would in, say, the UK.

School years here famously run from K to 12. The US grade numbers are one year fewer than those in the UK. The UK's Year 13, when you take A-levels, is Year 12 in the US. Year 1 in the UK is called Kindergarten here. As in the UK, most children start school one year earlier in preschool. Civics education in the US begins at Kindergarten, and children are taught the importance of self-control and being good citizens.

The main principle of education here is choice. In most large school districts, while you are zoned for a particular school, you can apply for another school if that better suits your needs. Unlike the UK, the catchment area does not change every year, depending on demand. If you live in a particular zone, you have the right to attend the school in that zone. If the zoned area has more children that year, it's the school that has to flex. Some high school students elect to take some or all of their college-level courses at nearby universities rather than their own high school. Other students choose to receive their education online but are still notionally attached to the school. When Daughter #1 was seriously ill a few years ago, she could complete a smaller number of virtual courses instead of attending school. When she needed to complete the final few classes to graduate from high school, she did these courses for one semester at a nearby university.

Students are over-tested. Most days, my children would have some sort of quiz or test that ultimately contributed to their overall grade point average. This creates a fairly stressful environment. Every evening you could tell how each daughter had performed in that day's tests by their mood when they opened the door.

The iconic yellow school bus is a feature for most students. All students are entitled to this free service, which fulfills two of the principles laid down by the first Board of Education. The bus picks them up every morning from their homes and returns them, usually safely, in the evening. Schedules are staggered to achieve this. Elementary children are collected first from just before 7 a.m. High schoolers just before 8 a.m., and students from junior high school, also called middle school, are collected just before 9 a.m. The bus drivers are mostly older. According to both daughters, the bus drivers are really nice, but they hit many curbs. States have strict laws on driving near school buses. If a school bus is stopped to pick up or let out school children, other drivers cannot pass.

Daughter #1 has a vivid memory of her first day on the US school bus. It was quite shocking for my Gap Kids-wearing twelve-year-old with her unshaven legs to see a boy in her grade sporting a full bushy beard. Both daughters describe the school bus experience as hell. A strict hierarchical system is in place, with the more popular and older children sitting towards the rear. It isn't written down, so you have to learn the hard way by sitting in the wrong seat. When students receive their driving licenses, they prefer to drive to school themselves. This means that most school car parks are enormous. It also concentrates many bad, inexperienced drivers in one place.

School uniforms are rare and mostly a feature of either private schools or schools in gang areas. In most schools, you can more or less wear what you want subject to decency standards. In practice, at least in our school district, most boys wear shorts and a t-shirt. Girls are a little more complicated and run closer to the dress code rules. Daughter #2 always ran close to the prohibitions on tops with spaghetti straps or shorts that didn't entirely fall below the length of her fingertips. Every once in a while, a boy would perform poorly in a school test and claim to his parents that poor performance was due to being distracted by a scantily clad girl in his classroom. The school would immediately police the uniform rules more assiduously.

In our school district, discipline is strict, reflecting the preferred parenting style of its community. At the junior-high level, students take only the twenty-two minutes state minimum time for the lunch break. Daughter #2 raged that, even at high school, she had to get a pass to go to the bathroom. Daughter #2 had more run-ins with school administration than Daughter #1, including school suspension for minor infringements of policy, for example, the phone ringing in class.

Like the UK, the vast majority of US students, 88 percent, are educated in state schools, which they call public schools here in the USA. Around two million US students, about 3.4 percent of the student population, are homeschooled. Home education was the norm in the USA's early days, but public school dominated from the time they were set up in each state. The popularity of homeschooling has increased since the 1960s and received a further boost when the internet made it easier for parents to access materials. The Supreme Court ruled in 1972 that Americans had a right to choose the appropriate education for their child. State regulation on homeschooling varies significantly by state, with some having almost no regulation and others insisting on curriculum approval and assessment. Academic studies have shown that the extent of homeschool regulation has no effect on standardized test scores.

The reasons why parents choose to home educate vary. The primary motivation for many is that you can include religious elements, which are banned at public schools. Other parents may have concerns about their local public school, either because of perceived low academic standards or because their child is being bullied.

Homeschooling doesn't necessarily mean that you are at home all of the time. Homeschooled children often congregate with each other in groups for a couple of days in the week. Harder-to-teach subjects like science or languages are often taught in these groups by an expert. These homeschooled groups can also provide children with non-academic activities. Homeschooled sports teams compete with other children; homeschool proms are organized; and local parades always feature a homeschool band, which is nowhere near as rehearsed as the local high-school band.

Homeschooling isn't always a permanent feature, and some parents home educate only for a period. We have met many parents who home educate during the impressionable ages until high school. They then proceed to join high school at fifteen when the subjects become more specialized.

In most states, parents self-certify grade books for their own children. You might think that all homeschooled children would receive straight As, which I understand is the Covid "Trust the Teacher" British standard. However, my children would likely have received lower grades had I been doing the marking.

There have been many academic studies that compare results on standardized tests. Homeschooled children score much higher on English and Reading, but comparably for Math. These results may solely be due to higher parental involvement. However, it's probably not surprising that homeschooled children are more disciplined and perform much better at college, with appreciably higher graduation rates and grade point averages.

What will probably not shock you is that the US Teaching Union opposes homeschooling. Their view seems to be that you should leave education to the professionals. When Lorna was a teacher in the UK, she had a similar attitude. However, exposure to many homeschooled children here has changed that view. We had US neighbors who homeschooled their children until college. Their curriculum was comprehensive and included many outdoor activities. Their children were well educated, well rounded, polite, and all successful at university.

The main reason against homeschooling has been widely debunked by academics. People believe that homeschooled children are less socialized. However, multiple studies have shown this not to be accurate; indeed, home-educated children have much higher socialization scores. Adults who were home educated are also much more likely to be involved in their community and civic life, much more likely to vote, and more likely to find life exciting. They are also more likely to be politically tolerant.

At two million years old, the Cascades Mountains are relatively young and have preserved their jagged nature as the mountain tops have not yet been worn down by fierce weather. The mountains, and accompanying valleys inside the park, harbor over ten times the number of glaciers of Glacier National Park, although these have lost half of their mass in the past hundred years. We enjoyed the tranquility of our three days in the park and vowed that we would return, probably to one of the lakeside cottages.

We loved the people we met in this park. In many ways, they were unlike the American stereotype. As you know, it's dangerous to generalize but long-winded if you discuss every one of the 331 million Americans one by one. Therefore, I asked my thirty recent immigrants to identify American stereotypes and ask whether they had any validity. They were surprisingly consistent in their responses. Let's start with the more positive stereotypes, but note that they are generally given with an air of downside.

First, Americans are obsessed with work. As noted in Chapter 7, the data shows this to be true. My sample also believed this to be true. The first question from almost everyone you meet is, "What do you do for a living?"

Second, Americans are confident and optimistic. This is self-evidently true. Which other nationality would hail "How are you?" or "What's up?" to everyone they met and walk on without waiting for a reply? An interesting question is where this confidence comes from. Is it an underlying belief many Americans have that somehow they are divinely favored and live in the greatest country in the world? Does it emanate from their education system that emphasizes verbal presentation? Or maybe it's a widespread bias where a whole nation consistently overestimates their ability? On this last point, two Cornell psychologists, Dunning and Kruger, showed that all Americans overestimated their abilities to some extent, but less competent people did so more. These less capable people tended to significantly overestimate their own skill levels, could not recognize skill and expertise in others, and failed to acknowledge their own mistakes and lack of skill.

Does American's confidence come from their history of invariably being on the winning side and (always/mostly/sometimes – delete according to your prejudices) fighting for the just cause? Does it come from their upbringing, where behaviors are always positively reinforced? As a bit of an aside, I was having one of my increasingly common off-days playing tennis with a mother from my subdivision this morning. Every time I hit the ball into the net, she would say, "Good Try," even though it was apparent to everyone that my endeavor was entirely hapless. Her children would have been exposed to maybe a hundred pieces of positive feedback from her every day. That's two-thirds of a million pieces of positive reinforcement by the time they have left school, just from her. Who wouldn't be confident with that feedback, even if you kept hitting the ball into the net? Digressing again, the average British child hyperbolically receives about ten pieces of positive feedback over their whole childhood. The research from Behavioral Scientists, Heaply and Losada, shows that the ideal ratio of positive to negative feedback is 6:1. Divorce academic John Gottman analyzed comments made by partners to each other. He found a similar proportion of positive to negative feedback (5:1) in successful relationships but found that couples whose marriage would later end in divorce had a ratio of less than 1:1.

While some would interpret this confidence and optimism as arrogance and superiority, it would seem that a nation is probably better to err on the side of overconfidence rather than the antonyms of confidence, such as insecurity, diffidence, fragility, and self-doubt.

Let's now move onto the more negative stereotypes of Americans. Third, Americans are fat. This one's definitely true, at least for the two-thirds of Americans who are overweight or obese. However, there are large communities of (rich) thin people for whom this isn't the case. Also, have you seen the rising obesity levels in Europe?

It also reminds me of a joke.

How many Americans does it take to fill the Grand Canyon? Four.

Fourth, Americans are loud and rude. Opinions differ on this from my sample group. On loudness, I'm not sure this is especially true, except at sporting events where Americans have a tendency to shout out inanities. Personally, I am still too self-conscious to do that. Elsewhere, Americans are louder on average than, say, the Japanese, but are they louder than a group of Italians? As for rudeness, I find Americans unfailingly polite, and my group of immigrants agrees. If you sneeze, for example, everyone around you will say, "Bless you." Incidentally, if a woman from the South says "Bless Your Heart," this may sound nice, but it is truly the opposite.

Fifth, Americans are racist. Opinions on this differ, depending on your country of origin. Certainly, the USA has a problematic history which it hasn't fully addressed. It also grants freedom of speech to its citizens, allowing people with unfortunate opinions to speak their minds. However, since the 1980s, a pretty consistent 86 percent of people approve of interracial marriage. This is more or less the same percentage as most European countries, and much higher than in most countries in Asia.

Sixth, Americans are gun loving. Our panel of immigrants agree with this stereotype; the gun is much more important to American culture than any other culture in the world.

Seventh, Americans are as materialistic as a Kardashian in the Oscar's gift-bag line. I will cover this topic in chapter 20. Some of the data may surprise you.

Eighth, Americans are not environmentally friendly. We will explore this subject further in the next chapter. Like most things, it is partly true and partly untrue.

Ninth, American's don't travel abroad; only 10 percent have a passport. All of our panel certainly had met people with very low or no knowledge of life outside the United States. The actual data part of this stereotype is a myth, however. It's actually 46 percent of American adults who have a passport. While this is lower than the average European country, the USA is a pretty big place. How many British people would travel so much if they could get snow, beaches, mountains, lakes, and guaranteed sunshine in the UK?

Tenth, Americans are as stupid as a lobotomized lemming. Nobody felt that this was particularly true. Obviously, there are many stupid, uneducated people in America. Some stupid people no doubt exist in the UK and elsewhere too. The data doesn't support the view that Americans are dumb comparatively. US figures are similar to other developed countries: 84 percent graduate from high school (equivalent to A level or Baccalaureate), 33 percent achieve a Bachelor's degree, and 80 percent of Americans read for pleasure.

By most metrics, the US tertiary education system is particularly strong. It has 34 of the top Global 50 universities and between 16 and 20 of the top 25, depending on the algorithm used. America educates well over a million international students every year at its universities, the most of any country. Finally, US citizens have been awarded more Nobel Prizes than any country, which is unlikely to have happened if all Americans were stupid.

Eleventh, Americans don't get irony. Contrary to common perception, Americans do understand irony but don't expect it in every sentence. There is sometimes, therefore, something of a disconnect with some British people who might overuse it. If, as a British person, you are going to use irony with an American, you should probably flag up that you are using it.

Twelfth, Americans have no culture. This is patently absurd. Not least, because it's often said by the very person who also goes on to accuse America of ruining other cultures in the world with American culture. You cannot have it both ways.

However, it does spawn a good joke.

What's the difference between the USA and yogurt? If you leave yogurt alone for two hundred years, it develops a culture.

A few qualities are left off the typical list of American stereotypes. Prison population notwithstanding, Americans are generally law-abiding. The most common expectation that Americans have for themselves and others is that they should respect the rule of law. Immigrants from less compliant countries often quote this as the most attractive feature of America. You know what to expect, so you can plan accordingly. Most immigrants come to America for better opportunities, sometimes for themselves but more often for their children. They understand that things will be different, and in most cases, they want things to be different from the less law-abiding societies from which they came.

Another is energy. Americans have a remarkable ability to regenerate themselves and their communities. Any visit to the diminishing number of bookshops will show that an enormous amount of space is given to self-help books. Lifestyle gurus across the nation show how you can improve your life. Cities improve themselves too. Countless US cities have declined, only to regenerate themselves. For example, New York was once a den of crime, but it's now a pretty safe city.

Finally, Americans are optimistic people who are invariably positive about all manner of things. I personally find this sometimes annoying, which only goes to show that I have not yet acclimatized sufficiently. You can join a group work call and hear everyone spouting positivity about every aspect of a topic when you know substantial downsides exist. The culture in America is to be mostly positive.

My perception is that Britain's press coverage of all things American is predominantly negative and often focuses exclusively on these American stereotypes' negative aspects. This isn't perhaps surprising as the British press is negative about most things. A recent study with six international PR agencies found that half of all British news stories had a negative angle, with a further 36% neutral.

I genuinely don't know if Europeans dislike Americans or whether dislike is confined mainly to people of a particular political persuasion who oppose capitalism. If there is a dislike of Americans, I will posit that this dislike is a combination of several factors.

Europeans value knowledge highly and see multiple examples of American ignorance. To be fair, these examples are not hard to find. A French friend meeting her Carolina-based trailer park in-laws for the first time was told that Paris must be an extremely long drive away. She told me that she felt awful to point out to such genuinely lovely people that an ocean was unfortunately in the way. Another person was told in a business meeting that this would work well in Spanish-speaking areas of Europe. When he clarified that they meant Spain, he was told yes, the Spanish-speaking regions of Europe. Another immigrant was once asked who Shakespeare was.

Examples such as this can be used to construct a case that all Americans are ignorant, and therefore all Americans must be stupid.

I have experienced a lot of misunderstanding of America. For example, many people don't take time to understand differences and therefore assume that the US political system is similar to the one in their own country. They are consequently flabbergasted that the US president doesn't just sort it out so that the US system is identical to their own country's attitude and policy on the matter under discussion. Some Europeans may be jealous or threatened by America's success, confidence, or can-do attitude. When you are less confident yourself, self-confidence in others can seem overbearing. Finally, a group of people is angry at the US's military gung-ho attitude, vexed by Murica's extreme patriotism, or disdainful at Americans' perceived lack of interest in "high" culture. The anger can translate into hatred of Americans. In my experience, these standards tend to be somewhat unevenly applied, however. Criticism of citizens from other countries with similar features might be described as racism. Somehow, it isn't when applied to Americans.

Chapter 16 – No Sunbathing on the Pacific

Our return boat trip from Stehekin did not reunite us with our rental car and the Washington State road system until 3 p.m. We then had a six-hour drive to the Pacific Coast, the first two of which regularly crisscrossed the mighty Columbia River following Lewis and Clark's route, and the last two of which were on narrow, tree-lined roads through various Native American Territories. We skirted south of Seattle. For some reason, many people think that Seattle sits on the Pacific Ocean. However, it is situated on the vast natural harbor of Puget Sound. Beyond Seattle, a myriad of islands and then the sizeable Olympic National Park peninsular awaits.

We arrived at the Pacific Ocean just as the sun had disappeared for another day over the horizon. We took the obligatory photo at the end of our sea-to-not-so-shining-sea drive across America. We were exhausted from the drive but still managed to celebrate our achievement by making a wood fire on the misty, damp beach. In normal times, we would have joined one of the half dozen or so other groups that had set up campfires. However, in these Covid times, everyone had their own campfire. S'mores – a contraction of "some more," a sandwich of two crackers with marshmallow and literally sickly Hershey's chocolate filling – were consumed, but not with any great joy as was usual with us when eating N'mores.

We sojourned in a wood cabin cottage on a bluff that overlooked the Pacific Ocean in the tiny Kalaloch community. This cottage had a perfect position, although the inside was undoubtedly designed and decorated by a man, and, one at that, who had likely never even met a woman. It had a kitchen and a wood-burning stove. It also had wall sockets out of reach of the average-sized woman on the sloping roof, no room to sit on the toilet for the non-yoga master, and décor that Freddie Mercury would have balked at in the 1970s.

Kalaloch is the Quinault Indian word for good place to land by canoe. Native American tribes here ceded their lands to the US Federal Government in 1855 and 1856, and some of these lands were immediately converted back into Native American reservations. Eight separate tribes now had their reservations along this stretch of coast.

The beaches were not the sunbathing variety. For one thing, although it was almost July, it was not warm. The rough sea pounded the gray-white sands below a seemingly permanent drizzly mist. We were used to this from our previous trips to the Pacific Coast. If you travel to anywhere north of, say, mid-California, you should not expect beach weather. For another thing, these beaches were also littered with hundreds of large, dead trees. These two-hundred-and-fifty-foot trees had uprooted themselves from Olympic Park's rainforests, and mighty rivers had carried them downstream into the Ocean. The Ocean had then spewed these trees back onto the mainland beaches.

The other feature of the beach we were on was a four-hundred-pound, seven-foot-long, deceased sea-lion. I had mistaken it for a tree trunk in my early morning run, but closer inspection later in the day revealed the flippers of a decomposing animal, the deep cuts of a propeller, and an unbearable stench.

The Kalaloch beaches were unimaginatively named Beach 1, Beach 2, Beach 3, Beach 4, and Ruby Beach. The next day we visited them all. There were few people on these magnificent, deep beaches and, on two of the beaches, we were its only visitors. Further up the coast, other reservations had closed. We, therefore, weren't able to visit the Quileute Indian Reservation beaches of the ever so slightly more imaginatively titled First Beach, Second Beach, and Third Beach.

Olympic Park was visited by Theodore Roosevelt in 1909, and he designated it as a national monument. It was left to his fifth cousin, President Franklin D Roosevelt, to name it as a national park in 1938. Its vast diversity of mountains, beaches, and rainforests attract more than three million visitors every year, the ninth-most-visited national park. In the space of a few miles, it features snowy peaks, dry oak, savanna, rainforest, and beach.

We saw a sign to Big Cedar Tree, which delivered what it promised. It was surrounded by a wide choice of other seemingly equally tall cedar trees, which we felt needed better agents.

We explored the nearby Hoh Rainforest. The Pacific North West is the only place in North America with temperate rainforests. These rainforests are the wettest areas in the continental USA and receive between twelve and fourteen feet of rain every year. This rain and persistent mist provide ideal conditions for these old and oversized trees. In Washington, these spruces, firs, and hemlocks are around 250 feet tall and 50 feet in circumference. As you travel further south, the trees become the taller-still Giant Redwoods.

The planet's tallest tree, a 379-foot-tall redwood, is called Hyperion. The tree's height was measured by a brave climber who ascended to the top of the tree and dropped an extremely long tape measure to the ground. Hyperion is situated in an undisclosed location to protect the tree from damage. For any arboreal sleuths out there, this sequoia is in Redwood State Park in California. However, it may be difficult from ground level to differentiate between Hyperion and the world's second and third tallest trees, Helios and Icarus, which are about three feet shorter. All three 600-year-old trees are still growing, though researchers have identified woodpecker damage at the top that may be inhibiting future growth.

California also boasts the world's heaviest tree, General Sherman, which is both 2,000 years old and 2,000 tons in weight. The Earth's oldest tree is a bristlecone pine, Methuselah, also located in California. It is 4,770 years old and predates both the Giza pyramids and Stonehenge.

These giant trees need a lot of water. The average, mature sequoia needs 500 gallons per day, the equivalent of 3,200 Starbucks Venti coffees per day per tree. When you have a whole forest of giant trees, this means that a lot of rainfall is needed as well as perpetual mist.

We took two curated self-tours of the different types of rainforest in the Hoh Indian Reservation and saw how life evolved here. Every surface had moss and lichen draped from each tree limb. Trees would eventually fall down; some would travel downriver to the coast, while others would lie on the forest floor with their decomposing trunks becoming nurseries that sprouted new large trees. We also saw Roosevelt Elk, not named after FDR but rather his older, distant cousin. We stopped to admire the mighty rivers' striking views that carried those dead trees to the coast. Bald Eagles hovered above the water for their next meal.

Time for a joke, I think.

Why didn't the dendrochronologist get married? Because he only dated trees.

There is a general view in the world that the USA is not environmentally friendly. I think it's easy to see how this view might be reached. After China, the USA is the largest emitter of carbon. It is a poor recycler, and the current executive has taken an extremely antagonistic view towards international environmental treaties and existing environmental regulations.

While not wanting to minimize the catastrophic negative message of the US Federal Government's policies, I think there is also another more positive way of looking at America's environmental record and intentions. You are probably getting fed up with me reminding you that America is not governed solely by its Federal Government. The legislature and judiciary's views were designed to be equally important, and, of course, individual states are the key decision-makers in most areas. About half of all US states and almost five-hundred US cities are committed to the Paris Climate Accord targets or better. Most large US companies say they are committed to this goal too. Regardless of the current administration's position, reducing emissions across the USA continues with or without federal support. The electorate says that it is supportive of aggressive actions on climate change. The majority of Republican voters are concerned about climate change, and three-quarters of their voters say they want to see more clean energy.

America has a strong record on clean air. It has almost the lowest percentage of fine particulate matter in its urban areas, only bettered by some Scandinavian countries. If California could improve some of its cities, it would probably be the best. As we have seen before, America protects just over a third of its contiguous land.

In many parts of the Western United States, forest fires' incidence and ferocity have worsened for many years. Power outages in places like California are now so frequent that the demand for generators is exceptionally high. One recent immigrant who had lived formerly in Indonesia told me that he had not expected to move to a country where the electricity infrastructure was less reliable.

Individual responsibility does need to improve. When we came here, we were astonished at how rare household recycling was. In our neighborhood, you have to pay extra for recycling, and at least half of households don't do it at all. This means that just over one-third of municipal waste is recycled, about half that of the best recycling country, Germany. Almost nine-in-ten US houses and every store is heated or air-conditioned, often to unsustainable temperatures.

We passed a large penitentiary near the park. As you know, America locks up a higher percentage of its population than any other country. At any one time, 698 people out of every 100,000 are incarcerated. That's 2.3 million people in some sort of jail. To give you an idea of scale, although America has only 4 percent of the world's population, it shelters just over 20 percent of the world's incarcerated people.

The justice system actually controls almost seven million people, about 2 percent of the entire US population. In addition to the 2.3 million people in jail or prison, a further 3.6 million are sentenced to probation, and 0.8 million are on early-release parole.

Of those in prison at any one time, state prisons hold the majority of prisoners, almost 1.3 million people who have been convicted of violent, property, drug, or public order offenses. A further 0.75 million people are in jails, and three-quarters of these have not yet been convicted of any crime. Of course, many are refused bail for public safety reasons or because of previous probation or parole conditions. Others, however, just cannot afford the typical bail of $10,000 to secure their release. I knew a Native American couple who were incarcerated for a charge that was later dropped. They spent four months in jail because they couldn't afford the bail. They lost their home, their children, and their jobs. A few states have decided to abolish bail or drastically reduce the level of bond payments, mainly as a tactic to reduce the high costs of incarceration.

Misdemeanors – minor offenses excluding speeding – clog the courts and, on any one day, account for about one in four of those in jail. A further one in four people in state prisons is there due to supervision violations of probation or parole. Unfortunately, it isn't true that non-violent drug offenders' release would solve the US's high incarceration level. About four-fifths of those in jail are incarcerated for non-drug offenses.

With the penitentiary in our rearview mirror, we were delighted to have our freedom, however, as we anticipated our drive down the Pacific Coast to California.

Chapter 17 – Misty Oregon Coast

We now had no defined agenda and no reservations and felt much happier without a schedule. It reminded us of our travels in our 20s. We would fly to somewhere in Africa, Asia, or South America with no plans or reservations of any kind. Often we would buy the guidebook at the airport and read about what was possible on the plane journey. We would make up our itinerary on the fly in our destination country. A combination of having children and an expansion in tourism had changed our habits, and we now planned our travel. Nevertheless, we loved the feeling that our options were infinite.

We spent the day driving along the beautiful but mostly misty Washington and Oregon coastlines. It was hard to believe that the rural idyll of the Washington we were seeing was also the land of Amazon, Costco, Microsoft, and Starbucks. I drove the first three hours on Route 101 along the Washington coast and rural inlands. This 1,550-mile road stretches from Los Angeles to Olympia, with the California section a popular road trip for bikers and other road trippers.

We hit the Columbia River again, at the point where some two hundred years hitherto Lewis and Clark had navigated down to the Pacific Ocean to complete their four-thousand-mile journey. The river marked the border between Washington and Oregon State and would have been a scary prospect in the early nineteenth century. A four-mile bridge built in 1966, with one lane of traffic each way, now spanned the mighty river. The northern part of the bridge lies low above the presumably shallower water, but then a scary ramp rises swiftly to around two-hundred feet towards the southern end to allow large ships to pass through without delay.

It was here where the Lewis and Clark party had voted on their winter camp location. This vote was notable as the first known time in American history that a woman and a slave were allowed to vote. They chose to set up winter camp on the Oregon side. Lewis had spent the winter writing his journal, recording what they had discovered, while Clark produced 140 maps of their journey.

We stopped further down the coast at a place called Seaside. Its claim to fame was that, on the beach here, some of Lewis and Clark's men had built a salt-making cairn, a pile of stones to you and me. As its name might imply, Seaside is a tourist-centric beach destination similar to any number of working-class beaches in the UK. There was a promenade, some hotels on the front, and tens of restaurants offering fish and chips, though almost all here in the USA with the inferior American version of French Fries. Indoor entertainment options distracted visitors on the plentiful occasions when the weather was terrible. Given Covid concerns, they were all closed or unused, including the only locally famous carousel. The town's many tattoo parlors were, however, open for business.

Seaside's average high is 65°F in the summer and 55°F in the winter. The day we visited was well below average for January, even though it was almost July. We ate lunch in a mild drizzle on a bench that overlooked the ocean and admired the bravery of the many people on the beach. A man wrapped in multiple layers of clothing had no business for his deckchairs. Ice cream-thieving seagulls were out in force, but alas, without any targets.

Mask-wearing in public areas was required all down the West Coast. With no apparent enforcement bodies, mask-wearing was close to 100 percent through a mixture of education, fear, and peer pressure. We compared the Seaside billboard picture with reality. It bore little resemblance. Nobody in the poster was wearing a mask, and neither sun nor swimsuit was on view in real life. Seaside used to have a Pacific Pier in the early part of the twentieth century. Unfortunately, storms regularly damaged it until after only a decade of use, they gave up repairing it.

The states along the Pacific Coast have pioneered the legalization of marijuana for both medicinal and recreational purposes. Marijuana stores abounded all down the coastal states. Americans' views on the legalization of marijuana have changed since the permissive sixties. In 1969, only one in ten favored legalization for recreational purposes. It is now two-thirds.

We continued down the coast, making little progress as the road roller-coasted from shore to high cliff and back again. Lorna drove the remaining three hours, and, tiring of these long journeys, we decided to stop at Nye Beach in the Oregon town of Newport. In clear weather, this would probably have been a spectacular drive. However, on the day we drove, there was almost continuous depressing drizzle, with every view shrouded in heavy gray mist or light fog. Meanwhile, the wrathful waves pounded the endless beaches.

We booked into a posh hotel with spectacular ocean views. Restaurants offered only takeout here. After too many veggie burgers and cheese sandwiches, I selected Thai in a white polystyrene container and a pathetic plastic fork. Lorna bought her Fisherman's Stew from a high-end establishment delivered in elegant boxes and almost proper silverware. We watched the sea from our balcony until it got too cold. Lorna ordered the fireplace's pilot light in our room to be extinguished, preferring no chance of carbon monoxide death to warmth.

Newport's motto is The Friendliest, but we doubted this sobriquet when we were awakened by some of the town's ten-thousand residents letting off fireworks on the beach, which we will come back to later in the chapter.

Throughout Oregon, each corner displayed political signs. The West Coast is, of course, now very much dominated by liberal, Democratic politics. When asked what one thing they would change about the USA, almost every recent immigrant that I spoke to said that they did not understand why American politics was so polarized. If they could change just one thing, it would be to reduce the polarization in US politics. Daughter #1 has noticed that many of her close friends don't like it when she rehearses the other side of an argument. She believes that most other young people are not interested in understanding why people have different opinions.

US politics has become extremely polarized, and substantial negative partisanship is commonplace. Liberals may have different political views within the Democrat Party, but they are united in hatred for Republicans. Similarly, conservatives may decry the madness of other Republicans, but they detest Democrats. Gallup, the polling organization, measures that around 40 percent of people consistently identify themselves as conservatives. People who identify as liberals represent a much smaller but growing group, approximately 25 percent. Moderates have been squeezed from the mid-40s to about 35 percent.

However, just under half of the American voters lean Democrat compared with around 40 percent who lean Republican. Moderates incidentally don't necessarily have centrist positions and are more typically ideologically inconsistent on their views taking viewpoints from both sides. Some seemingly liberal policies – including free public college tuition and medical insurance reform – are popular amongst all groups.

This might explain their respective policies. Republicans' unity historically comes from a commitment to small-government principle, which they know is popular with around 40 percent of the country. In the nineteenth century, this used to be a core Democrat principle. In contrast, Democrats represent a broad coalition of social groups who want policy changes favorable to their interests.

In primary elections to select the election candidate for each party, we have noticed in our state that Republican candidates are keen to portray themselves as the most conservative candidates on offer. In our state, these Republican primary elections are open to all but attract predominantly hardcore Republican voters. Republican candidates, therefore, tend to be at the more conservative end of the political spectrum. This, in turn, produces a more hardcore party. Republicans also compromise less, partly perhaps because compromise tends to expand the scope of government.

The rules on primary voting vary by state. Thirteen states plus Washington DC restrict voting in primaries only to those registered for that particular party; these are called closed primaries. A further fifteen states have semi-closed primaries, where both registered and unaffiliated voters can vote. Finally, the remaining states have various forms of open primary where a voter can choose to vote in either the Republican or Democrat primary, but not both. This can lead to something called raiding, where voters participate in the primary of their less preferred party in order to select a flawed candidate. This happened in a House of Representatives' primary in Vermont in the 1990s, where a local farmer, seeking to promote a documentary about his life, stood as a Republican candidate. He won the primary, partly through the help of votes from raiding Democrats, and then promptly said that he didn't want to live in Washington DC and endorsed his Democratic rival. In the UK, party candidates are chosen by a tiny number of party members. The Conservative Party tried a version of the primary for a couple of constituencies for the 2010 general election, but I think the wrong type of candidates were selected, and this experiment was discontinued.

There is actually a long list of parties for which you can register, not just Republican or Democrat. Someone I once worked with told me that he had registered for the Communist Party of America in the 1970s when he was eighteen to spite his father, who was nagging him to register for one party or another. His father believed that this assignation would be held against him by others for the remainder of his life.

Iowa, Kentucky, Nevada, North Dakota, and Wyoming have caucuses instead of primaries to select some of their candidates. These are much more complex; voters gather in large groups to hear supporters of each candidate. The group then has a debate and comes to a collective conclusion on who is the strongest candidate. It can take all evening.

In the USA, the whole electorate gets a say on every type of election. There are primaries for both parties to select candidates for President, Senator, and House of Representatives. Primaries occur for State officials of Governor, Lieutenant Governor, Secretary of State, Attorney General, Comptroller, Treasurer, State Senators, and State Legislators. There are then county primary elections to select a candidate for the majority of positions, and finally, there are city primary elections for Mayor and very many other positions. In all of these elections, at least in my state, if no candidate receives more than 50 percent of the vote, a runoff election between the strongest two candidates will be held to choose a winner.

From the above, I think you can probably visualize that the US has a bountiful number of elections, which is excellent news if you are a sign manufacturer or a student who likes time off from school. In case you didn't have enough elections, many states have referenda for particular political issues. In my voting lifetime in the UK, I have been able to vote in two referenda. In most years across the USA, there are more than one hundred and fifty. Most notably, in recent years, many have been on the subject of the legalization of marijuana. Referenda are definitely confusing if you don't pay close attention to the detail. Some propositions will be contentious and attract a lot of TV advertising. Vote Yes for Proposition 18 for a better future, followed by Vote No on Proposition 18 because it helps the wealthy. Neither advert will tell you what Proposition 18 actually proposes, though.

With all these elections, you would think that America would be skilled at organizing an election. However, you often see pictures of long lines at the polling stations in America. I think, also, everyone older than thirty recalls the hanging chad debacle of 2000, where the identity of the US president was determined by whether a relatively small number of individuals in Florida were deemed to have voted or not.

Despite what you see on TV, huge lines are not the norm, however. In the 2018 midterm elections, only 6 percent reported waits of longer than thirty minutes. Holding elections, of course, is a State responsibility often delegated to counties and cities. Much of the long lines are due to incompetence or equipment breakdown, but a minority appears to be a deliberate under-resourcing of polling stations in poorer districts. The primary cause of long-voting times is that you are almost always voting for multiple different types of elections on the same day. One trip to the polling station might see you have to vote for US president, US Senator, US Representative, State Governor, any number of State executive positions, County Commissioner, County representative, school board members, judges of many jurisdictions, and then any number of specific ballot measures. You could easily be asked to vote in twenty separate elections on the same Election Day. This takes time, especially if you haven't researched thoroughly in advance.

Around fifty million eligible Americans are not registered to vote through laziness, dissatisfaction with the political process, political Machiavellianism, or tactical reasons. I know some who refuse to register to vote because they believe, maybe correctly, that they will therefore not be chosen for jury service.

Democrats prefer compromise. Although a now small group of highly liberal – essentially socialist – Democrats exists, the party favors more centrist candidates for tight elections. The 77-year-old Joe Biden selection is a classic example of a compromise that offends the fewest people and potentially attracts the largest constituent audience. The hope amongst Democrats is that the election of any Democrat will advance social policies.

As we saw earlier with news networks, Democrats and Republicans struggle to understand each other. Democrats regularly compromise to reach an agreement on a policy and don't understand when Republicans show little interest in making a deal. Republicans assume that all Democrats are highly liberal and want to bring socialism to America.

In many states, citizens vote on specific potential laws too. There is a long tradition in both federal and state law of naming new laws after victims. Hundreds of these laws appear on the statute books. As most criminal activity is already outlawed, most of these laws typically attempt to close some perceived loophole. However, they more often overcorrect and end up creating more problems than they solve.

It is easy to see why parents want the new law. They want to prevent a reoccurrence of their tragedy. They also want to memorialize their son or daughter by leaving tangible evidence that their child once stood on the earth. Politicians respond to parents' demands by creating new laws to proudly announce that they have done something. To not accede to the parents' wishes would make them look callous.

Perhaps the most famous of these laws is Megan's Law, named after Megan Kanka, who was raped and murdered by a registered sex offender who had recently moved near the family. Her parents fought for a law that would warn communities about any sex offenders living in their neighborhood. President Bill Clinton required all states to establish sex offender registries that were accessible by the community. I can therefore see that thirty-one sex offenders live within five miles of my house. I can see the name and picture of each offender and their address. If I wanted to depress myself, I could read more details about each of these registered offenders. You may think this is a good law, but it was delivered so hurriedly that it included many downsides. For example, it doesn't distinguish between predatory sex offenders and those with lesser sex offenses, like public urination, consensual sex acts, and sexting between juveniles. It also punishes the sex offender's family.

In Georgia, Michael's Law prevents anyone under 21 from working as a bar bouncer after a twenty-year-old bouncer killed student Michael Gatto. The law was introduced even though the bouncer was sentenced to twenty years in prison under existing statutes.

Every new cellphone's default settings sound a loud, scary alarm every time a child is abducted. This is called an Amber alert. I have it turned off as it sounded too often for my mental health, and really what was I going to do about the child abduction? I thought this alert was not quite as severe as a red alert for several years, but it actually refers to Amber Hagerman, who was kidnapped and murdered in Texas in 1996. Dallas police and broadcasters replicated the early warning system used for severe weather events for abducted children. Seven years later, this system of amber alerts was used in every US state. Incidentally, there is a backronym, an acronym created after the fact, for Amber: America's Missing: Broadcast Emergency Response.

As a quick aside, Florida and some other states have Silver alerts. A brief description of their car and number plate flash on digital roadside signs to inform drivers that a senior with dementia is missing. We once saw one of these warnings on one of our many trips to Florida and then, minutes later, saw the station wagon in question hurtle towards us going the wrong way on an interstate. It's all a matter of perspective, however. The driver of the station wagon probably saw the same warnings and thought, "There's not one, there's fifty of them."

New Jersey rushed through Pamela's Law banning synthetic stimulants after speculation that a felon had murdered his girlfriend under these stimulants' influence. You still can't purchase these synthetic drugs in New Jersey, even though it was long proven that the killer had never taken these drugs. These name laws are pretty ubiquitous in the USA. There are, for example, three Jacob's Laws and three Laura's Laws.

And, of course, there is Cole's Law. This is finely shredded cabbage in a vinaigrette or mayonnaise sauce.

There is some evidence that these child victim memorial laws are finally becoming less popular. The main reason is that more states resist them due to their high implementation costs, especially incarceration costs. The Three Strikes law in California – introduced in 1994 after heavy parental lobbying – costs tens of millions of dollars every year but was softened in 2012 after a statewide referendum.

Many obvious loopholes have already been closed. Newer first-name laws typically impose higher costs on society for lesser gain. Sheena's Law would have allowed victims of crime to break their leases, but it was thwarted by landlords who believe that this would be abused by other tenants who wanted to get out of their lease. In New Jersey, Christina's Law would have required employers to review all applicants' social media accounts for inappropriate postings.

Anyway, all of this was a big digression away from fireworks. Although fireworks were actually, unintentionally, invented by the Chinese in 200BC, they weren't a big thing in the nineteenth century. Hence, they are clearly a State responsibility because nobody would have thought to include fireworks in their 1783 deliberations. Every state, therefore, has its own rules on fireworks. One state, Massachusetts, prohibits the sale of any fireworks, even sparklers. Some states ban their use in particular places or times, others limit the spec of what can be sold or used, and a few allow pretty much anything that doesn't contravene the now-defunct Anti-Ballistics Weapons Treaty.

Now you could research every state's firework laws, but the easier way of determining is just to take a major highway that crosses state lines. If you see lots of firework stores on your side of the border, this means the state you are in has more liberal firework rules. If not, it's vice versa.

Chapter 18 – A Big Crater

We'd had enough of the misty Oregon beaches, so we headed inland towards Crater Lake National Park. We were surprised to pay twice the price of gas that we would in Georgia and put this down to temporary Covid regulations that mandated full service to pump gasoline for you. However, we later read that it's always illegal to pump your own gas in Oregon in city areas. A few years ago, legislators had eased state laws to give some dispensation to pump your own gas in Oregon's rural areas during the hours of darkness. Essentially though, Oregon and New Jersey remain the last two US states that persevere with full-service gasoline. In Chapter 480 of Volume 12 of the Oregon Revised Statutes on Drugs and Alcohol, Fire Protection and Natural Resources – I read it, so you don't have to – the Oregon legislators give seventeen reasons why a trained person must fill your gas tank. The main reasons given were safe use of dangerous class 1 flammable liquids; equitable treatment of seniors and disabled people; economic justice for those on lower incomes, who otherwise might have to undertake this perilous activity themselves; and job retention. With these as the main reasons, you can probably imagine that the remaining thirteen arguments were quite light.

You may wonder why Americans use the word "gasoline" while we in the UK call it petrol. The origin of the name gasoline is, of course, British. What you probably wouldn't have guessed is that it doesn't come from the word gas. John Castellan, a coffee merchant from Manchester, imported crude oil from the USA into the UK in the 1860s. He called his product Caseline after himself. This was later corrupted to gasoline. In the UK, we call it petrol as a shortened form of refined petroleum.

My paramour, Lorna, gave the server a tip for his service. The elderly man – sorry, highly trained gasoline dispenser and safety officer – looked perplexed. This was a non-tippable service. After almost a decade of living in the USA and three decades of travel here, we are still uncertain about which services you should tip for and which not. I frequently ask American friends for advice but find that they are just as confused as me. There is an expectation that any personal service might receive a tip, even though most earn much higher salaries than minimum wage. Hairstylists, tattoo artists, animal groomers, massage therapists, hotel workers, and taxi drivers all regularly receive tips. There used to be no expectation that you should tip for fast food or pick up food. However, Covid has clouded this rule, as more restaurants have moved to curbside collection. I notice that people tip the restaurant the requisite 20 percent even when it is they themselves who have done the service. The general rule used to be 10 percent for OK service, 15 percent for good service, 18 percent for great service, and more than 20 percent for excellent service, but I always feel bad if I don't tip 20 percent. Some Americans – and I guess this holds for other nationalities – are not naturally able to calculate percentages in their head, so usually helpful guidelines on how much tip to give are included at the bottom of the bill. In most cases, this guidance starts at 20 percent.

The European in me would prefer to dispense with tipping altogether and pay servers a proper living wage. However, I was surprised to learn that tipping is originally a British concept. It was introduced shortly after the US Civil War and was a practice that wealthy new Americans had learned from their British friends. The Anti-Tipping Society of America tried to discourage the practice, and this was partly successful in the South, where presumably, many providing the service were African Americans. In the 1960s, Congress formally recognized the practice by setting a lower minimum wage for those jobs which typically received tips. Our frankly, low-skilled, not-exactly-service-oriented daughters both work as servers and regularly earn at least twice the minimum wage pay rate. It may not surprise you that they are strong advocates of tipping and believe that you should not eat out if you can't afford at least a 15 percent tip.

We passed through a town called Philomath, which means love of learning rather than pastry-wrapped arithmetic. This town was named after a church-based university located here until its demise in the Great Depression. It was a town whose wealth was founded on the timber industry, but it was gradually modernizing its industrial base.

The town was the subject of a 2006 documentary called *Clear Cut: The Story of Philomath, Oregon*. We downloaded the movie to watch later. This skillful documentary by a former Philomath High School graduate is ostensibly about the town's reaction to social change in the community's school system. The documentary highlights the cultural differences that divide conservatives and liberals in the USA. This town's recent history seems to be a microcosm of the broader divisions in American society.

The founder of the leading sawmill in town had formed a foundation to award free four-year university scholarships for Philomath High School graduates. Generations of local timber workers' children had benefited from this scholarship. As we mentioned earlier, college tuition is expensive in the USA, and this benefit had attracted new, more liberal residents to the town, often only for the last year of their children's studies.

Out-of-state school administrators were hired to modernize the school system in Philomath. They had been somewhat skilled in their culture change but had managed this change relatively poorly with the foundation's trustees. They had changed the football team's name (from the Warriors to the Cadets), encouraged gay rights groups at the school, and changed the curriculum to explore the negative impact of the logging industry on the environment. All of this, plus the bungling of a property transaction with the foundation by the Chicago-born superintendent, had annoyed the socially-conservative trustees. The foundation made an ultimatum to the school board that the administrators be replaced, or they would withdraw free-college education. Public hearings and the selection of people with pre-existing viewpoints worsened the divide. Ultimately, polarized views led to a pretty poor outcome for everyone concerned. Parents and students took a fairly-entitled perspective, and the school board supported the superintendent they had hired. The foundation changed its scholarship criteria so that it applied nationally, but only to children of timber-industry parents. The residents lost out on a great benefit, the foundation lost respect, and the school administrators left to join the Seattle Schools System.

The documentary makers took great care to give everyone the time to make their points in their own way, and all the participants had the opportunity to show their true motives. Ultimately, I suspect that the viewers' original sympathies will determine how they see the rights and wrongs of what happened in Philomath, Oregon. The reviews I have read suggest that many reviewers end up completely empathizing with one side while villainizing the other, just as this played out in Philomath and in Everytown, USA.

We stopped for lunch at a lake resort in the middle of Oregon. During our travels, we had come across many servers with limited experience. Tourism had been so low that they just hadn't had enough experience to know what they were doing, and service was slow even though there were rarely many customers. When I asked the waitress at this restaurant whether they had a menu, she accurately replied yes. After a few seconds, I then had to ask if we could see it. Similarly, when she brought the food out to us, we asked if they had silverware. The answer again was yes, but it was not brought to us until we had explicitly requested if we could have some.

We passed through many other small communities, which typically had a few dozen houses, no stores, but always a church. As you know, the USA is predominantly a Christian country. The latest data shows that 83 percent of Americans believe in God, and 71 percent describe themselves as Christian. They are active worshippers, too, with 69 percent having attended their church in the last month and 41 percent belonging to a prayer group. Religion is self-evidently much more important in the USA than in Europe, where, in most countries, fewer than one in five say that belief is essential to them.

The First Amendment to the US Constitution prevents the Government from having any authority on religion. This means that public institutions, like schools and the military, are not permitted to promote religion in any way. In the UK, where only one in ten say that religion is important to them, it's common for schools to come together for assembly and prayer. This can only happen in private schools in the USA. Despite this, the culture is one where religion is central to US daily life. In response to atheist Soviet Union, the USA did not change its constitution. Still, it did amend both the Pledge of Allegiance to include the words "under God" and change the national motto to "In God We Trust."

Every US president and vice president in history has described themselves as Christian. Of current Congress members, 88 percent say they are Christian, with the remainder reporting that they come from another religious group.

Freedom to practice, or not practice, religion is a cornerstone of the Bill of Rights. Most Americans still don't want the church involved in politics. Churches have an added incentive to stay out of politics because they cannot endorse a candidate or risk losing their tax-exempt status. However, a strong link definitely exists. Evangelical Christians, the largest denomination, tend to support the Republican Party. Some other denominations have historical ties with the Democratic Party. One close neighbor tells me that he votes Republican solely for the Republican stance on abortion. He isn't necessarily typical, though. Just over one-third of Republicans and just under one-third of Democrats disagree with their party's respective position on abortion.

US church attendance and daily prayer have both edged downwards for decades. Over the last decade, the number who attend a religious service at least every month has dropped by 7 percentage points. Just over one-quarter of US adults never participate in religious services, up from 11 percent in the 1970s. The number of Americans who now describe themselves as atheists or agnostics is also rising but is still small: 4 percent atheists and 5 percent agnostic. As an aside, Pew Research administered a religious knowledge survey and found that the atheists were the best performing group in the test and were at least as knowledgeable on Christianity-related questions as those who identified as Christian. Atheists are perceived negatively by Americans, who rank them alongside Muslims in the Pew Research feeling thermometer. Another poll reports that more than half of American adults would never vote for an atheist as president. This is very different from most of Europe, where we usually have little idea about our political leaders' religious views, nor would it affect how most people would vote.

A couple of factors seem to drive this gradual disengagement. First, some young adults are turned off organized religion because they associate it with conservative politics with which they passionately disagree. Second, married people have a higher degree of religious affiliation, and marriage is now happening later or not at all. More adults in today's America cohabit rather than marry. As a married man myself, my wife tells me that I should point out that these same polls show that married adults are much happier in their relationships and trust more than those just living with their partner.

America may provide most missionaries to the world – 127,000 at any one time since you ask – but it is also the country that receives most foreign missionaries, 32,400. The USA is the largest essentially Christian country, but adherence to Christianity is falling. Since 1990, there has been a 15 percentage point drop in the people who classify themselves as Christian. Therefore, overseas missionaries travel to the USA to attempt to prevent the USA from falling into secularism as Europe has done.

We didn't know what food would be available at the park, so we stopped to buy some milk, cereal, and drinks. This was a very low-density part of the world, and no towns of any type appeared on the map. We, therefore, stopped at a motel that had a grocery section in the reception area.

I have no idea who would select this particular motel to stay in. It was the type of motel where you would envisage yourself being murdered by the morning. Police would have likely said, "well, what did they expect?" Indeed, no living customers were staying on the day we visited. It was a fifties drive-in motel that hadn't changed much in seventy years, although the sign outside now boasted that it had Wi-Fi.

The store was peculiar. Most stores organize themselves by product line, a few organize by manufacturer, but this one seemed to manage its products by sell-by date. Not that any of the food was in date. This was a nightmare in stock keeping and organization. Everything was probably there, but it was like a junk shop. Produce was everywhere, including what used to be the aisles. There was no way to shop here except to ask the motel owner where to find something. She knew where everything was. It was as if Daughter #2 was running the shop. She knows where everything is, so she doesn't need to tidy up.

There was a microwave to heat things up, which looked a bit like the one my parents had proudly bought in the 1970s. The sign outside informed us that the motel was under new management, but the lady inside told me she had run it since 2013. A massive bank of VHS videotapes stood by the checkout desk. I asked if there was a big demand for these videos in an as innocent manner as I could muster. She told me that some guests liked to watch them in their rooms. Incidentally, you might want to know that Oregon is also the home to the last remaining Blockbuster store. Readers of a certain age will remember that Blockbuster was once dominant in providing video rentals for the family. At one point, more than nine thousand stores worldwide dominated high streets. They missed the trend towards sending DVDs by mail in the noughties and went into bankruptcy in 2010 before being purchased by a satellite TV provider. Stores have regularly closed since then until today, where only one store remains, in Bend, Oregon. They still rent out videos and DVDs, but most of their turnover is from Blockbuster merchandise.

We had followed the guidelines on only having one person in the store, but this was too interesting a site for Lorna to miss out on. I called her in and noticed that she had reversed her car to just outside the shop and that the engine was still running. She told me that she had taken a picture of the place and was ready to flee if I didn't come out again.

We got talking to the lady who ran the motel. Unlike most women we came across, she was unkempt and without a trace of makeup. She was also exceptionally friendly. She recognized our English accents from the many years she had spent living on the England/Wales borders. It was difficult to imagine how a globetrotter could end up here in the middle of Oregon. It could be you. We looked at the Trip Advisor reviews later when we returned to the land of cellular data connection. The reviews were mixed. Many said that they wouldn't touch the motel with a figurative barge pole, while others said it was excellent value and that the manager had a heart of gold. We wished we had stayed there.

We drove on to Crater Lake National Park, which was established as the sixth national park by our old friend, Theodore Roosevelt, in 1902. We got out of the car at the first sight of the lake inside the ancient volcano. I believe this must be the best view that I have ever seen. Against the bright snow of the volcano top, the lake inside the volcano was so deep and the water so clean that the color was an unbelievable pristine blue. It was easy both to see why this lake was named Deep Blue Lake originally and why three-quarters of a million people traveled to see this view every year.

The crater was formed from the inside of Mount Mazama when it erupted around eight thousand years ago. For those who were paying attention in Chapter 15, you will recall that Crater Lake is the USA's deepest lake. The lake is filled mainly from the forty-four feet of snow that hit Crater Lake every year. The lake has no rivers in and no outlets either, and the amount of evaporation is now exactly equal to the new precipitation. The lake has more than five trillion gallons of water, enough for 556 billion showers. The lake also has an island, Wizard Island, a vain attempt by the mountain to rebuild itself.

I had experienced considerable difficulties in booking this accommodation at Crater Lake. Lodges at national parks are extremely popular. They go on sale 365 days in advance but can be canceled for usually no cost up to the day before travel. They typically use no revenue management system to maximize income but are extremely expensive for the low-quality accommodation they provide. However, the alternative is usually either camping or a hotel a long way from the national park.

During the planning stage, our trip's exact dates changed according to the latest travel regulations in each state. This meant that I had to amend the dates for some of our accommodation. Crater Lake had a simple online booking system. You went on to their website to see any availability. Usually, there was none, but occasionally someone had just canceled. To modify or cancel a reservation was not so straightforward. There was no online facility that enabled it, and you needed to phone the reservation line. No matter when you called this number, you would always have a long wait. The shortest I experienced was 105 minutes, but it was often 300 minutes plus. The automated voice told you every minute or so that you could use their website to make reservations, which grew tiresome after minute 200 or so. The other thing this voice did was to apologize for the delay, explaining that due to the Covid outbreak, waiting times were likely to be longer than usual. I can imagine that Covid had caused significant disruption to, say, hospitals or the unemployment office. However, I had observed that this excuse was being used everywhere by all sorts of companies not obviously affected by the virus. I suspect that companies had seen an opportunity to reduce their customer service costs, especially in areas where they might have to return money.

We took several stunning hikes around the volcano's rim. The view of the lake just got better and better with each corner. We had a great night's sleep at the Crater Lake Lodge, another Swiss-style lodge, and woke up to a fresh lake view in the morning.

The next day, we traveled to Lassen Volcanic National Park in California, a range of large snowcapped volcanos set south of the Cascade Mountain Range. Apparently, this is one of the few places in the world where you can see all four types of volcanoes. We didn't have a lot of time, so we took a drive through the park, marveling at its lava fields and hiking around Manzanita Lake. An aggressive river otter had attacked and bitten a man swimming in the lake there recently, so most of the recreation around the lake was closed. A picture of a woman with otter injuries adorned many signs, which made me both see otters with new respect and allow Lorna to go first on the narrow paths around the lake.

Chapter 19 – A Napa Haircut

We had shared the driving fifty-fifty, but Lorna still concentrated hard when I was at the wheel, making sure that I could benefit from her advice. Just after I had observed something ahead, she would tell me that the car in front was braking, or that she had detected a vehicle on the slip road, or that there were traffic lights a thousand feet in the distance. As we came towards five thousand miles driven, she was therefore tired because in her mind, at least, she had driven the whole way. Consequently, I decided that we should go to Napa Valley for some relaxation for a couple of days.

At first, we drove along the North California backroads in awe at the number of fields of fruit and vegetables. We both grew up in farming communities, but the scale of this agriculture dumbfounded us.

Agriculture has changed dramatically in the USA over the last few centuries. Pre-independence, the focus was on self-sufficiency and household independence. Consequently, agriculture was mixed farming, mostly corn, grain, and some grazing. The economy was predominantly bartering. When someone wanted more space, they traveled a little further to the West, where more land was always available.

From 1789-1815, agriculture became much more export-oriented. The USA was reliant on foreign economies for much of their goods and services and had to provide something in return. A cash economy developed, and many stores started to open. Single cash crops were cultivated, at least on a three-year rotation basis. Farming became more intensive, often with the help of new technologies of the time.

Our familiar conflict, the War of 1812, made it inescapable that the USA could not rely on other countries for other goods and services. From 1815, the USA made a concerted attempt to become more self-sufficient. The Mid-West, and increasingly the West, developed more agricultural capacity to feed a growing country. Factory cities were set up in Boston, New York, Waltham, and Providence to produce the goods which previously Europe had provided. Agricultural products moved eastwards, and industrial products moved westwards.

As the US population grew into the hundreds of millions, farmers needed to produce more food. They did this through better technology and more agricultural workers.

Mega-farms – those with more than a thousand acres – now represent fewer than 10 percent of total farms but provide more than half the output. Two million smaller farms hang on, but this is five million fewer than in the 1930s. Mass Covid infections have demonstrated that meat production is concentrated in the hands of a tiny number of meat processing facilities. Consumer concern on food safety is also growing, with more choosing to shop at organic supermarkets and farmers' markets.

Technology continues to improve productivity in agriculture. Agricultural output tripled between 1948 and 2015; that's around a 5 percent improvement every year, and today's agricultural worker now provides enough food for almost a hundred people. Some of the most recent productivity improvements have been via GMO seeds and advanced pesticides. However, even greater improved productivity comes from new equipment. In 1970, one farmer could plant 40 acres of crop and harvest 4,000 bushels per day. By 2005, the same – slightly older – farmer could plant 420 acres and harvest 30,000 bushels. Being a farmer is a hard life. Historically, it had the lowest divorce rate of all professions, but the 1980s farm crisis saw this rate move to the national average of 40 percent. Maybe because of this, suicide rates of agricultural workers are amongst the highest of all professions and outnumber murder rates in the USA.

Today, the USA is a net exporter of food but does rely somewhat, about 30 percent, on fruit and vegetable imports, notably from Mexico. About 40 percent of US land is used for agriculture, roughly half for crops and half for pasture. In the nineteenth century, around half the population was employed in agriculture. This has now fallen to only 1.3 percent, with up to half of these illegal workers. Americans spend only 10 percent of their income on food, less than in any developed nation in the world.

Knowing I am vegetarian, you would probably expect me to point out that only seventy-seven million acres – the size of Indiana, Illinois, and half of Iowa – is needed to grow the food we need to live, while ten times as much land is used for feeding cows and other livestock. So, I won't disappoint you.

It is mainly cattle that take up all the pasture space. The USA has 95 million cows at any one time, one cow for each 3 Americans. By way of contrast, the UK only has one cow for every 7 British residents. Americans don't eat much lamb at all; I've never seen it on a menu here, and it's not sold in mainstream supermarkets. Consequently, America has only just over 5 million sheep, one for every 63 Americans compared with the UK, which has one sheep for every 3 British people. Although they take up much less space, Americans pig out on 120 million hogs every year compared with the British comparatively low consumption of only 10 million swine. If you are talking about animals that sadly take up very little space, each American eats a whopping 27 chickens each year compared with the average Brit, who only eats 15. According to the National Chicken Council – the meat association, not the ultra-dangerous freeway car dodging society – fewer than 5 percent of processing plants use any chlorine at all in chicken processing. It will be no surprise that turkeys are a rare treat for British people. 14 million are eaten, almost all of which are at Christmas. America, with its 5x population, eats 250 million turkeys. These are consumed throughout the year, with the special occasions of Thanksgiving (46 million), Christmas (22 million), and Easter (19 million) accounting for just more than one-third of all turkey consumption. Guests at Disney alone consume annually 1.6 million of those enormous, 720 calorie turkey drumsticks.

Most US agriculture occurs in the Corn Belt and Wheat Belt of America in those mid-western states between the Great Lakes and the Rocky Mountains. The Central Valley of California is known as the Salad Bowl of America, producing much of its fruit and vegetables.

Although California had been hit early by Covid, it had avoided the worst of Covid infections seen by other states. While Governor Cuomo in New York had received widespread praise for his handling of the Covid crisis, there were few plaudits for Governor Newsome in California, who had clamped down earlier and presided over a relatively low infection rate. Governor Newsome had recently allowed Napa's four hundred wineries to open under tight regulations. All tastings had to be booked in advance, be outdoors, and tasters be distanced from each other. As we had seen elsewhere on the West Coast, people here were cautious. In normal times, Napa is a pretty expensive place to stay. We chose a charming B&B in the heart of Napa town that usually costs $450 per night for the price of a cheap motel. The owners had shown a lot of ingenuity to minimize their risk. We did not see a single person during our stay at the B&B. Their breakfast and evening wine tasting had been canceled. However, the B&B had a pleasant garden, and we could have our breakfast or takeout there.

In addition to the sixteen appellations of Napa, there is also the adjacent wine district of Sonoma. These inland areas of Northern California are ideal terroirs for growing wine. The soil in the northern part of the valley is predominantly volcanic, while that of the southern area comes from the original San Pablo Bay. Although the coast is mostly cold and misty, a few miles inland, the weather is hot but still benefits from gentle breezes. The hilly terrain enables the growth of diverse grapes at different elevations. Finally, the variety of mesoclimates in the valley ensures that the wine quality can be high. Compared with the other famous wine-producing areas in the world, Napa is a fairly new winegrowing area. In 1976, Stag Winery surprised wine experts when they won a blind winetasting competition called The Judgment of Paris. They won both best red and best white. This famous win subsequently attracted winemakers from all around the world to set up vineyards in the region. In the past fifty years, this area had become a Wild West for winegrowing as traditional horse ranches were replaced by wineries.

A few ranches have hung on, but you could see that the writing is on the wall for them. Not that it is an easy process to set up a new appellation. The approval process itself takes about seven years, and then you had to grow the vines, which take a further five years. Once you have the wine, you finally have to build a reputation.

The geometric design of vineyards appealed to me like a Mondrian painting. They were perfectly straight lines that suddenly took another direction as they veered up or downhill. As we traveled through the region, we observed the winemakers at work. Their attention to detail was extraordinary, as they inspected each vine, each bunch, and each grape. Every winery had a marginally different climate, maybe 0.5°F temperature difference or slightly higher elevation. According to sommeliers, these factors made a big difference to the final product. Unlike other wine areas we had visited in the world, everything was shiny and brand new here. Napa had used technology to produce world-class wines, and this had worked.

In 1989, Orley Ashenfelter, a Princeton economist, found that he could predict the quality and price of Bordeaux wines via a mathematical formula.

$$Q = W + H + T - 12.145 \qquad (3)$$

Where Q = quality; W = winter rain, measured in millimeters; H = Harvest rain measured in millimeters; and T = Average summer heat, measured in centigrade

This calculation, he said, explained 80 percent of the variable in the price for each year.

Just as in Moneyball for baseball, a decade or so later, professional wine tasters were appalled. How could analysis of data be better than the expertise they had gathered over decades?

From the data he had collected, Ashenfelter predicted further that 1989 would be a stunning vintage and that, from the winter rain, 1990 looked promising too. Most wine experts at the time disagreed, but there is now almost unanimous agreement that these two years are two of the outstanding vintages of the last fifty years. The prices have demonstrated this too.

The wineries here are not unusually large. They are mostly independent wineries, but about one-quarter are owned and run by foreign companies. Diageo and Fosters both have high-end brands here, and Mumm and Beringer also have vineyards. Some wineries have also replicated the idealized French chateaux. Perfect in every way, except perhaps in authenticity.

The business models of Napa wineries are different from others around the world. They aim to sell most of their product to their own wine club members, ideally the spectacularly wealthy from Silicon Valley. Winetasting is a channel for this wine club as well as being big business too in its own right. In other countries of the world, winetasting is mostly a free loss-leader. It can cost big money in California to taste wine. In normal times, designated drivers or organized tours took people to about five wineries throughout the afternoon. This had been disallowed due to Covid restrictions. Wineries were only allowed to take reservations now. We poured over the hundred or so options. We were mainly used to European wineries, where you showed up, and they plied you with free wine until you were so mellow that you bought a case.

The new Covid regulations had increased costs. Those wineries with indoor tasting rooms had to create outdoor tasting areas. We were astonished to see that many tasting sessions cost more than $150 per person. I don't drink alcohol. This makes me an excellent designated driver for winetasting, but $300+, the cost of two people, for Lorna to taste a few wines is a bit pricey. However, we found a winery that had a reservation slot for only $20 per person, and that also allowed you to take a picnic. We went into Wholefoods to buy our picnic: the best French cheese, bread, olives, and some rocket, which they call arugula here.

Benessere Winery had an excellent outside tasting facility. Set in the vineyards, they had wicker sofas and plump cushions with awnings overhead that protected you from the powerful sun.

Over the four decades we have been together, I have invested heavily in Lorna's wine addiction, or as she calls it, wine appreciation. Every other Christmas, she has received winetasting lessons as presents. She loves these lessons, but I think it's safe to say that she isn't a natural. She approached each of the six wines with the same air of professionalism.

First, she looks at the wine. She picks up the glass by its stem and swirls the liquid around in a metronomic fashion. She gazes at the wine from every angle. First from above, then from each side. She places the wine against the whitest background she can find. She attempts to determine something about the grape from these visual tests. What's its age? Does it have legs? If it's a red wine, is it more purple (young) or is it more orange (old)? As a color-blind person, I have to say that they all look red to me. Apparently, Napa Cabernets have a rich ruby color. If it's a white wine, they will acquire a darker hue with age. Dark yellow or mustard is perfect but brown, and it has probably gone bad. Can she determine the grape variety from this visual inspection?

She then smells the wine. She places her small nose as far into the glass as she can. First, she takes several short sniffs of the wine. Then a longer whiff. She tests for flaws in the aroma. Maybe mildew or vinegar? Then she tries to pick out the dominant fruit aromas. If white, is it citrus, tree, or tropical? If red, is it red fruit or blue fruit? Then she endeavors to elicit secondary aromas, such as spice or flowers.

After about ten minutes of looking and sniffing, she then tastes the wine for the first time. She focuses on the immediate taste. Is it sweet or dry? Is it light, medium, or full-bodied? What are the primary fruit flavors? Are they red fruits, black fruits, or desiccated fruits? If a red fruit, is it raspberry, strawberry, currant, plum, pomegranate, or cherry? She then swirls the wine across her palate. Are there secondary flavors present? Vegetables, flowers, or spice? Are there signs of the terroir: chalk, clay, or slate? Does her mouth feel gritty from the tannin? Lorna likes a tannin, at least in a red wine. How complex is the wine? Is there just one taste, or are there multiple flavors that change with the wine's position on the palate or over time?

The thing is that – despite doing all the right things and all the lessons purchased – Lorna is genuinely terrible at winetasting. On the positive side, she can now differentiate between a red and a white. Rosés are more problematic. Otherwise, she is almost 100 percent wrong in my experience. On this occasion, I had commandeered the winetasting notes of the six wines being tasted. I tested her knowledge of each wine. What were the dominant, primary fruit flavors? Can she specify what these tastes were? What were the secondary floral and herbaceous flavors? Not a single match in six wines.

Unlike most pros, Lorna doesn't believe in spitting out the wine she is tasting. She likes it when her deductive reasoning becomes impaired, as it gives her an excuse. Today was a great day for her. She not only had to drink her glass, but she also had to drink mine too.

We had a wonderful three hours at the winery, eating our picnic outside by the vines under the deep blue sky, but protected from the roasting sun. Lorna loved her wine, and I liked quizzing her. We didn't buy any wine or join their wine club. It was challenging to think of a better $20 per head entertainment.

Lorna was drunker than a frat boy at a free bar and in no fit state to drive or – even better – give me the benefit of her driving guidance, so I drove through wine and horse country to Bodega Bay, the setting for the second half of Hitchcock's The Birds. The bay was unspoiled but windswept and somewhat rustic. A small number of people were there on vacation. We recognized key vistas from the film. We then sought out the school from the movie. Deceptively, this is inland from the bay in a village called Bodega. The school is now a private house but looks exactly the same as in the film. The playground has gone, but the fences and the wires on which the birds sit are still in place. The odd bird tottered on a wire, hoping for a part as an extra in the remake. We wondered how they filmed the escape to the coast scene, as it really is many miles from the ocean, and we could not locate the gas station.

I have this thing where I don't get my haircut in the same place that I live in. It started accidentally almost twenty-five years ago when I traveled nearly every week for a global company and had little time for leisure. The only time I seemed to have for a haircut was when I was traveling on business. One day, I realized that I hadn't had my haircut in the UK for over five years. I have tried to keep that run going since then. When we moved to the USA, I changed the rules a bit. I didn't need to get my haircut in a different country, but I did need it to be in another state.

Over the years, I have had some genuinely terrible haircuts. Often I don't share a language with the cutter or don't know the specialized word for, say, clippered. A few haircuts were famously bad. A man in Central Dubrovnik showed me a picture of a haircut that he was going to administer. It looked terrific, and I was looking forward to looking pretty smooth. The haircut bore absolutely no resemblance to the picture. Another time, in Istanbul, the lack of symmetry in the haircut reminded me of Gaugin's asymmetrical balance. Twenty-one years ago, I had my hair cut in a small town in North Carolina. The woman had never cut the hair of anyone out of state before, and she had never heard of my state of the UK. She was so nervous that she cut her finger with her scissors. I swear to you that this is true; I had her blood in my hair. Nevertheless, I was sufficiently American even then to give her a good tip.

On the positive side, I have met approximately 288 different hairdressers and barbers of varying backgrounds and nationalities over the years. I also know the words for "cut," "weeks," and "over the ear" in many foreign languages.

I wasn't sure when we would travel outside the state again, so I thought I had better have my hair cut. Regulations on haircutting had recently been relaxed in California. You had to make a booking, wait outside until your turn, and wear a mask during the whole procedure. I found a barber on Napa's outskirts, a refined town in a well-heeled area of Northern California. Although my barber was wearing a mask, it was evident that all of the other rules were already being flouted.

I seldom go to male-dominated places, but this place was a man's refuge. Men milled around the shop. It wasn't apparent that they were there for a haircut, but they liked other men's companionship. They talked about sport, though none was being played. They talked too about beer, but mostly they spoke about their recent sexual conquests, all of them in great detail. There was other bragging, too. One person bragged about how he had almost traveled overseas, but the $3,000 airfare had put him off.

My barber was OK. I had chosen him because he was rated 5/5 after 19 ratings on some hairdresser website. A lousy haircut makes a good story, but I do prefer to look vaguely normal. Like most other hairdressers, he was an immigrant who had a skill from his home country that he could use anywhere. It is said that barbers are more or less recession-proof. However, this virus had deprived him of his trade for almost three months.

Lorna likes to judge each haircut, and high marks are unusual. This haircut received a 9/10.

Chapter 20 – A Journey's End in Every Step

Lorna wanted to drive over the Golden Gate Bridge, so we took the route through Marin County. In San Francisco, the roads were eerily quiet, and almost nobody was on the street. An occasional masked runner wheezed up and down the challenging, hilly streets. We wanted to stop for breakfast, but nothing seemed to be open. The cable cars were running, but they were reduced in number and as empty as an American's wallet the day before payday. On a whim, Lorna decided to drive down Lombard Street.

Lombard Street is an unusual one-lane street that winds down a steep hill with great views over San Francisco and the Bay. The hill on which it sits has a 27-percent-natural grade, so a winding road had been constructed with multiple switchbacks. According to IMDb, twenty-six films and TV shows have featured this road.

It's usually a popular tourist destination with about two million visitors every year driving down the road. In normal times, it has long traffic lines, waiting up to ten hours to make the short journey. In 2019, the City of San Francisco agreed to install a reservation system and charge each car $10 for the brief drive, but the city hasn't implemented this yet. As we were almost the only tourists in San Francisco, we were able to stop our car on the road and take photos. We noticed for the first time that the street was an affluent one. Usually, residents have to put up with a steady stream of traffic down their road, but we were the only car that hour.

In the Bay, we could see Alcatraz, a fascinating place to visit in normal times, but it was closed along with everything else. The guided tour of the island and its prison is captivating. I recall that, contrary to public opinion, Alcatraz Prison had hot showers for its inmates. Wardens feared that cold showers would toughen up the not-so-good people of Alcatraz and enable them to complete the one-and-a-half-mile swim to the mainland.

Another San Francisco feature that seemed to be much less prominent were the homeless people. My previous visit to San Francisco had disturbed me due to the monstrous numbers of homeless people on the street. I had walked down a wide sidewalk that was carpeted with homeless people who had settled down for the night.

Like most other US cities, San Francisco had leased large numbers of hotel rooms to shelter the vulnerable during the pandemic.

Much of America's expansion and history are tied to gold discovery, in the same way that many modern-day countries' history and culture are tied to oil. We saw earlier in our trip how the Georgia Gold Rush had led to the Trail of Tears and the removal of Native Americans from Georgia and elsewhere. We had seen the foundation and quick decline of communities in Rainy Lake, Minnesota, and Wallace, Idaho. However, the really big gold rush was in California.

The 1848-1855 gold rush was the original California Dream. At the time of the discovery of the first gold in Northern California in January 1848, California was technically still part of Mexico. The outcome of the Mexican-American War transferred California to the USA the very next month.

As we saw from Lewis and Clark's experience a few decades earlier, it was challenging to travel to California. There were few '48ers, as it took a minimum of six months to reach California. However, by 1849, ninety-thousand miners seeking their fortune poured into the state. Roughly half were Argonauts coming by sea, and the other half broadly followed Lewis & Clark's route across America. The California State Constitution was written in 1849, and – following the inevitable Compromise of 1850 – California became a state in record time. Its state motto is Eureka – I have found it.

Gold mining around the world follows a predictable pattern. Initially, easy gold is panned from rivers by the early miners. Some investment in river sluices is then needed, and so large companies are required for their specialists and more considerable capital investment. Usually, once gold has been depleted, miners move on to silver and other metals.

As with many industries, most money is made from people offering infrastructure services. The owners of saloons, brothels, transportation, and stores made the most money from the California Gold Rush. Although he originally planned to sell tents, Levi Strauss started offering denim overalls in San Francisco in 1853, and his company did pretty well.

The earlier miners earned good money, perhaps ten times what they would have made elsewhere. It was a tough life, however. There was little in the way of rights' ownership, so you had to capture and then protect your own patch. Miners who arrived later in the rush struggled to make money. While the '49ers were genuine pioneers, they were often also thugs. Around fifteen thousand Native Americans died from 370 separate massacres, as the '49ers deprived them of their land. Attacks on foreign-born miners, including twenty-thousand Chinese, were funded and encouraged. The first state government was dominated by miners' interests. Although American miners paid no tax, foreign miners were taxed $20 per month. The first California Governor proclaimed that Indians had two options: extermination or removal. The misleadingly named State Act for Government and Protection of Indians 1850 provided for settlers to capture and bond Native Americans and their children.

California is now the most populated state in the Union, with around forty million people. By 1860, the population had grown to almost four hundred thousand, still mostly miners and infrastructure businesses to support those miners. While there were a few female miners and female business owners, California was overwhelmingly male. San Francisco had transformed itself from a thousand-person coastal village in 1848 to twenty-five thousand by 1850. It was known as the city of bachelors, and the lack of women began its long and proud history of homosexuality. The US economy as a whole was also transformed by the discovery of gold in California and stayed recession-free until 1855.

This accession of free-state California to statehood followed by the 1850 Fugitive Slave Act, which required US citizens to aid the capture of fugitive slaves, would put the United States on the path to civil war and ultimately end slavery in the USA. I thought this would be a good moment to explore the history of slavery on the American continent.

It is unknown when slavery started in Africa, but it was undoubtedly many centuries before European contact. The first slaves were mostly prisoners of war from one of the many tribal conflicts.

In 1455, the Roman Catholic Church granted Spain the rights to colonize America, and Portugal the exclusive rights on West African trade. This included the right for Portugal to "reduce their persons to perpetual slavery." By 1494, Portuguese kings had negotiated trade agreements with rulers of many West African kingdoms. In essence, Portugal received raw material and people in exchange for European manufactured goods. Initially, the traded people were predominantly prisoners of war and the occasional criminal. The first slaves went to Portugal to labor on infrastructure projects.

The Atlantic slave trade effectively began at the beginning of the sixteenth century. The Spanish likely transported the first slaves to Spanish colonies in the American continent from about 1503. As the sixteenth century progressed, even though African tribes were in a near-continuous state of war with their neighbors, the supply of prisoners of war could not keep up with the European demand for slaves. Therefore, many African kingdoms began to raid neighboring interior tribes for slaves that they would sell on to Europeans. This started the Triangular Trade. Europeans traded their exported goods with African Kings in exchange for enslaved Africans. Europeans transported these slaves to the American continent, and Europeans then imported the American continents' goods to Europe.

At a time when the world's population was increasing, Africa's population did not increase between 1500 and 1900. Numbers are imprecise because record-keeping was not a priority. However, it's likely that just under twenty-five million Africans were forcibly removed from the continent in this four-hundred-year period. Around half were taken across the Atlantic to the American continents. A similar, or maybe slightly lower, number of Africans was taken to the Arab World. Some historians calculate that a further four million Africans died awaiting trade, and there were an additional eight million intra-Africa transfers.

There are multiple estimates from historians, but I will use the estimates from the Trans-Atlantic Slave Trade Database run by historians from the Universities of Emory and California. They estimate that 12.5 million Africans made the journey across the Atlantic to the American continents. The two to three-month voyage to the Americas, often called the Middle Passage, was hell. Each ship's hold would contain several hundred Africans, who suffered from lack of food and water, physical abuse, disease, and severe overcrowding. Historians have estimated that around 14 percent, some 1.8 million, did not survive the journey. Conditions were so bad that one in ten ships had some form of mutiny.

These Africans came from many diverse tribes and different parts of Africa. Most came from the modern-day countries of Angola and the Congos (39%) and Benin (20%). The remainder were widely dispersed, reflecting the range of European nations involved in the slave trade. Biafra, now part of Nigeria, provided 15%; Cote d'Ivoire, Liberia, and Ghana 12%; Senegal & Gambia 5%; Mozambique and Madagascar 5%; and Sierra Leone and the Guineas 4%.

There were four waves of the Atlantic slave trade. The first wave saw Portuguese and Spanish traders ship Africans to South America in the sixteenth century. This accounted for just 2 percent of the total 12.5 million. The seventeenth-century wave, accounting for 15 percent of the total, was by English, Portuguese, French, and Dutch traders, mainly to the Caribbean for sugar growing and Brazil for mining. The third wave, from the beginning of the eighteenth century until Britain and the USA banned the slave trade in 1808, saw more than half the total slave trade. Almost seven million Africans were transported against their will, mainly by the British, Portuguese, and French. After slavery was officially banned by most countries, the final wave saw a further 3.5 million slaves forcibly relocated.

Many people might be surprised that – which I think is code for I was surprised that – only 4% of these unfortunate Africans were shipped to the USA. Most of these 0.4 million or so Africans were transported directly to the USA, but some were initially mentored into slave life in the Caribbean. The vast majority of Africans went to Brazil (47%), British West Indies (26%), French Americas (11%), Spanish Empire (8%), with the Danish and Dutch territories making up the remaining 4%.

Seventeenth-century America already had many indentured servants. These were individuals who had their Atlantic fare paid by their "master" in exchange for typically five years of service. At the end of their service, these indentured servants would be given their freedom, a gun, and a pre-arranged termination bonus. In case you think this might be a good deal for a poor British serf, only two out of five indentured servants lived to see the end of their contract.

The first twenty and odd African slaves arrived in Virginia in 1619. They were survivors from the Spanish ship, Sao Joao Bautista, attacked by British pirates searching for gold. These pirates were disappointed to find mainly Kongo or Ngongo slaves destined for Central America and decided to take these slaves to British America. Virginia initially classified these 20 or so as indentured servants to be freed after seven years.

Slaves were not admitted into the USA in large numbers until well into the eighteenth century. Tobacco, cotton post invention of the cotton gin, and other plantations needed a lot of workers. African slaves were a cheaper source of labor than indentured servants from Europe. America transformed slavery by making it permanent, hereditary, and racialized. Children of slaves were born into slavery, having never known freedom. They were chattel to be sold at the whim of their "owner."

For all of the Founding Fathers' wisdom and passion for individual freedom, they were mostly blind to the injustices of slaves. The US Constitution notably counted each slave as three-fifths of a person for taxation and representation purposes. Had the Founding Fathers been wiser and, for example, banned hereditary enslavement, the USA would probably have had no civil war and a substantially less acute race issue today.

The Age of Enlightenment led to European countries banning the slave trade. The Portuguese were first to ban the slave trade in 1761. The French banned it in 1794, only to un-ban it in 1802, and then re-ban it in 1848. The Danes, the Spanish, and the Dutch stopped it in 1803, 1811, and 1863 respectively. Wilberforce banned the UK's substantial role in the slave trade in 1807. Still, slavery was not entirely abolished in the British Colonies until 1838, when all slaves in the Caribbean were given their freedom. The forty-six thousand British slaveholders received the equivalent today of $21 billion in compensation for their loss. All these nations have more successfully covered up their role in the slave trade than the USA, presumably because the slaves' descendants didn't generally live in the countries responsible for the slave trade.

In the USA, slavery was never widespread in New England due to their Quaker and Puritan views, and the Northern states abolished slavery shortly after independence. The US Congress outlawed the international African slave trade in 1808 but still permitted a large domestic trade. This saw about one million slaves move to the Deep South in the first half of the nineteenth century. Congress only had authority over USA territories, and slaves continued to be imported via Florida and Texas.

At the time of the US Civil War, just over one-quarter of white Southerners owned slaves. However, these slaveholders had almost three-quarters of the total wealth and the majority of government influence to maintain that wealth. The proposal to ban slavery altogether threatened to remove all their wealth. By the start of the Civil War in 1861, the African American population had grown from its 0.4 million forced immigrants to 4.4 million descendants, of whom only about 10 percent were free.

The US Civil War was ultimately won in 1865 by the Union side with the loss of 620,000 men, more than any other conflict in US history. It left the South bankrupt and its infrastructure in ruins. Republicans pushed through reconstruction, which delivered three constitutional amendments: the Thirteenth, which officially abolished slavery, except as punishment for a crime; the Fourteenth, which supposedly conferred citizenship and promised equal protection; and the Fifteenth, which gave men of all colors the right to vote. Republicans also delivered a host of reconstruction laws. Union troops policed reconstruction efforts in the South for just over a decade until the compromise that surrounded the presidential election of Republican Rutherford Hayes, which I will detail later in the chapter.

Ultimately, reconstruction did not deliver its promise to African Americans in the South. However, it did offer some freedoms that have enabled African Americans to make outstanding contributions to the USA. Carter Woodson created Black History Week in 1926 because he noticed that African Americans were mostly absent from the history books. It's now a month-long celebration that recognizes African Americans' achievements and their central role in US history.

African Americans excel in so many walks of life today, but, of course, they stand on the shoulders of those Black Americans who were pioneers in their industry. I would like to take a few paragraphs to celebrate some of these pioneers.

In the sporting world, there are few sports where African Americans don't make outsized contributions. The Williams sisters did not have an easy road to world domination in tennis. However, their success was made possible by eleven-time Grand Slam tournament winner Althea Gibson, who had been prevented from playing in premier tournaments until 1950. Some of the greatest baseball players are African American, and it's fitting that every year on April 15, players celebrate Jackie Robinson Day by wearing his retired number, 42. Jesse Owens may be more celebrated, but the son of a former slave, John Baxter Taylor Jr, was the first African American to win an Olympic Gold medal in 1908. He died five months later of typhoid fever at the age of twenty-six. Mohammed Ali is probably the greatest of many great black boxers, but the first African American to become heavyweight champion was Jack Johnson, also in 1908. He retained his crown until 1915 when he lost a twenty-six-round fight in Cuba.

There have been almost four hundred African American generals in the US military, but the first was Chicagoan Benjamin Davis, who served first as a volunteer in the Spanish-American war of 1898. He was appointed as General in 1940 by FDR.

Phillis Wheatley was transported to colonial America at the age of seven or eight in 1761. She was sold to a Boston merchant family. She took her first name from the slave ship and her second name from the family who "owned" her. The Wheatley children educated her and, by twelve, she could read Greek and Latin poetry in their original languages. After her first book of poems was published at the age of twenty to the plaudits of London critics, she was emancipated by the Wheatley family.

Unfortunately, the story did not end well. After the Wheatley family died, she fell ill when working as a scullery maid and died at thirty-one.

There are numerous African American pioneers in business. I would like to recognize Mark Dean, the computer engineer who, along with his IBM colleague Dennis Moeller, designed the IBM personal computer in 1981. In a recent blog post, he said, "When I helped design the PC, I didn't think I'd live long enough to witness its decline." He now uses only a tablet.

We breakfasted in a less salubrious area. These areas exist in seemingly every part of America, and they always feature the same icons. There are stores offering bail bonds for families desperate to get their loved ones out of jail. Pawnshops also flourish, and you can deposit valuables in return for cash loans. These items of value could be anything but are usually jewelry, guns, electronics, and musical instruments. Pawnshops are quite interesting places to visit but are built on others' misery. A pawnshop customer typically receives about one-third of the item's value in cash and has two months to repay the debt at interest rates in excess of 100% APR. Three-quarters of these loans are never repaid, and the shop can then sell the item. Around ten thousand pawnshops thrive in America. A surprising 7.7 percent of Americans are unbanked, which is about the same percentage of Americans who have deposited items at a pawnshop. Incidentally, and contrary to public perception, only about one item in a thousand at a pawnshop is stolen property.

Writer L Robert Kohls defined materialism as the predisposition "to value and collect more material objects than most people would ever dream of owning." The US clothing store, Kohl's, has a slightly different take on this. Their desire is for you to buy an entirely new wardrobe every week through a bewildering discount system which appears to give you clothing for free.

The USA is commonly held to be very consumeristic. I see signs of this regularly. Americans don't seem to like to keep spare cash in a bank account. As soon as they receive money, most Americans like to purchase something. Actually anything: shoes, clothes, a vacation, or a car. Except that they seldom buy a new car, they procure it on a lease or with a loan. When you go to a car dealer's lot, vehicles are advertised by their monthly leasing cost, not their purchase price. You have to ask what the cost is to purchase the car with cash, and when you do, the car dealers are evasive because they prefer you to lease it or obtain a loan because that way they make more money. The USA has a tax system where most people overpay their income tax. Americans seem to like this arrangement, as this means that they receive a tax refund when they submit their tax return. For many, this is the only way they can save money.

The average fifty-year-old American has more than $120,000 of non-mortgage debt. They have personal loans against house equity of $50,000, student loan balances of $40,000, car loans of $20,000, and credit card debt of just under $10,000. Americans will readily tell you how much they earn, but much less commonly how much they owe.

Most Americans have massive houses with huge closets. The immigrants I spoke to loved that they had vast homes, the likes of which they would never have been able to afford in Europe. My real estate agent looked at me strangely when I said that I didn't want a large house. We ended up with the smallest we could find in our district, a whopping 4,000+ square feet of house, some 400m2, of which we now use less than a third. All houses have a lot of closet space. My wife has a double room for a closet for her clothes, and I have the equivalent of two single rooms for mine.

Despite this enormous amount of space, one in ten households also rent self-storage space for things that won't fit in their large houses, and they pay an average of $88/month for this storage. They visit these self-storage spaces only to put new things in them, and stuff is only withdrawn for episodes of storage wars.

I know many sales directors who tell me that they like to hire people who are in a lot of debt. They will work harder, I am told. To be fair, this attitude appears to be true for sales directors all over the globe. Are Americans more materialistic than other nations? Actually, the answer seems to be no. Indeed, there is evidence to suggest that they are slightly less materialistic.

The polling company IPSOS asked people from multiple countries two questions. First, "Do you measure your success by the things you own?" 21% of Americans said yes, lower than the global average of 34% and about one-third of that of countries such as China, India, and Turkey. You may be pleased to hear that only 16% of British people agreed with this question, but Sweden, in turn, is half that of the UK. The second question was, "Do you feel under a lot of pressure to be successful and earn a lot of money?" About 46% of Americans agreed with this statement, which was precisely the global average. China, Russia, and India topped this poll, with the UK slightly lower and Sweden again the lowest.

So the Chinese appear to be the most materialist country on earth, which is perhaps why they purchase one-third of all the world's luxury products and why the overpriced fashion houses and watch companies have such strong bases there.

Despite these international comparisons, the level of materialism in America does seem to have increased over time. Monroe Friedman from Eastern Michigan University studied the incidence of brand names over generic names used in thirty-one bestseller books, twenty-eight long-running Broadway plays, and lyrics from more than two-hundred-and-fifty pop songs from the 1950s to today. He found that the ratio of brand names to generic names – for example, Cadillac to car – is six times higher than it was in the 1950s.

Some argue that America's culture encourages materialism. It emphasizes individualism rather than collectivism. This encourages material things rather than more esoteric elements like equality and social responsibility.

Material goods, of course, are not necessarily harmful. It's useful to have a vacuum cleaner, washing machine, or TV. But do we really need a cordless vacuum, industrial washing machine with a built-in steamer, or 3D TV? It is rare indeed to see an American child without the most modern iPhone. Air Jordans – made for $16, retailing at $200 and up – are preferred to other sneakers. These are status symbols that identify their owner's place in the social hierarchy, and there's little indication that Generation Z will change its desire for material goods.

I suspect that we all know that no link exists between possessions and happiness and that any joy we receive from, say, buying a new car is transitory. Actually, it's worse than no link. Many academic studies have demonstrated a negative correlation between material possessions and social wellbeing. Daughter #1 believes that Americans are not as concerned with happiness as they should be. She believes that a selfish, winning mentality is too predominant in the average American life.

Mass production of goods and GDP growth need consumers to fuel them. It isn't surprising that any country will encourage consumer spending and not seek to dissuade people from making unnecessary purchases. Advertising is everywhere you look and is increasingly influential. There are more TV ads than ever. If you watch YouTube or view a webpage, you will see an advert tailored to your interests. If you have viewed some garden furniture or talk about it near your Alexa, you will be bombarded with garden furniture ads even after you have bought it. The job of the marketers is to manipulate you into thinking that a luxury is, in fact, a necessity. Increasingly, products are made to endure for shorter periods. A new laptop will only be effective for two years to encourage the next, bigger purchase in two years' time. Your older model iPhone seems to mysteriously slow down when a new version is available.

None of this is especially American, of course, but it started here and continues to this day. In this particular way, I am not American. I always choose the purchase of experience over a product. My favorite saying is that "this will see me out." I believe I will never have to buy any new clothes, pens, kitchen equipment, or shoes. I do need sandals, however.

Independence Day fell on a Saturday, so Friday, July 3, was judged a public holiday. One American word I find difficult to remember is that a holiday refers to one of the public holidays and not the time you take off from work, which is called a vacation.

In normal times, Independence Day is fun. If you can time your US vacation with the fourth of July, it's the easiest holiday to participate in. Most towns will have a parade, where many hundreds of organizations will march the streets to adoring crowds. Those parading will hand out goodies, usually candy, which is one reason children love a parade. The UK does not have a strong tradition of parades, and this is a pity.

Every community organization takes part. The fire service drive their large firetrucks, doctors and nurses sport their scrubs, and police proudly showcase their patrol cars. Every school is represented by its principal and other administrators, its marching band, and its teacher of the year. Increasingly, school clubs show off their robotics, drama, or chorus activities. Librarians dance with their bookcases on wheels, and dentists and orthodontists parade but can't hand out candy. Local businesses, like rock schools, clubs for gymnastics, dance, unicyclists, Pilates & yoga teachers, and real estate agents demonstrate their services. Local children's sports teams, whether baseball, soccer, basketball, track, or lacrosse, find some way of proving their skills while on the move. Regional cultural institutions abound; in the South, elderly twirlers march and twirl, Civil War enthusiasts reconstruct, while Southern Belles show off their finery and promenade. Local charities of every cause recruit, and churches of every Christian denomination march onward. Buddhists also march, but it's a typical day for them. Every brownie and scout group participates. Finally, every candidate who stands for political office must attend… if they want to be elected. As we have discussed before, that's a lot of politicians. Despite the partisanship at every other time of the year, the crowd is friendly towards all political candidates on Independence Day, even the small contingents from Moms against Guns or the even smaller group of Women for Trump.

A couple of years ago, Lorna won our city's Mom of The Year and was given a place in the parade. Daughter #1 drove an open-top sports car, with Daughter #2 in the passenger seat. Lorna sat elevated in the back, accepting the plaudits from most of the large crowd and throwing candy at children. Some mothers asked, "How come she gets to be Mom of the Year?" in an accusatory tone to their husbands. The answer is that Daughter #1 nominated her and wrote an essay on why Lorna deserved to be Mom of the Year, so you should be looking at your children.

After a couple of hours, the morning parade and its hundreds of paraders reaches its end. Independence Day, though, is about to hot up. An overflow of pool parties proliferates in the afternoon, either private or neighborhood. The evening brings firework displays, first the official one and then the unofficial ones going late into the night.

It won't surprise you that Covid canceled pretty much every single Fourth of July activity across the whole of America in 2020. As people didn't even see each other, even the traditional "Happy Fourth" greeting was lost. This is a real shame because it's my second favorite holiday. However, it is Daughter #2's least favorite holiday, as apparently, the only people who got independence were white men.

There are ten official USA federal holidays. Every non-essential federal agency closes on these ten days, along usually with the stock and bond markets and banks. Private sector companies, however, choose which holidays they want to celebrate. Pretty much all of them have a holiday for New Year's Day, Memorial Day, Independence Day, Labor Day, Thanksgiving, and Christmas Day. The other federal holidays of Martin Luther King Day, Presidents' Day, Veterans Day, and Columbus Day are optional. Some companies prefer to give their employees holidays instead on

Black Friday or the eves of Christmas, New Year, or Independence. While we are mentioning Christopher Columbus, neither Columbus, credited for discovering America, nor Amerigo Vespucci, after whom America is named, actually visited any part of the USA.

As with all things American, there is a holiday season. It forms part of the rhythm of the year where the same type of activities happens in more or less the same way every year. This season of parties begins on Halloween and ends with New Year, having Thanksgiving, Christmas, Hannukah, and Kwanzaa in between. This is also a baking season, where American women – fortified by the latest episode of the enormously popular and slightly renamed Great British Baking Show – try to demonstrate that they too could impress Paul Hollywood.

My favorite holiday is Thanksgiving. Originating as a harvest festival to thank Native Americans, it falls on the fourth Thursday of November. Like Christmas, this is predominantly a family holiday, and it's based around food and football. If you think Christmas dinner has bounteous food, you should count the sides on offer at the Thanksgiving meal.

It was time for us to go home. When we had planned this trip, I had wanted to carry on driving eastwards back towards Atlanta, but Lorna had insisted that we fly home after a month away. She did not want to leave Daughter #2 on her own for any longer. We returned our rental car to the good people of Alamo, who will undoubtedly have to rename themselves in due course. We had traveled 5,700 miles in this rental car, more than in some cars we had owned.

As Daughter #2 drove us home from Atlanta airport, election signs for primaries were ubiquitous. There are one hundred US Senators to vote for, two from each state. With its forty-million population, California, and Wyoming, with its half-a-million population, both elect two senators. The design was that these individuals should be a "temperate and respectable body of citizens." Up until 1913, US senators were chosen by their respective state legislatures. The Seventeenth Amendment changed this so that US Senators are now elected by voters for a six-year term, roughly one-third every two years. The amendment also allows the state's Governor to appoint a new Senator if a Senator retires or passes. This new Senator then has to stand for election at the next election opportunity.

There are 435 members of the House of Representatives. The distribution of these seats by state is calculated, by a surprisingly complex formula, according to census population numbers every ten years. As the US population has risen, the number of people per representative has grown to around three-quarters of a million, the highest by far of any OECD country. California has 53 representatives, while Alaska, Delaware, Montana, North Dakota, South Dakota, Vermont, and Wyoming only have one. States with rapid population growth, for example, Texas or Florida, have seen an increase in their number of representatives. In contrast, states with declining or stagnating populations – Illinois, Ohio, or Pennsylvania – have experienced the opposite.

By deliberate design, US Representatives are elected every two years in the belief that they should remain close to public opinion. In practice, these politicians are thus more or less in a permanent state of election. They represent the constituents of their district, the shape of which is decided by the individual state.

While the states' shape either follows natural boundaries or are straight lines, the edges of districts can be bizarre indeed. This is a result of gerrymandering, the name of which comes from its early proponent, Massachusetts Governor Elbridge Gerry, who apparently looked a bit like a salamander. Gerrymandering can be carried out by the ruling state party on either a partisan basis or by the two parties colluding to exchange citizens from one district to another. The third district of Maryland, designed to favor Democrats, has been described by a federal judge as a "broken-winged pterodactyl lying prostrate across the state" and by others as a "blood spatter at a crime scene." Ohio's fourth district, designed to favor Republicans, is nicknamed the duck.

Some states require representatives to live in their district. My favorite story is when boundaries were redrawn in the shape of a thin finger which placed the longtime home – but not where he parked his car – of a popular Democrat into a new district.

A few forms and examples of gerrymandering have been held unconstitutional by the Supreme Court, but in general, the judiciary leaves district design to the states. A few states have instigated bipartisan commissions, but most states have a fresh round of gerrymandering at each census's closure.

Gerrymandering can make a big difference. In 2012, Republicans in Wisconsin won sixty of the ninety-nine state assembly seats despite not winning a majority of the state's votes. They packed likely Democratic voters into districts that were won by landslides.

Presidents are elected every four years. Neither US Senators nor US Representatives have limits on the time that they can serve. However, the Twenty-Second Amendment in 1951 imposed a term limit of two terms on US presidents that previously was just a gentleman's agreement. The only president to serve more than two terms was Franklin D Roosevelt, who served 3.05 terms before his death in 1945.

You have probably seen that presidents are not voted by popular vote, but rather by something called an Electoral College, which is state-based. This is a complicated body which meets just once every four years to elect the president. The simple version is that 538 electors are chosen by political parties. The 538 number comes from one for each of 100 senators plus every 435 representatives plus 3 for Washington DC residents. In the vast majority of states, all of the Electoral College votes in a state are required to go to the candidate for the party with the plurality of votes in that state. In both Maine and Nebraska, they divide the electoral votes according to the majority of votes in each congressional district.

There have been five presidents who won the presidency despite losing the popular vote. The first was John Quincy Adams, who won the 1824 election, which was contested by four Democratic-Republican candidates. The second was Rutherford Hayes, who was trounced in the popular vote by Democrat Samuel Tilden in the 1876 election and led the Electoral College vote by 184 votes to 165, with 20 disputed electoral votes. Under the Compromise of 1877, the Democrats agreed that all 20 remaining electoral votes could go to the Republicans in exchange for Hayes agreeing to serve only one term and the withdrawal of federal troops from the South. This allowed the Democrats – who were then dominant in the South – to continue many of their antebellum policies. The third was the 1888 election of Republican Benjamin Harrison, who beat Democrat President Grover Cleveland. The 1892 rematch saw Cleveland win both the popular and electoral vote. Incidentally, Grover Cleveland is the only president to serve non-consecutive terms and accordingly is both the twenty-second and twenty-fourth president of the USA. Democrats Al Gore and Hilary Clinton lost the Electoral College vote in more recent times even though they won the popular votes by 0.5% and 2.1%, respectively.

This morning, I received a short call on my mobile phone from the Republican Party. The woman asked me how I thought the president was doing on a scale of 1 to 5, with 5 being very well and 1 not very well. My response should mean that I am not bothered by any further calls from her. I plan to do something similar when I receive a call from the Democrats. If you are in a Swing State, you will be bombarded with such calls. The admittedly small number of people with a landline report that they never answer their phone during the election period.

What did we learn from our drive across America? I don't believe I had any eureka moments, but we reminded ourselves about some key features.

First, the USA is big. It's the third-largest country in the world, about the size of the continent of Europe. It's forty times larger than the United Kingdom, and there are eleven US states that are larger than the UK. The distance between attractions can be huge. Americans think nothing of driving four hours to get somewhere. When we arrived, the four-hour drive from London to Devon seemed a long way. Now, we were happy to drive 5,700 miles across the country.

The vistas are big too. The US has at least 73,000 named mountains taller than Ben Nevis and abundantly more mountains without names. At 220 miles, the longest river in the UK is the River Severn, but thirty-eight American rivers are five hundred miles or longer. Both the Missouri and Mississippi Rivers are well over two thousand miles in length. If you fancy a lake view, you have an estimated four-million choices.

Business is big also. President Calvin Coolidge once said that the business of America is business. The USA is very successful in business. With only 4 percent of the world's population, America is responsible for about 24 percent of its economic output. Nine of the largest ten companies by market capital have American HQs, and one US Company, Apple, has a market capitalization greater than the combined top 100 companies in the UK.

The second thing we were reminded of is America's diversity. We have traveled to more than a hundred countries in the world and have liked most of them. However, the diversity in landscape and experience is extraordinary in the US. If we were to be locked down and only allowed to travel within any one country, this would be the country we would choose because it is so diverse.

Contrary to the American stereotype, there is a diversity to the people. Of course, some Americans do conform to the stereotype, but this stereotype doesn't describe most Americans we know. There is a diversity here of fat and thin people; an assortment of ultra-conservative and ultra-liberal; highly educated and happy to be ignorant; conventional and maverick; rich and struggling to make ends meet; and patriotic and embarrassed.

The third thing we reflected upon is the USA's future. I know that many believe that America is at the start of a decline seen by previous all-powerful empires. I take a different view. I think that the USA is still on the ascent. The USA will continue to dominate the twenty-first century and end up more robust at the end of this century than it began post-disintegration of the Soviet Union.

Due to its nineteenth-century achievements in controlling most of the North American continent from sea to shining sea, the USA has a powerful geopolitical position. It has two friendly neighbors: in small numbers to the north; and more significant numbers to the south. Unlike most other countries globally, it's unlikely to have external conflicts on its own mainland territory. The USA will have to guard against internal conflict. Previous wrongs will need to be appeased and opportunity more evenly distributed. However, I believe that America will belatedly address these issues, not necessarily because it's the right thing to do, but because the cost of internal conflict is so high.

As we explored in North Dakota, the USA spends more on its military than the next ten largest spending countries combined. Although the USA spends more money than is necessary on the military, the military plays a vital role in the United States' wealth. There's an adage, from Rear Admiral Alfred Mahan, in case you are interested, that whoever controls the seas controls trade. The powerful US military will ensure that the USA continues to control both the Atlantic and Pacific Oceans.

Increasingly, the USA controls space too. While there are probably no species to trade with in nearby solar systems, this control of space should ensure that the USA controls its own destiny. The USA will also secure the US's position to exploit resources from space.

The military also provides an important Research & Development function for the US. Along with the excellent American university system, the level of military investment in technology will eventually transfer to the private sector, which will, in turn, find new industries to dominate or old industries to disintermediate. After World War II, this happened with rocket technologies when America recruited German scientists – many of whom had been active in the Nazi party – to join their rocket development program. This happened again with the microchip. The microchip was developed in a 1959 invention through NASA's massive investment for the Gemini and Apollo space programs in the 1960s. This technology ultimately created the computer and mobile industries, which, in turn, revolutionized every other sector.

DARPA, the Defense Advanced Research Projects Agency, is instrumental in managing these military investments. It was founded by President Eisenhower in response to the Soviet launch of Sputnik 1, the Earth's first satellite. It has been instrumental in developing the internet, the cloud, electronic mapping, GPS, GUI interfaces, robots, stealth vehicles, video conferencing, and voice recognition, to name just nine. Many technology companies get their start with defense contracts before migrating to a broader consumer or industrial client base.

The next game-changers are probably a combination of the inter-related areas of artificial intelligence, robotics, and nano-technologies. Again, the military and universities have invested heavily in the development of these areas for decades. The large US technology players and a myriad of startups are now investing in these areas. With the exception of China, it's difficult to see any other country or region compete in this space. Ultimately, developments in these three areas will create new industries and greater productivity for America in the future.

The US technology and medical R&D ecosystems are self-perpetuating. Much of the best American talent is filtered through the excellent university system into these areas. It is supplemented by top talent from around the world, who are attracted to America for this technology ecosystem and the American Dream. It's this immigration that America needs to continue to attract.

The final area we reflected on was whether we wanted to stay in the US. We like the people, the lifestyle, and its physical geography. We had barely scratched the country's surface on this long journey and had so much more to see and do. We believe America still provides the best opportunity for our children, and maybe one day, grandchildren. Like the hundred million first-generation immigrants before us, we will never entirely be American. Our grandchildren will be, though.

Chapter 21 – Postscripts

While writing the book after our US trip, there were a few updates relevant to what was discussed in the book that I thought you might enjoy.

High School Graduation

Two weeks after our road trip, Daughter #2 finally attended her high school graduation. It was held two months late, but in person on a football field, rather than online, which her classmates had feared.

Covid was prevalent in the community at that time, but the school administrators did an excellent job creating a fully socially distant event. The stadium field sported one thousand seats for the seniors, all at least six feet from each other. Four thousand seats in the stands were marked so that family groups could attend substantially apart from any other. Everybody wore a mask.

There was an accidental British theme to the whole event. The graduates entered the arena to an extended version of Elgar's *Land of Hope and Glory*, the British patriotic anthem. They exited to Walton's *Crown Imperial* initially and then finally to 1985 hit *Walking on Sunshine* by British band and later Eurovision winners, Katrina and the Waves. It was raining.

As with every American event, it featured the singing of the American national anthem. Everyone would stand for the Star-Spangled Banner with their right hand or cap over their heart in normal times. However, the Black Lives Matters movement had started to change the cultural landscape of the USA. I noticed that about one in six students – but conspicuously none of the parents – took the knee or remained seated during the rendition. This defiant act would have been unthinkable three months previously. Of course, Daughter #2 was one of the defiant ones who defended their right to protest peacefully as part of the First Amendment.

Many speeches were orated. One of the Board of Education elected officials gave an address, a version of which presumably he had been providing for more than a decade. We knew him reasonably well, as he seemed to go to every school event in his fifteen-school constituency. He was obviously committed to the wellbeing of children but was highly conservative in his views and attitudes. His speech seemed out of touch with many from Generation Z on the field. He proclaimed that the graduates were lucky to be born into the greatest country on earth that there had ever been. This viewpoint was pretty standard fare, and we had heard this sentiment a hundred times. However, it now seemed a little out of place in a humbled country struggling to come to terms with past injustices.

One by one, each student then marched on stage to collect their graduation scroll. We had been asked not to shout out as our loved ones received their award so that parents of the following graduate did not miss their child's name being announced. It was easy for us Brits to adhere to this rule. However, Americans just can't help themselves shouting out their good wishes. Whether it's a general cheer, a whooping noise, or the ever-annoying "In the Hole," it is just part of what they do. The whole process of graduating every student took a long time.

Americans do these events exceptionally well. It provided a fitting moment for Daughter #2 to celebrate her passing from school to university and from adolescence to adulthood.

Funeral

My ALS-suffering friend died on a ventilator alone in a hospital, probably one of the few on a ventilator not struggling with Covid. He had spent his last four months alone in a dementia care home, with next to no in-person contact with others and only FaceTime connectivity with his family and friends. I had sensed from our recent video calls that the seemingly boundless optimism he possessed had lessened each month that he was deprived of contact with others.

He would have wanted a joyous memorial service that focused on the joy he had experienced in his life. However, his funeral was a somber affair. We all knew that this was not the way for anyone to leave this world.

Covid

The second wave hit Georgia and other Southern states hard. The number of positive Covid tests was over six times higher than when Georgia came out of lockdown. It was primarily driven by young people who had tired of restrictions. Although warned to the contrary, they preferred to believe that they would likely be asymptomatic or experience only mild symptoms.

It was no surprise to us when Daughter #1 contracted Covid in July. She worked in a busy bar in her college town; what did she expect would happen? As one of her roommates has a serious underlying health condition, Daughter #1 had to come home to us. She entered via the basement backdoor and remained in the basement with its own air conditioning unit for two weeks. We left food for her at the top of the stairs.

Daughter #2 dodged Covid for a while. Although some of her friends tested positive, her tests were always negative. She caught Covid too when at college but suffered only a temporary loss of smell and taste.

Travel Restrictions

At the time of writing, nineteen states have quarantine measures for any visitors from other states. They requested that visitors quarantine for fourteen days on arrival in their state. We could not have made the same journey that we made in June and July, at least without regular fortnightly periods of quarantine. This would undoubtedly have made a different type of book.

The east entrance to Glacier Park is still closed, as the Blackfeet Nation refuses any travel through their territory.

Cannonball Run

The Cannonball run has since been broken twice by others also taking advantage of lower police presence. Fred Ashmore completed a solo run in 25 hours and 55 minutes, at an average speed of 108mph. He used a rental Ford Mustang and made only one fuel stop by removing all but the driver's seat to make space for additional fuel tanks.

However, the world record was reclaimed by another set of three men who completed the journey in an Audi S6 Sedan modified to look like the more unobtrusive Ford Taurus. Their journey took a mere 25 hours and 39 minutes, or an average speed of 110mph. It took just over four minutes to get out of Manhattan.

College Move-In

Daughter #1 and Daughter #2 moved into university in consecutive weeks in early-August. Daughter #1 swapped one apartment for another in her luxury block. The new apartment had more space and a pool table. It was hard work to move all of the accumulated junk she had collected. Another forlorn group of adults stood around a huge sofa that was stuck in one corridor corner. They couldn't seem to shift it either forward or back. We didn't like to tell them that, even if they transported it around the corner, they would never get it through the apartment front door.

Daughter #2 moved into a high rise block with a thousand of her closest new friends. She shared a small double room with another girl, let's call her Dorm Room Girl #1. It's normal to share a room at college. Some roommates are preselected; others are random. Some go on to be best man or maid of honor at their weddings; others never speak to each other again. Daughter #2 had selected wisely. They liked to come home and tell each other about their respective days. Others were less fortunate and counted down the days until they would never have to see the other again. In 2020, there was an additional area of contention: covid carefulness.

The move-in was well organized. Lorna had been thwarted from her plan to enter earlier. "We can just sneak in" did not work on this occasion. Each student was allocated a one-hour period to park their vehicle and transport their belongings to the room. Some, the boys, had driven their saloon cars and hauled their one bag up the stairs. Some, including Daughter #2, had driven their SUVs with stuff packed to the ceiling. And there were those – like Dorm Room Girl #1 – who had rented a U-Haul van for the day.

Our girls were on the eighth floor of the high rise, so we had to line up six feet apart for the elevator. Each journey was a fifteen-minute wait, but it gave you a chance to survey what everyone else had bought. My summation was that Ikea must have had a bumper week. Although everyone had to wear a mask, I hoped that the aunts and father of Dorm Room Girl #1 were Covid-free because it was a tight squeeze with seven-masked adults in one small double room.

The girls had spent a good deal of money on their dorm rooms. Everything must match, and the dorm room must have everything. Their place was pre-stocked with two elevated bunk beds, stairs to reach said bed with each step doubling as storage space, wardrobes, desks, and chairs. It was already quite full. We had bought a fridge freezer. Dorm Room Girl #1 had bought a big TV, microwave, plants, wall coverings, rug, lights, velour curtains, and poles.

Dorm Room Girl #1's father immediately set to work on assembling the Lunnarp Ikea Coffee table. One aunt had to assemble the various lights. I'm one of the least practical people, and I was summoned to put together the posh, white-suede futon sofa bed with integrated drink holders.

I will congratulate the girls. The room had been planned to the nearest millimeter, and everything did fit in the room…just. Having spent eighteen years living with Daughter #2, I wish Dorm Room Girl #1 the best of luck in keeping the place tidy.

Each girl had brought very many pairs of shoes. In addition to the white trainers they were wearing, both had an additional four pairs of similar trainers. When we saw the girls rushing down the hill for sorority rush, we instantly saw this was the footwear of choice for girls. Every single one of the thousand girls sported white sneakers, with individuality demonstrated only through their selection of Nike, Adidas, or Asics.

The bad news for our heroines was that the RA's room was right next to theirs. The RAs made it clear that mask-wearing would be mandatory, visits from others to their dorm rooms forbidden, and drinking not tolerated. All these rules were ones which we believed Daughter #2 planned to break.

University Goes Online

Entirely predictably, after only two weeks of college, fifteen-hundred students tested positive for Covid. These students were isolated from others in emergency university accommodation. Many more had symptoms but refused to get a test. Nearly all of my daughters' classes were held online. The university was undoubtedly relieved, though, at having received all the tuition payments for the semester.

The bar in which Daughter #1 works is still open, along with all other bars. The bar owners challenged through the courts any ruling for them to close.

Surprisingly, the college football games took place, albeit with limited crowds of twenty-thousand people. Tailgating was prohibited for everyone except those people with a game ticket.

The Post Office

The US Post Office hit the newspapers' front pages worldwide when a recent political appointee to run the post office was accused of implementing changes that might slow down the delivery of mail-in ballots for the November election. The issue was eventually resolved when the disputed proposed changes were delayed until after the election.

Incidentally, do you know why presidential elections are held on the first Tuesday in November? In the mid-nineteenth century, most Americans were farmers. November was chosen because it was after farmers had completed harvest but before the worst of winter. A Tuesday was selected to give a full day of travel after Sunday, the day of rest.

Tokyo Valentino

Following the ordinance's approval, which defined what a sex shop was, this newly defined sex shop had its license suspended again in September 2020. It was subject to appeal in October 2020, and the businesses would have until 2021 to move, which could be extended by up to one year in the event of hardship.

Gretchen Whitmer

In October 2020, the FBI thwarted a plot to abduct and overthrow the Michigan Governor, Gretchen Whitmer, whose unpopularity we had seen while traveling through Michigan. According to the FBI, six Michigan militia men – some from trailer parks – were arrested for planning to put Ms. Whitmer on trial for treason for exceeding her authority on the issuance of state executive orders.

Big Storm

As I struggled to finish the final edit before copyediting, Tropical Storm Zeta hit Atlanta in late October. Fourteen separate trees felled the power lines on our road, and we lost power for four days. I was forced to borrow power from a neighbor with a generator to meet the deadline.

Immigration

Immigration Services finally opened up again after a prolonged Covid shutdown. The likely completion date for our citizenship application moved from May 2020 to February 2021. We had only the citizenship test and swearing-in to complete. After having written this book, I felt I was well-prepared.

If you have enjoyed the book

Thank you for purchasing *High, Wide, and Handsome*. I understand that there are just under fifty million books that you could have picked, but you picked this book and, for that, I am extremely grateful.

All first-time authors need the help of their readers to promote their books to others. I'm no different. If this book has improved the quality of your life in any way, I would be grateful further if you could share your enjoyment via your favorite social media site. Amazon reviews are particularly helpful to new authors.

You can stay in touch by following me on Facebook, Instagram, Twitter, or Amazon. You can also subscribe to my website, www.julian-bishop.com, where I will talk about future books.

Until next time.

Julian Bishop

About the author

Julian Bishop and his family have lived in three continents and traveled to over a hundred countries. For the last decade, Julian has lived in Atlanta, Georgia. Julian has a wide range of eclectic passions, including how history affects culture, the foster care system, bridge, installation art, cricket, of course, and fatherhood to name but a few.

Printed in Great Britain
by Amazon